Business Ethics for Future Leaders

First Edition

Edited by

Victor L. Heller
University of Texas San Antonio

Jacob A. Heller and Nathan A. Heller
Tarleton State University

Bassim Hamadeh, CEO and Publisher
John Remington, Executive Editor
Gem Rabanera, Senior Project Editor
Alia Bales, Production Editor
Emely Villavicencio, Senior Graphic Designer
Trey Soto, Licensing Coordinator
Natalie Piccotti, Director of Marketing
Kassie Graves, Vice President of Editorial
Jamie Giganti, Director of Academic Publishing

Copyright © 2021 by Cognella, Inc. All rights reserved. No part of this publication may be reprinted, reproduced, transmitted, or utilized in any form or by any electronic, mechanical, or other means, now known or hereafter invented, including photocopying, microfilming, and recording, or in any information retrieval system without the written permission of Cognella, Inc. For inquiries regarding permissions, translations, foreign rights, audio rights, and any other forms of reproduction, please contact the Cognella Licensing Department at rights@cognella.com.

Trademark Notice: Product or corporate names may be trademarks or registered trademarks and are used only for identification and explanation without intent to infringe.

Cover image copyright © 2019 iStockphoto LP/MicroStockHub.

Printed in the United States of America.

Contents

Acknowledgments ix

Introduction xi

Section I The Role of Business Ethics 1

Pre-Reading Questions 2

Reading 1.1 A Method for Embedding Business Ethics into Traditional Business Analysis 3
John L. Keifer and Mary Carter Keifer

Reading 1.2 An Introduction to Ethics: Framing and Key Themes in Business Ethics 13
Andrew C. Wicks, Bidhan L. Parmar, R. Edward Freeman, Jared Harris, and Jenny Mead

Reading 1.3 The Moral Advantage 21
William Damon

Post-Reading Questions 30

Section II Ethical Challenges in Today's Multi-Generational Workplace 37

Pre-Reading Questions 38

Reading 2.1 Altogether, Now: Engagement and Multigenerational Workplaces 39
Jessica McManus Warnell

Reading 2.2 Organizational Ambidexterity and the Multi-Generational Workforce 59
Kathryn Woods

Post-Reading Questions 80

Section III Mind-sets for Ethical Leaders 87

Pre-Reading Questions 88

Reading 3.1 One Bad Apple: The Role of Destructive Executives in Organizations 89
Alexa A. Perryman, David Sikora, and Gerald R. Ferris

Reading 3.2 Ethical Leaders: Trust, Work-Life Abundance, and Treating Individuals as Unique 109
Tammy Cowart, Ann Gilley, Sherry Avery, Afton Barber, and Jerry W. Gilley

Post-Reading Questions 122

Section IV Ethical Challenges Relating to Cyber Security/Internet 129

Pre-Reading Questions 130

Reading 4.1 Proper Distance: Toward an Ethics for Cyberspace 131
Roger Silverstone; ed., Gunnar Liestøl, Andrew Morrison, and Terje Rasmussen

Reading 4.2 Privacy Is Freedom 141
Robert Scheer

Post-Reading Questions 158

Section V Redefining Internal Environmental Ethics 163

Pre-Reading Questions 164

Reading 5.1 Ethics of Business Decision Making 165
Paula Alexander

Reading 5.2 Sustainable Environmental Management 179
Paula Alexander

Post-Reading Questions 196

Section VI Redefining the Role of Corporate Social Responsibility 203

Pre-Reading Questions 204

Reading 6.1 Ethical Climate and Safety Performance 205
E. Andrew Kapp and K. Praveen Parboteeah

Reading 6.2 Using Safety to Introduce Ethics into Operations Management Courses   213
Wayne Buck and Jeffrey Schaller

Post-Reading Questions   232

Section VII   Public Affairs and Ethical Business   237

Pre-Reading Questions   238

Reading 7.1 Strategic Stakeholder and Ethical Public Affairs, Issues, and Crisis Management   239
Robert N. Lussier and Herbert Sherman

Post-Reading Questions   282

ACCESSING WEB-BASED RESOURCES

This book has QR codes available to complement your reading.

The author has selected additional web-based content for further engagement using QR codes, which are intended for those who have purchased print copies of the book. Those who have purchased a digital copy may simply click on the corresponding hyperlinks. Please check with your professor to confirm whether your class will access this content independently or collectively.

Cognella maintains no responsibility for the content nor availability of third-party links. However, Cognella makes every effort to keep texts current. Broken links may be reported to studentreviews@cognella.com. Please include the book's title, author, and 7-digit SKU reference number (found below the barcode on the back cover of the book) in the body of your message.

Acknowledgments

We would like to express our heartfelt thanks to our wives, Andrea, Carley, and Lisa Heller, and to our children, all of whom sacrificed their time and interests in order for us to pursue our interests. Thanks also to Dean Wm. Gerard Sanders, Department Chair Jonathan Clark at the University of Texas at San Antonio, and Dean Chris Shao and Department Chair Reggie Hall at Tarleton State University. Finally, we owe a great deal of gratitude to Gem Rabanera, Project Editor, her staff, and the leadership at Cognella.

Introduction

Today, there are numerous well-written traditional business ethics textbooks found in the marketplace. They provide a wealth of classical and historical content that is of enduring value to the reader. The primary value of *Business Ethics for Future Leaders* is to supplement these works with worthwhile contemporary readings designed to fill content gaps not addressed in these texts, which are impacting everyday ethics in the workplace—academic readings that will raise today's student's awareness of the changing dynamics in the discipline that they will find useful as tomorrow's leaders.

We had three criteria that governed our selection of readings in each chapter. First, we wanted readings that are relevant to the changing dynamics of ethics in today's business world, readings that will bring new awareness of the ethical dynamics in the workplace. Second, we wanted readings of significant value in the realm and discipline of ethical business leadership, readings that would challenge the traditional leadership mind-set. Finally, we wanted readings that would be understandable by business and non-business students alike. Business is part of everyone's lives; we hope this anthology will make the discipline easier to understand.

The novelist Marcel Proust is quoted as saying, "The real voyage of discovery consists not in seeking new landscapes, but in having new eyes." We hope these readings will give the reader new eyes for business ethics.

Happy reading!

Victor L. Heller, Ph.D.
Associate Professor
University of Texas at San Antonio

Jacob A. Heller, Ph.D.
Assistant Professor
Tarleton State University

Nathan A. Heller, Ph.D.
Professor
Tarleton State University

Section I

The Role of Business Ethics

*"I believe firmly that in making ethical decisions, man
has the prerogative of true freedom of choice."*
Corliss Lamont

IN CHAPTER 1, WE INTRODUCE YOU to three articles that address (a) how ethical behavior can contribute to organizational success, (b) why individuals see ethical behavior differently, and (c) how leaders can incorporate ethics into their decisions. These articles are intended to help you better understand the complexities of ethics within an organizational setting.

The first article, "A Method for Embedding Business Ethics into Traditional Business Analysis" by John Keifer and Mary Carter Keifer addresses the need for an organization's activities to include environmental and social responsibilities. The article is divided into three sections. First, the article advocates that ethics cannot be taught as a standalone concept. Second, they discuss the traditional approach to decision making that is embedded in cost-benefit analysis and that pushes ethical issues out of the decision making process. Finally, the authors note the only way to incorporate ethical concerns into the decision-making process is to require organizations to consider the social and temporal implications of their decisions.

The authors present a model of ethical decision making that incorporates environmental and social sustainability into the traditional business analysis that uses Porter's Five Forces and SWOT analyses. They conclude that business schools are not developing instructional models that incorporate ethical issues and strategic thinking on a global scale.

In the second article by authors Wicks, Parmer, Freeman, Harris, and Mead, "An Introduction to Ethics: Framing and Key Themes in Business Ethics," the authors note that the concept of ethics refers to a theory of living that addresses the question "How should we live?" This question relates to individuals, organizations, industries, societies, and nations. It assumes that individuals are accountable for their actions in addressing what is right and/or wrong. However, all individuals see the world through different lenses. Even if individuals can agree on the facts of a situation, there still maybe differences on how one should handle a situation. For business leaders, ethics can be seen as a restrictive tax being imposed on them as opposed to being perceived as building trust and honesty among all individuals.

The authors discuss the relationship between ethics and the law. Laws articulate how individuals must not behave but do little to help individuals determine how they should behave. Laws are ambiguous, constantly changing, and reactive. Ethics help individuals determine how they should plan their goals in a way to advance their careers and develop patterns of cooperation. Finally, the authors discuss how business leaders must accept and address ethical challenges.

In the final reading, "The Moral Advantage" by William Damon, the author discusses the multiple ways that morality (ethics) contributes to business successes. His four dimensions of business morality are generative, empathic, restrictive, and philanthropic.

> Generative morality arises from a deep inner understanding of one's purpose in life and how it is an inspiration in his or her work.

> Empathic morality reflects the "Golden Rule" principle of treating others as you would like to be treated.

> Restrictive morality regulates ethical behavior according to society's norms. It guards reputations and provides safety from legal attacks.

> Philanthropic morality reflects a charitable approach for altruistic ends. It enhances the reputation of individuals and businesses.

Finally, the author notes that an individual's moral identity is the best predictor of why an individual selects a particular course of action.

Pre-Reading Questions

As you read the chapter articles, reflect on the following:
- How do the articles integrate with my understanding of ethics from other classes?
- What concepts in the readings resonate with me regarding ethics in organizations?
- Where do I see the need to implement the articles' concepts in the organization where I work or have worked?

Reading 1.1

A Method for Embedding Business Ethics into Traditional Business Analysis

John L. Keifer and Mary Carter Keifer

I. Introduction

By historic design regulation of corporate governance in America has been largely feckless when it comes to the public good. This approach has been largely driven by economic thought and particularly the notion of the "invisible hand" which posits the public benefits of self-serving, productive behavior and a corresponding belief in the self-regulating nature of markets.[1] Recent events have called into question such beliefs especially in situations where globalization of markets has created systemic risks which go well beyond the welfare of individual firms. In fact, it has resulted in calls from unlikely places for moderating economic incentives in a deliberate effort designed to moderate risk-taking going forward.[2] Even before the current economic debacle, there were signs that economic thought and its focus on monetary gain was having an overly dehumanizing and increasingly detrimental impact on firm decision making to society's detriment.[3]

The authors are not looking simply to find fault with management education over its heavy reliance on economic thought and the importance of incentives.[4] They argue instead that the rightful place of economics is as a filter by which managers test the strategic fit of their ideas against an assortment of metrics including their social and environmental impact and sustainability from both a temporal and spatial perspective. The authors argue prescriptively that the scope of managerial consideration should be broadened to include the firm's environmental and social footprint, which is strictly governed by the two maxims: (1) do no harm[5]; and, (2) look, where possible, to do good.[6] Economic considerations, in other words, should be relegated to a final benchmark (1) to justify or reject a decision after it has been made, (2) to aid in the derivation

John L. Keifer and Mary Carter Keifer, "A Method for Embedding Business Ethics into Traditional Business Analysis," *Southern Journal of Business and Ethics*, vol. 1, pp. 141-150. Copyright © 2009 by Southern Academy of Legal Studies in Business. Reprinted with permission. Provided by ProQuest LLC. All rights reserved.

of a decision as a result of an iterative process, or (3) to provide a rational explanation for a decision once made.[7]

The paper is divided into three separate but interrelated propositions. First, it posits that ethics cannot be taught as an aside or as an additional consideration and be effective when it comes to moderating future behavior. This is true because the compelling nature of the profit incentive is simply too great when it comes to doing business. In other words, unless doing the right or good thing lies at the center of a person's approach to decision making, it is foolhardy to think that any instruction in ethics will have a significant impact on future decision making as born witness from experience. Second, as commonly taught across business schools worldwide, the traditional approach to decision making which assesses the merits of an idea largely on a cost-benefit analysis focusing primarily on the anticipated revenues and expenses has the effect of pushing issues of ethics largely to the periphery. The net effect of such relegation has been the ancillary development of the concept of negative externalities and the concomitant call for regulation to force the internalization of certain costs otherwise born by the public, a solution that has proven to be totally inadequate in the multiple jurisdictions of the global economy given the power wielded by multinational corporations. Finally, the paper posits that the only way to put ethical concerns at the center of decision making is to require firms to consider both spatial and temporal implications of their decisions (i.e., their social and environmental footprints) from the standpoint of their social and environmental sustainability.

We would like to make one additional comment. Ethics is a complex matter when viewed from the perspective of the firm. This complexity can be minimized by treating ethics from the multiple foci of micro (individual level), meso (group level), and macro (firm level) perspectives. While wonderful materials exist that look at ethics from the micro and meso perspectives[8], firm level treatment of ethics has begun only recently, but has not been adequately addressed from a pedagogical standpoint. The paper looks to address this shortcoming since what may happen at the individual or group levels will surely be constrained by firm level decisions of a strategic nature.

II. Ad Hoc Approach to Ethical Instruction

Agency law and its fiduciary obligations have been the dominate paradigm when it comes to identifying the role of firm management and its primary responsibility to maximize firm profits. "The only business is business," reminds Milton Friedman, and the only social [read moral] responsibility of a business general manager is to "increase its profits."[9] While this has been tempered somewhat beginning with the New Jersey Supreme Court decision in 1953 holding the corporate philanthropy in moderation was authorized and consistent with their obligation to "acknowledge and discharge social as well as private responsibilities as members of communities in which they operate,"[10] the amoral argument still holds that firms should not internalize costs beyond those expenses mandated by law when it comes to their operations. For instance, McKinsey & Company, the premier management consulting firm globally, argued in the third edition of its famed publication,

> This book is about how to value companies and use information about valuation to make wiser decisions. Underlying it is our basic belief that managers who focus on building shareholder value will create healthier companies than those who do not. We also think that healthier companies will, in turn, lead to stronger economies, higher living standards, and more career and business opportunities for individuals.[11]

While the advent of the Internet and cable news has upped the ante considerably for firms which fail to take into consideration the external effects of their operations, *The Economist* magazine reported as late as January 2008 that only sixty percent of 2000 firms surveyed actually required codes of conduct of their suppliers, and only forty-two percent even regularly assessed ethics risks in their supply chains.[12]

The influence of economic theory on the profession of management has not gone without its critics. Ghoshal and Moran (2003), for instance, argue persuasively that the "issue of intentionality" must be included in any systematic analysis of social phenomena or "sidestepped." In suggesting that sidestepping has largely been the order of the day, they say,

> In most causal theories, sidestepping is accomplished by making some assumptions about human nature—assumptions that are often not explicitly in the theory but remain implicit, hidden from causal logic. Our more pragmatic ground for making the distinction between good and bad theories relate to the nature of the assumptions that underlie much of management theory.[13]

For them, the assumptions are all too "negative, pessimistic, and empirically unsupported, lacking not only in moral grounding but also in common sense."[14]

More recently, Khurana (2007) has called for putting the teaching of ethics in business schools within a "holistic, institutional context."[15] Criticizing business schools for their poor handling of the topic of ethics in the wake of corporate scandals, he stated,

> The effect of these corporate scandals on business schools has been confined mostly to debate and, to some degree, action with respect to the subject of business ethics. In the wake of Enron and Tyco, some business school deans argued that the scandals reflected the presence in the corporate world of a few "bad apples," not any systemic problems that reflected in any way on business schools, which, they maintained, should not be held accountable for the moral failings of their graduates. At other schools, deans recycled their talking points about business ethics from the insider trading scandals of the 1980's, describing what their schools were doing to strengthen the ethics component of their curricula, which in some cases entailed the creation of new centers or programs on business ethics. Debates about ethics in the business school curriculum centered on whether instruction in ethics should be provided in a single, freestanding course or integrated into the entire MBA curriculum.[16]

Ironically, his call for action was predicated on what he calls "investor capitalism" which has placed enormous pressure on managers to show increases in quarterly earnings each year as a result of the dynamics of the market for financial control. The current financial meltdown, we would argue, raises a whole different genre of concern when it comes to the management of agency costs.

Newly initiated social science research questions the negative assumptions made about human beings and offers great insight into our ability to tap into the creative energies of people. For example, behavioral economists have shown that people can be trusted experimentally to do the right thing when reminded on their responsibilities as principled adults.[17] Even more interesting is the work being done in cognitive psychology that people have evolved an universal moral instinct, "compelling us to render judgments of right and wrong independent of race, gender or education."[18] This research stream needs further development but the strong suggestion there that formalizing ethics instruction may well lead to better decision making is not just Pollyanna-type thinking.[19]

III. The Peripheral Nature of Business Ethics

The traditional approach to decision making pushes issues of ethics largely to the periphery as students are taught to assess the merits of any proposal largely on a cost-benefit analysis and various ways to measure a firm's return on investment. This is especially true when it comes to management education given the pervasive influence on economic thought on strategic theory. Both Porter's value chain analysis and the Resource-Based View of the Firm (RBV) are undergirded by economic thinking or marginal analysis. As currently taught, business ethics is an anathema to questions of strategic fit or competitive advantage. As further proof of this fact, Dranove and Marciano's very popular book, "Kellogg on Strategy," makes a compelling case linking the firm's financial footprint to its strategic drivers.[20] The topic of ethics is not even covered in the book.

The law itself offers little reason for a firm to look beyond its own interest and the interest of its shareholders. First, as explained previously, for much of their existence, American corporations have been under a fiduciary mandate to act solely in the best interest of their shareholders. While this has been tempered by both court decision and state legislation in some instances, top managers and boards are under no illusions when it comes to the reason for their retention. In the absence of a positive case being made for taking a broader view of a firm's obligation to the larger community of stakeholders or otherwise compelling legislation, the safe course for managers and boards to take will remain looking after the best interest of their shareholders. Secondly, states have vied to attract business to their borders with Delaware doing the best job when it comes to offering lenient corporate governance regulation. As it stands, boards in Delaware are protected under the business judgment rule to the extent that they seek to be informed and otherwise act in good faith even if they fail to follow best practices.[21] In the case of Wall Street's financial collapse, it is not clear that liability could be established even though a warning of potential systemic collapse was sounded as early as 1999.[22]

The feckless nature of American law offers little hope that managers and boards will respond consistently in a positive fashion to social and environmental concerns short of some form of mandatory regulation. Given political exigencies, they may well find that to be the case. In the meantime, business schools can seek to require their students to engage in analyzes that serve for a firm and society's interests.

IV. Moving Ethics to the Center of Decision Making

Historic developments have brought to the forefront the need for firms to consider their social and environmental impact. In 1971 the World Economic Forum first identified the stakeholder concept—the idea that a firm has a clear responsibility to the community beyond just its shareholders.[23] This was followed some twenty years later by the 1992 Rio Conference of the United Nations on Environment and Development (UNCED), which began the discussion on global warming and sustainable development which has now become a centerpiece in the discussions of world business and governmental leaders at the World Economic Forum in Davos, Switzerland each year. While it began with a focus on the natural environment, it now has broadened into the topic of corporate social responsibility which "incorporates a host of concepts and practices, including the necessity for adequate corporate governance structures, the implementation of workplace safety and standards, the adoption of environmentally sustainable procedures, and philanthropy."[24] This now has further broadened into the relatively recent topic of corporate social entrepreneurship which involves transforming socially responsible principles and ideas into commercial value.[25] For instance, it has been reported that Hindustan Unilever actually profits more from shampoo sales to rural India in small, individual packets than they do from bottle sales.[26]

These developments beg the question as to how business school curriculum should be adapted to capture the benefits of these developments. The question comes down to how students should be trained to analyze business situations. Presently, the choix du jour is to have students do both a macro (PEST)[27] analysis and a micro or industrial (SWOT)[28] analysis of the firm environment in an effort to determine its existing and prospective circumstances and the changes needed to maximize its financial performance.

A problem has been that there has been little discussion within the academy relates to how ethics can be incorporated systemically into business instruction[29]. Khurana notes,

> As things stand, there is little sustained discussion among business school faculty and administrators about whether new technologies, the globalization of trade, demographic trends, the growing inequality between rich and poor, and sustaining social norms may be rendering the investor capitalism model unsustainable, if not obsolete. Yet these and other developments in the world since the rise of investor capitalism suggest that a new model—one akin to the stakeholder model ... one that recognizes legitimate economic and social interests of many members of society other than shareholders—may be called for.[30]

We propose that social, environmental and economic sustainability be added to the traditional analysis done in business schools. Students should be expected to add to their macro/micro analyzes a sustainability analysis in which they consider social and environmental sustainability in addition to a project's economic sustainability.

What follows is our model for decision making that business schools should adopt when it comes to matters of firm strategy.

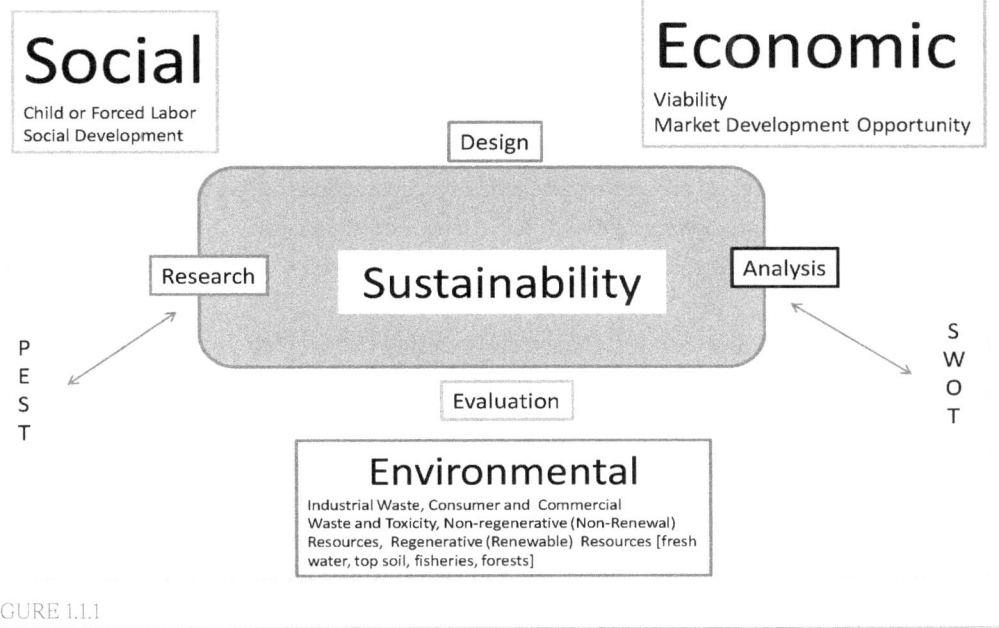

FIGURE 1.1.1

This model would look to incorporate traditional analysis into a sustainability model which looks to focus the attention of students on the critical issues when it comes to both innovative opportunities and possible threats or hazards from a sustainability standpoint.[31]

V. Conclusion

Business schools are not keeping pace with the changes happening in the world when it comes to their instructional models. We know that courses in ethics have not been effective when it comes to modifying the effects on behavior that ethicists find desirable. While it may be impossible to eliminate malfeasance altogether, we certainly can create instructional models that force future business leaders to think through the consequences of their decisions from the stand point of their firm's footprint on society and the environment. This could greatly aid innovative thinking and lead to positive changes in the law especially when it comes to the business judgment rule. With such analysis, it would be more difficult for directors to benefit from the presumption of good faith when it comes to their decisions.

Notes

1. *See* Adam Smith, *An Inquiry into the Nature and Causes of the Wealth of Nations* (Prometheus Books 1991) (1776).
2. *See* statement of Lloyd Blankfein, chief executive of Goldman Sachs Group Inc., as reported on April 7, 2009, that the financial industry needed a "renewal of common sense" and pay standards to "discourage selfish behavior, including excessive risk-taking." Walter Hamilton and Tiffany Hsu, Executive-pay overhaul gets backing from Goldman Sachs CEO, *Los Angeles Times*, April 8, 2009 <http://www.latimes.com/business/la-fi-execpay8-2009apr08,0,3574531.story>.
3. See Ghoshal, S. & Moran, P. "Towards A Good Theory of Management." Birkinshaw, J. & Piramal, G. Sumantra Ghoshal on *Management: A Force for Good*. Prentice Hall, 2005, 21.
4. Friedman, M. "The Social Responsibility of Business Is To Increase Its Profits." *New York Times* Magazine, 9/13/70: 32
5. Paine, L. *Value Shift: Why Companies Must Merge Social and Financial Imperatives to Achieve Superior Performance*. Tata McGraw-Hill, 2003.
6. See Prahalad, C.K. *The Fortune at the Bottom of the Pyramid: Eradicating Poverty Through Profits (Enabling Dignity and Choice Through Markets)*. Wharton School Publishing, 2005.
7. A principal benefit of economic theory lies in its ability to adapt to changing phenomena and provide a coherent explanation. For instance, technology has permitted specialization along an industry's value chain due to a technically enabled ability to organize and coordinate business activity effectively across intermediate markets. This would be consistent with Coases' transaction cost approach since technology better enables greater monitoring of related firm activity and therefore reduces the threat of transaction costs related to market failure.
8. For a comprehensive set of materials (articles and cases) developed in collaboration between the Center for Business Education at the Aspen Institute and Yale School of Management for the macro and meso perspectives, see: http://www.AspenCBE.org.
9. *Supra* note 4.
10. *See A.P. Smith Manufacturing Company v. Barlow*, 13 N.J. 145, 154 (Sup. Ct. of N.J. 1953).
11. Copeland, T., Koller, T. & Murrin, J. *Valuation: Measuring and Managing the Value of Companies*. 3rd edition. Wiley, 2000, 3.
12. *See* "A Stitch in Time: How Companies Manage Risks to Their Reputation", The Economist (January 17, 2008)
13. *Supra* note 3, 21.
14. *Id.*, 21.
15. Khurana, R. *From Higher Aims To Hired Hands: The Social Transformation of American Business Schools And The Unfulfilled Promise of Management As A Profession*. Princeton, 2007, 365.
16. *Id.*, 364.
17. *See* Ariely, D. *Irrational Predictability: The Hidden Forces That Shape Our Decisions*. Harper, 2008.
18. *See* Hauser, M.D. *Moral Minds: The Nature of Right and Wrong*. Harper Perennial, 2006.

19. *Supra* note 15. Skepticism can dominate sometimes the business school agenda unfortunately when it comes to ethics instruction. As reported by Khurana (365):

    > One dean made the case for treating ethics in the context of the existing curriculum by noting that the most intelligent MBA students would not get much out of an ethics course because the subject could not be reduced to equations: 'unless the student is really interested in the issue [ethics], it's not effective because it's too easy to blow off. It's not like there's a formula that you absolutely have to learn. If you're not interested in a required course of this kind, you don't have to spend much time on it if you're a smart student, and you don't get anything out of it and the whole thing is lost.'
    >
    > He then goes on to say, however, "Other schools have a more optimistic view about their ability to educate students on ethics and have incorporated ethics courses either throughout the curriculum or through required courses."

20. *See* Dranove, D. & Marcinano, S. *Kellogg on Strategy: Concepts, Tools and Frameworks For Practitioners*. Wiley, 2005: Figure 1.1, Economic Profit and Its Sources, page 12:

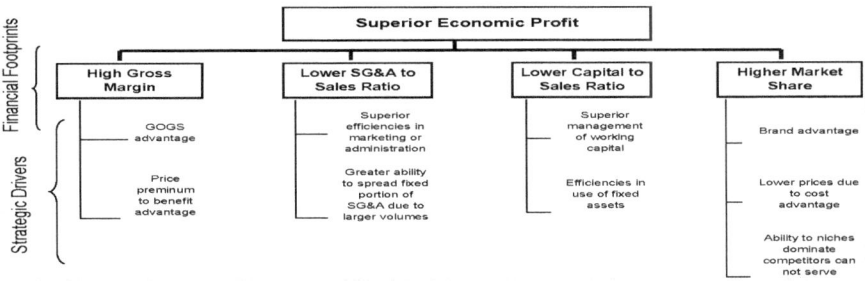

21. *See* In re The Walt Disney Company Derivative Litigation (Del.S.Ct. 411,2005)
22. Steven A. Holmes, Fannie Mae Eases Credit To Aid Mortgage Lending, *New York Times*, September 30, 1999, http://query.nytimes.com/gst/fullpage.html?res=9C0DE7DB153EF933A0575AC0A96F95
23. *See* Schwab, K. Global Corporate Citizenship: Working With Government and Civil Society. Foreign Affairs, January/February 2008, 107–118.
24. Id,107.
25. *See* Prahalad, C.K. *The Fortune at the Bottom of the Pyramid: Eradicating Poverty Through Profits (Enabling Dignity and Choice Through Markets)*. Wharton School Publishing, 2005.
26. *Id*.
27. The acronym stands for political (regulatory), economic, social and technical analysis of the firm's environment and their expected trends.
28. The acronym stands for the strengths and weaknesses of the firm and the opportunities and threats provided by or present in its external environment.

29. A suggestion by Ghoshal and Moran is to think of employees as "voluntary investors" in the enterprise. Our concern is that that would result in little more than a feel good concept at times of real stress in the organization. Also, it fails to take into consideration necessarily the impact that the firm's activities socially and environmentally.
30. Khurana goes on to say, "if university business schools … are to continue to play a role that could not be filled equally well by corporate training programs or for-profit, purely vocational business schools, they belong in the forefront of the decision now taking place among informed and thoughtful citizens all around the globe about the shape that capitalism should take in the twenty-first century."
31. For an absolutely wonderful book detailing how the environmental component of the model can be taught, see: Peter Senge, Bryan Smith, Nina Kruschwitz, Joe Laur and Sara Schley. *The Necessary Revolution: How Individuals and Organizations Are Working Together To Create A Sustainable World*. Doubleday, 2008.

Reading 1.2

An Introduction to Ethics: Framing and Key Themes in Business Ethics

Andrew C. Wicks, Bidhan L. Parmar, R. Edward Freeman,
Jared Harris, and Jenny Mead

You represent a small investment firm in country X. You want to gain access to a business in another country where business is based on relationships. You met with a potential broker whom you are led to believe is both trustworthy and could connect you with the kind of organizations that are vital to the success of your firm and doing business in country X. During the meeting, which the broker has arranged at his home, he tells you that trust is vital to doing business with him and that he needs to know that you can be trusted. He asks you to deposit $80,000 in a bank account he specifies within 24 hours. Once he receives the money, he will wire it back to your account. He says without trust and your show of good faith, he will be unable to do business with you. You ask around and find that requests such as this are common practice. What do you do?

MOST PEOPLE HAVE ONE OF TWO reactions to this kind of situation. Either they have a strong moral intuition toward one of the options, or they experience conflicting moral intuitions and cannot decide between the two. They ask themselves: "Is this person honest and simply testing me and then will be the broker I hope for, or is this a set-up and I'm being asked to pay a bribe—or simply give away $80,000 for nothing?" Moral intuitions or sentiments (as Adam Smith called them) are our gut reactions to situations as to what is right or wrong. They are developed over time from our past experiences and social interactions. We may regret decisions that are based just on moral intuition when we find they missed the mark or don't stand up to scrutiny. It is only when we do the hard work of analyzing a situation and meshing intuition with reason that we can be confident that we are making the better choice. Turning to analysis and using reason are critical ways to build on moral intuitions and ensure that they stand up under the scrutiny supported by ethics.

Andrew C. Wicks, et al., "An Introduction to Ethics: Framing and Key Themes in Business Ethics," pp. 1-6. Copyright © 2009 by Darden Business Publishing. Reprinted with permission.

What Is Ethics?

Translated from ancient Greek, ethics means "theory of living." In answering the question: "How should *we* live?," one engages in a consideration of ethics—thinking about what is right and wrong. Ethical deliberation is the process of reasoning about what is right and wrong, specifically giving defensible reasons for actions. Ethics requires that we engage others in conversations regarding our concerns and offers a check on our moral intuition as well as on opportune action to find better ways to live. The process of moral judgment—deciding what is right and wrong and refining moral intuition—is a critical tool for managers, particularly in challenging situations where others might question their judgment.

It is important to point out that ethics is more than an individual's view of things; it is also tied to a larger communal context—an organization, an industry, a community, a nation, or the globe. Ethics is about how one should live as an individual as well as how to get along with others. Ethics assumes that people are accountable for their actions, both to themselves and others. Every day, managers make decisions that can affect customers, employees, financiers, partners, the community, and the world in powerful ways. Since managers are accountable to these groups, they should have good reasons for their actions that go beyond mere intuition and be able to explain why they make the choices they do.

Disagreements in Ethics

People see the world in different ways. These differences can lead to disagreement about what is right and wrong, so people often associate ethics with conflict or disagreement. To offer morally defensible reasons for an action, one must understand where disagreement occurs in the conversation about morality. People can disagree about the facts of a situation, the values and principles involved, or about the language and framing.

In the paragraph that introduces this note, one might doubt the claim that the broker is trustworthy and will return the money. Believing or not believing this information can drastically change the options that one would consider. There may also be critical pieces of information missing. In addition to clarifying the facts about which there is disagreement, it is important to clarify the facts about which there is agreement, because these can provide a starting point for a constructive solution.

Even if there is agreement regarding the facts of the situation, there may still be disagreement about what one should do. This is disagreement about values and principles. In the situation at the beginning of the note, even if one accepts all the factual parameters, one may still disagree about the values and their priority. Should I focus on self-preservation as my primary value and think about how my choices do a better or worse job of realizing that value? Or should I be focused on doing what is best for the company and my being a loyal employee?

Finally, there can be disagreement on the framing of the situation. One might question the either/or framing of it. Would one really be fired if he or she made (or didn't make) the payment? Couldn't one reason with the broker or one's boss, to avoid this sticky situation? It might be that the broker can be persuaded, and there may be a way to satisfy both the values of self-preservation and company loyalty—or not. How a decision is framed delimits the options and considerations given to it. Is this a decision about duty to the shareholders or about duty to oneself? Each framing guides the manager toward certain conclusions. Being clear about the framing and language of the situation can go a long way in understanding one's own beliefs and values as well as those of others.

Putting Business and Ethics Together[1]

Questions about right and wrong matter, and they can be asked in all areas of our lives. In the context of business, managers can think about the connection between business and ethics in two ways. The first and most common way is to conceptualize business and ethics as two distinct disciplines. Business is usually seen as being only about the numbers and is hard, analytical, and factual, so the right thing to do is usually apparent from the analysis— do that which maximizes value for the shareholder. Ethics, on the other hand, is seen as soft, subjective, and relative. In this view, ethics affects business like a tax: it is imposed by outsiders, usually government. It holds back a manager's maximization of profits and can encumber good managerial practice. Along with this view is the idea that ethics is only about curbing illegal business practices—the usual don't lie, don't cheat, and don't steal view of ethics called *separation fallacy*.

The second view is that business and ethics are fundamentally connected. Both are semisoft, meaning that they are more like an art than a science, but that there can still be agreement on the fundamentals. In this view, every decision a manager makes has some ethical content, just as each decision can affect the financials of a business. Ethics is seen as fundamental to trade, rather than peripheral. Without the norms of trust and honesty, trade and business are not possible. Ethics is about more than just avoiding illegal actions; it is about choosing between alternatives in a way that benefits rather than harms stakeholders. This view is called the *integration thesis*.

Many managers have been socialized and inculcated into one or another of these views. Each view guides managerial action in different ways, and managers have a choice as to which view they will subscribe to. The question of how to frame a situation is also a moral question. Regardless of which view managers subscribe to, they must have morally defensible reasons for doing so, as opposed to merely relying on gut reactions.

Ethics and the Law[2]
Similarities and Differences

The law and ethics are interrelated but distinct. At a basic level, the law—referring primarily to criminal law—can be described as socially enforced standards of minimally moral behavior. Although people often focus on laws or specific legal rules, the law is best described as a dynamic and evolving code in which minimum standards of behavior are continually defined and revised. Because of its pervasiveness and the formidable sanctions behind it, the law is a significant source of guidance for managerial decisions.

Laws articulate a code of behavior the violation of which can result in a loss of basic rights and freedoms. At its most basic, the law tells people how not to behave. Thus while the law is based on ethical ideas, it is focused primarily on things we ought not to do and sets a standard below which one's behavior should not fall. It does not go very far in telling people how they should behave or what sort of standards and aspirations they ought to have. These positive considerations are the domain of ethics. Ethics provides resources to help individuals order their activities in ways that advance their goals as well as the goals of others and to create agreements and arrangements that enable all to live a better life.

Given this rough distinction between the two fields, it is important to point out that there is often a substantial gap between what is legal and what is ethical. Within the realms of possible legal choices, the subset of ethically sound choices may be significantly smaller. Just because there are no laws governing an activity does not mean that it is ethical.

Problems with the Law

Relying on the law or using legal reasoning as a primary mode of thinking can be problematic for a number of reasons:

1. *Ambiguity*: Because law evolves through a process rather than merely a static set of rules, defining laws and specific statutes is only the first step in discerning what is and is not legal. Laws and statutes are often stated very generally and can be interpreted in a variety of ways. Even when there is significant case law to establish precedents, a variety of factors can affect how laws are applied—judges, juries, changes in the political climate, or how a case is argued. While there are often some guidelines on what activities to avoid, there are few positions to take that will guarantee that one will not be sued or be held liable.

2. *Changes in the law*: Laws and the law are not static. They are subject to changes in public sentiment over time. They often lag behind new technologies, procedures, and developments. In some cases, law is created or articulated by judges even though no formal statutes exist. Just because something is legal today doesn't mean it will be legal tomorrow. Absence of a specific law does not mean that one won't be sued. For example, A. H. Robbins met the existing legal standards of the FDA in testing the Dalkon Shield, yet when consumers experienced serious health hazards from the prescribed use of the product, the courts held the firm liable to customers, and it had to pay millions of dollars in damages. In the face of activity that the public finds irresponsible, it may press state and federal legislators to pass laws to both punish and prevent such activity.

3. *Reactive and adversarial*: Shaping one's response to a situation in legal terms typically means one is reacting to a situation that has become problematic. In general, this is a suboptimal strategy for managers. Instead of trying to resolve conflicts that arise, it is often more beneficial for managers to search for proactive strategies that prevent confrontations with stakeholders and offer mutually beneficial arrangements. Frequently, the adversarial posture of legal thinking creates a divide where disagreements become greater and differences are exacerbated.

Overlaps Between Ethics and the Law

Ethical problems that emerge may occasionally provide the basis for legislative action, both in the form of specific statutes and other forms of regulation. The environmental movement provides an illustrative example. Numerous environmental issues that began as moral concerns among the public or a particular stakeholder group have led to a wide array of regulative organizations and laws. Thus today's moral problem could end up as the basis for future legislation or public policy.

Ethics as Sanctioned by the Law

The U.S. Sentencing Commission guidelines passed in 2004 by Congress make ethics an important consideration for all corporations. These laws tie corporate liability for misdeeds, as well as the degree of punishment, to the ethical climate of the firm (e.g., whether there are explicit codes of ethics, standards of behavior, mission statements, and so forth, which are comprehensive and enforced). Where such activity is present, courts are more likely to see misdeeds by employees as isolated events for which the firm as a whole is less likely to be held liable. In instances where firms are liable, the existence of effective ethics programs is specifically factored into the determination of fines and penalties.

The law is clearly an important source of guidance for firms, both in the operation of day-to-day business and in facing complex and difficult dilemmas; however, the above considerations suggest that it is inadequate as the sole or even primary source of direction. While at one level doing ethics is inescapable—given that one's choices and priorities reflect certain values whether they are consciously adopted or not—these considerations would indicate that it can be extremely beneficial to incorporate an explicit use of ethics or ethical thinking in how firms set their priorities and deal with difficult situations.

What Difference Does My Decision Make?

One of the potentially frustrating aspects of ethics is that the exercise of discussing cases and debating how to proceed can sometimes leave people more confused and uncertain than they were when they started. Rather than getting answers or coming closer to the truth, some case discussions make it seem as though these goals can be more elusive than before the discussion began. Frustration can lead to apathy, raising the question of why one should engage in the process at all—if there is no clear right answer, what difference does my choice make? How is my answer any better than anyone else's? Why "do" ethics at all? These are important and sensible questions, but the following considerations suggest why a particular decision matters.

Managers Are Held Accountable by Various Stakeholders

The decision made must be defensible to various stakeholder groups, particularly those to which the firm is most committed and those that have the most power to influence the fate of the firm. In many instances, a job could be at stake, the success of a particular product or project could be involved, possible legal action or public outcry could be at issue, and so on. In such circumstances, managers must pay careful attention to how they approach the problem, whom they decide to include, how and when they decide, as well as what they choose. The ability to defend a decision, its rationale, and the process of deliberation are vital to business success. Stakeholder groups that are relevant include superiors/colleagues in your firm, communities/customers and society as a whole, and other stakeholder groups who have an interest or stake in the outcome.

Ethical Problems Are Part of the Job

Managers are asked on a daily basis to weigh or balance responsibilities to various stakeholders. Resolving conflicting demands and obligations is part of a manager's responsibility. Just because these choices are difficult and complex doesn't mean they can be handed off to others or to "ethics experts." Ethics and the process of resolving ethical dilemmas is embedded within each person's responsibilities (in personal life, in an organizational role, or both). Ethics is everybody's business.

Personal Integrity

Managers' decisions should matter to them personally, particularly if there are important values or commitments at stake about which they have strong feelings (i.e., particular decisions may make them feel very uncomfortable or violate their sense of integrity). The movie *City Slickers* has a scene highlighting this issue. In a conversation between Billy Crystal and one of his friends, the friend describes a scenario where Crystal could have one night of pleasure with the woman of his dreams, and no one would ever find out. If he had the chance, would he do it? Crystal responds by saying he would not, not because he was worried his wife might find out, but because *he* would know (i.e., he could not live with himself if he were unfaithful to his wife).

Legal Reasoning Is Often Inadequate

Doing what the letter of the law says could still leave a firm open to civil and or criminal suits. Adopting a law-based approach puts firms in an adversarial posture with respect to others, which may be counterproductive to other objectives in facing a crisis, such as public trust (e.g., compare Johnson & Johnson in the Tylenol case with Burroughs Wellcome and the Sudafed tampering case). The U.S. Sentencing Commission guidelines create incentives for firms to aim at ethical performances rather than legal compliance. Taking the high road can be both cost-efficient and important for satisfying basic objectives of the firm.

The Indispensability of Ethics to Leadership

Ethics is an inescapable part of management and leadership. All managerial decisions involve weighing harms and benefits to stakeholders, considering core principles, asking questions about character, and maintaining healthy relationships with stakeholders. The challenge for leaders is thinking about how they want to manage and direct their organizations. Business management necessarily occurs in the realm of humans and human relationships. Ethics pushes managers to think about their goals, core principles for action, and who they are trying to be on the way to creating organizational excellence.

A critical leadership test is to make decisions in challenging circumstances where the right thing to do is not obvious. Making a decision and simply saying it was the right thing to do is not enough for leaders. They must understand the nuances and complexities involved in making good choices and be persuasive in convincing others that their decision is the best for the organization. It is precisely in those situations where the right thing to do isn't obvious that critical analysis and valid reasons for our decisions are especially important. Keeping credibility, maintaining confidence in our judgment, and convincing stakeholders we understand the issues and care about what is going on may be vital to our effectiveness as leaders, especially if they disagree with our choice.

Unfortunately, ethics is not easy. What separates leaders from managers is their ability to energize and motivate themselves and others around moral goals and means, as well as their ability to be thoughtful in complex situations. Those managers who take ethics seriously are poised to enter into the realm of real leadership. The complexity of our lives can be an obstacle for those looking for a quick and easy path, but for those who choose to rise to the challenge of leadership, it provides great opportunity.

Notes

1. R. Edward Freeman, "The Politics of Stakeholder Theory: Some Future Directions," *Business Ethics Quarterly* 4, no. 4 (1994); Philosophy Documentation Center: 409–21. doi:10.2307/3857340 http://philpapers.org/rec/FRETPO-10 (accessed Dec. 1, 2015); R. Edward Freeman, "Managing for Stakeholders," UVA-E-0383 (Charlottesville, VA: Darden Business Publishing, 2013).
2. We wish to thank Tom Brucker, JD, senior lecturer in business law, University of Washington Graduate School of Business, for his suggestions on this section.

Reading 1.3

The Moral Advantage

William Damon

The Four Dimensions of Business Morality

As a shorthand, I call the four dimensions of business morality the *generative, empathic, restrictive,* and *philanthropic* modes. *Generative* morality hinges on the use of moral imagination to create innovative initiatives that reflect noble purposes. *Empathic* morality hinges on the use of perspective-taking and the Golden Rule to build strong collaborative relations with employees, partners, investors, clients, and customers. *Restrictive* morality hinges on the use of ethics to prevent damaging and disreputable practices. *Philanthropic* morality hinges on the use of charitable giving to share part of one's profits with worthy causes. Some distinctions among the four are drawn in Table 1.3.1.

Generative morality arises from deep inner purposes and beliefs. Not everyone feels such purposes and beliefs, or sees how to connect them to their career choices. But those who do often find these core beliefs to be a valuable source of inspiration in their work. Deep purposes and beliefs provide the sparks of imagination that can give birth to a new business concept. They also can provide a sense of commitment that can sustain the concept during inevitable periods of doubt, stress, and temporary reversals. They provide a reason to go to the mat for an idea, a steel foundation for the persistence always needed to implement any innovation. I place this dimension first because it is the mode of morality that people tend to be most in tune with when they first choose a career and set their goals. People who enter business to make positive contributions to the world (the "what" and "why" questions discussed in the Introduction) are motivated by purposes and beliefs that can form the basis of a highly generative morality. The key to success […] is to nurture this fertile source of creative imagination rather than allowing it to fade away over the course of a career filled with compromise and burnout.

William Damon, "The Moral Advantage," *The Moral Advantage: How to Succeed in Business by Doing the Right Thing*, pp. 48-59, 163. Copyright © 2004 by Berrett-Koehler Publishers. Reprinted with permission.

TABLE 1.3.1 The Four Faces of Morality in Business

	Generative	**Empathic**	**Restrictive**	**Philanthropic**
Function	Inspiration	Collaboration	Protection	Promote worthy cause
Source	Deep beliefs	Perspective-taking	Traditional codes	Charitable impulse
Instrument	Imagination	Golden Rule	Conduct	Earned profits
Venue	Products, services	Relationships	Management	Outside institutions
Outcome	Innovation, sales	Trust, morale	Reputation, safety	Reputation, satisfaction

Empathic morality is an approach to business relationships that reflects the Golden Rule principle of treating others as you yourself would like to be treated. It fosters trust, collaboration, understanding, and communication. [...]

Restrictive morality is the widely shared societal code of ethics that protects people from trouble, regulates their behavior according to the traditional norms that society demands, guards their reputation, and provides them with safety from legal attack. It is the mode of morality most strongly emphasized by business-school ethics courses and corporate ethics training. Important though such training can be, its effectiveness often suffers by taking ethics out of the context of the broad personal and social concerns that are included in the other three moral dimensions. [...]

Philanthropic morality reflects a charitable impulse, donating a share of profits for altruistic ends. It requires the same sense of purpose, diligence, and humility that is required by the business success that brought the profits in the first place. When done properly, philanthropic morality reaps benefits beyond pure altruism, such as enhancing the reputation of the business leader and the company in the communities in which they operate. When done poorly, however, philanthropy causes more harm than good, damaging both the community and the donor's reputation. [...]

Using the Four Moral Dimensions to Build a Rewarding Career

In our interviews with top business leaders, we found frequent mention of all four dimensions of business morality. The men and women differed in which of these aspects they personally emphasized, but there was virtually no disagreement about their importance. [...] I illustrate how each dimension is used in a real business life, quoting some of the business leaders as they offer details about how they employed their moral convictions in the service of their work. [...] I have selected cases that represent especially relevant examples of the moral dimension discussed therein. But the set of interviews as a whole contains many other cases that I could have used to illustrate the same points, because all of the business leaders in our study expressed commitment to these moral modes.

Approximately two-thirds of the business leaders reported use of generative morality, in the sense of drawing on beliefs and purposes for inspiration. Many talked about how they used their moral imaginations to produce innovative business concepts, and to muster the persistence and commitment needed for sticking with a new idea despite skepticism and the risk of the unknown. Some said they actively train their minds to nurture this kind of moral creativity.

Many interviewees reported relying on religious or spiritual faith to spur creative inspiration and sustain their mental discipline, a characteristic not typically evident among business leaders because they tend to keep their faith private to avoid being perceived as imposing their own religious beliefs on employees. In our study, however, more than 90 percent of the people interviewed expressed a devout spiritual or religious faith of some kind. Few executives try to use their businesses to advocate for a particular religious or spiritual doctrine. Rather, they take their own inspiration and commitments from their faith, and keep it to themselves in their day-to-day business operations.

I first realized the power of generative morality a few years ago when I met with Sir John Templeton, the legendary business leader to whom I have dedicated this book. It was clear to me that Templeton's business accomplishments reflected a deeper sense of purpose, a purpose closely linked to his spiritual beliefs. For him, it was faith that fueled his moral imagination. Connecting the dots, I could see that this had been the primary wellspring of Templeton's daring and creative path to success.

When Templeton was active in business, he was an investment manager who gained international renown, a vast fortune, and a British knighthood for his distinguished service to the Crown. He was the first investment manager to create a global family of mutual funds. As early as the 1930s, before the advent of the personal computer or international jet travel, Templeton found economic value in places where few Western investors had thought to look—in Asia, the Middle East, Australia, even remote parts of Africa. The value was there. The Templeton funds grew from a one-room operation over a local police station into a multibillion-dollar corporation. The way that Templeton came up with this concept reveals how business leaders use generative morality as a source of innovative business concepts.

What gave him the vision to explore global investing and the fortitude to gamble in such little-known territories? One answer to this (not the only one, but a key piece of the puzzle) lies in Templeton's commitment to his particular faith. He devoutly believes in the love of all humanity, without discrimination of any sort. As a young man, Templeton first considered becoming a minister, but while in college he decided that his gifts were in financial analysis and that he could best serve God and humanity in this way. (He told me that his only regret is that he did not start his mutual funds earlier "because I would have served many more people.")

Central to Templeton's belief is the idea that all people are "only the tiniest part of God." Therefore, "each of us should try to love every human being without *any* exceptions, and not just a little bit, but unlimited love for every human being with absolutely no exceptions." Separating people by tribe, race, club, or nation is "probably not as healthy" as thinking of all humanity as one. Templeton is not a fan of narrow, overly chauvinistic sentiments that divide people. His purpose of celebrating the infinite worth of all people, and his belief in the essential unity of humanity, led him directly to the notion of global mutual finds. Although this notion has become commonplace in the financial world by now, it was radical and untested when Templeton first introduced it. Who, after all, could imagine that companies in strange, faraway places might be worth investing in? But the risks that he took on his faith's behalf were richly rewarded.

Templeton never used his companies to proselytize for his particular faith. He did not expect his employees or his customers to join his own church. What he *did* do was express his vision by founding a truly international, boundary-crossing approach to investing, an approach that seemed risky and audacious at the time but that ultimately proved brilliantly successful. Material success followed from Templeton's spiritual inspiration in ways that would be hard to trace without knowing his innermost sense of purpose.

A powerful concept lies at the heart of every successful business. In the most spectacular cases, the new business concept—a car in every garage, airplane travel for the masses, a computer on every desk—transforms the way people conduct their lives. How do businessmen and -women come up with powerful new ideas? Where do they get the nerve to commit themselves to an unproven idea when people who seem to know better say that they are crazy? Where does the spirit of innovation come from, and the mettle required to venture down a new road? Templeton gave me my first inkling of where successful businesspeople find this kind of inspiration and strength.

The other business leaders whom I interviewed filled in the rest of the story. […] I will present some further examples of the moral imagination at work.

Once a concept is born out of an inspiring sense of purpose, it must be communicated to those necessary to make the concept a reality: partners and investors, coworkers and employees, clients and customers. The communication must keep the company focused on the concept and see that it is executed with conviction. Such communication rests on the trust and respect of all those who must buy into the concept. Building trusting relationships among disparate groups of people is a serious accomplishment in itself, because each group—whether partners, employees, investors, or customers—has its own special interests at stake. The only way to get all of these people to trust what a leader is saying is to gain a reputation for decency and honesty in one's dealings with others.

Among the business leaders we interviewed, we found that many look to the age-old principle of the Golden Rule as their way to ensure that their behavior conforms to such standards as decency and honesty. At the heart of the Golden Rule is empathy, the sense that everyone shares in one another's joys and pains and therefore that everyone must care about the conditions in which others find themselves. In our study, almost all of the men and women expressed an active commitment to building trusting relationships through empathic understanding and other principles consistent with the Golden Rule. Without prompting, more than one-fourth invoked the Golden Rule itself to explain how they manage relations with partners, clients, and employees.

Closely tied to empathy is the capacity to take the perspective of the other, to "step inside another person's shoes." This capacity can be cultivated to great effect in one's business relationships. [...] I will present examples of how businesspeople employ empathy, perspective-taking, and the Golden Rule to cultivate the productive and trusting relations that they must build with colleagues, employees, and customers.

What applies within companies also applies among companies. In addition to fostering trusting communication within their own companies, business leaders today say that they must establish good collaborative relations *across* organizations, even in cases where those organizations have a fundamentally competitive relationship with one another. Some interviewees in the high-tech corridors of Silicon Valley and Boston, for example, called this "co-opetition," although others outside of those regions spurn this term as New Age jargon. Yet by whatever name this trend is called, most try to practice it, because they believe that in today's ever-shifting business world, this kind of cross-company teamwork provides a decisive advantage, an advantage that hinges on a leader's reputation for decent conduct and trustworthiness.

Beyond empathy, stringent ethical conduct—what I have called *restrictive morality*—is a key element in a reputation for trustworthiness. More than four-fifths of the business leaders in our study placed an extremely high priority on restrictive morality. Their commitment revolved around such values as resistance to corruption and refusal to cut corners in truthfulness, fairness, and respect for the law. These values guided their relations with partners, employees, customers, competitors, and society at large. The interviewees reported that these values had enabled them to reject frequent pressures to give (or take) bribes, to put out deceitful public information, to renege on contracts, to manipulate share prices, to cover up defective products, to steal other people's inventions, to cheat vendors or customers by unfair pricing, or to harm their communities through irresponsible environmental policies—any of which could spell trouble if practiced and then revealed.

This ethical sense also helped these business leaders establish dependable relations with colleagues and competitors. They see this as an urgent challenge in today's fluid marketplace. Because of globalization, technological innovation, and conglomeration, companies rise and disappear quickly. Jobs are created and lost overnight, and workers move on the instant they spot a new opportunity. What does this mean for working relationships within a company, including the bonds between leader and staff? Are traditional notions such as loyalty still useful, or even viable? Is teamwork possible among people who may become competitors by the time of the next paycheck? The business leaders in our study used ethical principles to create a spirit of cooperation in their intensely competitive environments.

Finally, philanthropic morality is a widely followed path of public service in the business world, as four-fifths of the business leaders in our study subscribed to such a practice. Philanthropy enables business leaders to define relations with the broader community in ways that yield benefits for both the community and the company, especially providing the company with compelling and legitimate public relations material. In certain cases, philanthropy can feed back to a business's founding mission, thus serving the generative function as well as the community-relations one. For example, a computer company that donates equipment to schools not only aids the worthy cause of education but also expands its future market by enlarging its consumer base and building brand recognition within it.

Although philanthropy rightly occupies an honored place among the four dimensions of business morality, it is not as certain a means to doing good as it may first appear. Believe it or not, simply giving away a bunch of money does not always improve the lot of those who receive it, as many philanthropists discover, to their regret. The same moral qualities that lead to success in business—purpose, insight, empathy, humility, honesty, trustworthiness—are also required for effective philanthropy. For this reason, among many others, philanthropy should never be seen as a sure-fire salvation for a corrupt and ruthless business career. Although careful philanthropy can bring many good things to the world, it is neither redemptive nor certain. Andrew Carnegie once said that it is harder to give money away well than to make it.

The Development of Moral Identity

The four dimensions of morality that I just described each serve an important function (outlined earlier in Table 1.3.1). In an operational sense, there is a time and a place for each one, because the moralities operate differently, solve distinct kinds of problems, and produce different sorts of results. But in a personal sense, these four dimensions develop together, as part of the person's never-ending quest to build an admirable character.

This is not to say, in reality, that anyone ever manages to act perfectly with respect to all four moral dimensions. Indeed, the reason that one's quest for character is never-ending is that everyone is far from perfect, and even the most reputable people will behave inconsistently at times. These dimensions themselves can stand in conflict, as when a creative idea that reflects a driving purpose (an example of generative morality) is misrepresented to best market the idea (a restrictive morality breach). Or any one of the moralities may be neglected for periods of time, as when a rising business leader decides that the time for philanthropic giving has not yet come.

In the long run, all four moral dimensions contribute to a full life in business, and a person fully armed has an enduring moral advantage. When integrated in a person's character, the four enhance and reinforce one another. The way that this happens in the course of development is by forging a strong *moral identity*. This process usually begins when young, often as early as adolescence (although it is never too late for someone to start), and it continues throughout life. Identity is a person's sense of who he or she is, and who he or she would like to become.[1] Moral identity is the part that revolves around the person's moral convictions—the sense that I am honest, compassionate, responsible, fair, and trustworthy, and that these are important defining features of who I am and what I want to be like.

The development of moral identity begins with the discovery of what convictions most matter to you. (This is what Robert Greenleaf meant by the "act of self-discovery" [...].) These convictions, once fully realized, directly lead to purposes to which you can dedicate yourself. For example, if you have a conviction that people have a right to food and shelter, you might dedicate yourself to purposes that provide these essential commodities to the poor. Of course, there are any number of ways that you might go about doing this, including new ways that others haven't thought of. When you dream up new ways of accomplishing a moral purpose, you are using your moral imagination, or engaging in an act of generative morality. In this sense, the drive to accomplish a moral purpose is the trigger for both the formation of moral identity and the acts of creation that generate new solutions to moral problems.

Once convictions are found and purposes established, they need to be pursued in a manner true to the moral nature of the conviction. Killing all poor people would not be a moral solution to eradicating poverty. The *means* of the act must be just as moral as the *ends.* No matter how lofty our goals, they have little moral worth unless we pursue them with decency, honesty, compassion, and respect. For this reason, developing the capacity (and the will) to act empathically and ethically is critical to the forging of a strong moral identity. Empathy and ethics ensure that moral purposes will be pursued by moral means. In the case of empathy, we follow moral means out of concern for the other, as expressed by the Golden Rule. In the case of ethics, we follow moral means out of conformity to the codes of society. The two together create a powerful incentive to act in an upstanding manner.

Capping the development of moral identity is the sense of the self as a responsible citizen in one's community and society. This sense of citizenship develops gradually over the adult years, as a person takes on responsible social roles such as worker, spouse, parent, and active community member. In business, a prime way to express a sense of responsible citizenship in the broader society is through philanthropy. Business leaders usually wait to begin their philanthropic efforts until after they have established their businesses, and they accelerate them only when profitability grows. But, as I noted previously, even though philanthropy tends to grow later in life, it draws on the same moral convictions and virtues used in the earlier achievement of business success. In this sense, philanthropic morality is linked to all other components of a person's developing moral identity.

Figure 1.3.1 indicates the ordering of the four dimensions of business morality in the course of a person's development of moral identity. The logic of the pyramid shape is that the direction of development (beginning with purpose and moving up through the empathic, restrictive, and philanthropic moralities) also reveals the practical relationship of the moralities to one another in the business world. Although each moral dimension plays an important role in itself, some are more fundamental than others in the sense that they drive and sustain the others. The foundation of business success is a sense of moral purpose (at the bottom of the pyramid). Without purpose, a person tends to see the other dimensions of morality merely as rules and proscriptions: they are to be followed when necessary (or convenient), but they do not have a compelling rationale of their own. A lack of purpose will always put the other moral dimensions on shaky ground. Only when shored up by a constant focus on purpose can they be reliably counted on.

Moving up the pyramid, all dimensions of moral action draw on prior dimensions for their meaning and sustenance. Restrictive morality, for example, can be no more than a negative force—and consequently a weak one—without a concern for purpose, fairness, and compassion. When based on an awareness of these fundamental moral concerns, the restrictive ethical codes that constrain illegitimate behavior come naturally, because they feel internally generated rather than externally imposed. Similarly, philanthropy can be an empty

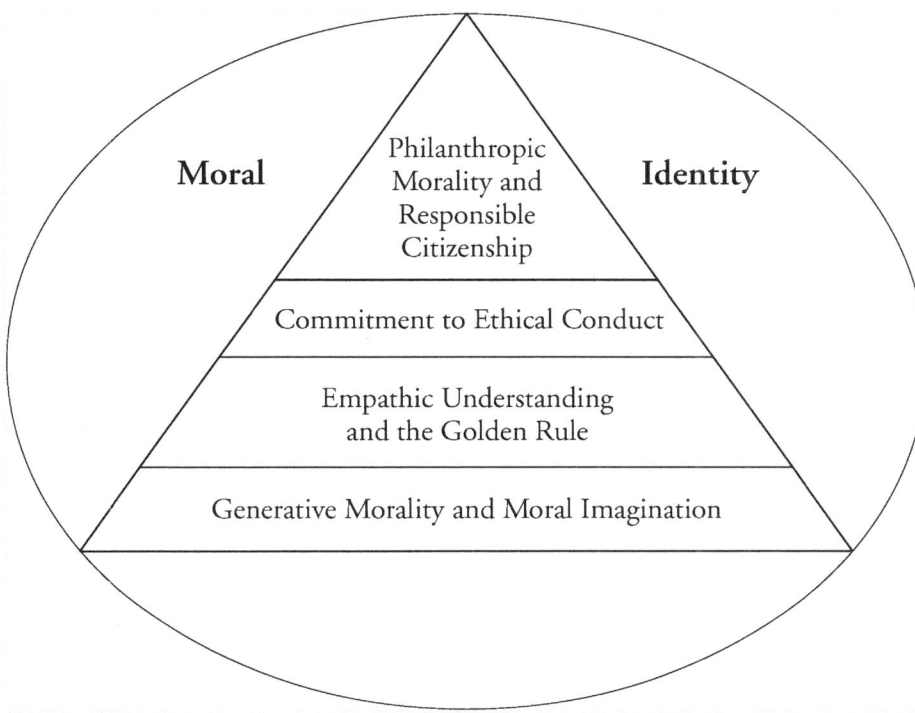

FIGURE 1.3.1 The pyramid of business moralities

shell, possibly doing more harm than good, unless it is based on a sense of moral purpose and conducted in an empathic and ethical manner.

Surrounding the four moral dimensions in Figure 1.3.1 is moral identity, from which all moral commitment springs. As a rule, a person acquires the elements of moral identity in the same order as indicated by the direction of the pyramid, with purpose coming first (often in late adolescence), followed by commitments to empathic understanding, ethics, and philanthropy (or other acts of responsible citizenship). But the order is not a rigid one, and there is always interaction among the moral dimensions as they develop. They play in to one another, growing organically as they feed the person's moral identity. In the end, in the best cases, the four dimensions become fully integrated, as part of a mature personality. This integration is what I refer to as "integrity," the heart and soul of moral character.

Note

1. E. Erikson, *Identity: Youth and Challenge*, New York: W. W. Norton, 1968.

Applied Ethics Case: The Heinz Dilemma

Heinz's wife was dying of a rare form of cancer. There was only one available medication that her physicians thought might cure her, but it was an advanced formula that XYZ Pharmaceutical Company had only recently obtained FDA approval. The drug was extremely costly to produce due to expensive production equipment and singular production techniques. Thus, the pharmaceutical company was selling the drug at 100 times the production costs.

Heinz went to everyone he knew to obtain the funds to purchase the drug but could only collect half of what the drug cost. He sought an audience with representatives of XYZ Pharmaceutical Company, told them of his wife's illness and his inability to raise the needed money to purchase the drug. The representatives refused to sell him the drug at a discounted price, as the company had invested massive funds in research, development, and equipment. It was essential that the company make a profit from the drug. Making a profit was the top priority for the company. Heinz was devastated.

Did XYZ Pharmaceutical Company make the appropriate decision in the Heinz case? Discuss the case from the perspective of the organization's values.

Post-Reading Questions

"A Method for Embedding Business Ethics into Traditional Business Analysis"

1. The authors argue that "unless doing the right thing or good thing lies at the center of a person's approach to decision making," instruction on ethics will not have a significant impact on future decision making. Defend or refute this position.
2. The authors wrote that the law does not provide sufficient reason for an organization to look beyond its own interests and the interests of their stake holders. Do organizations have an ethical obligation beyond their own financial interests? Defend your response.
3. The concluding argument is that business schools are not keeping pace with the changes happening in the world. Based on your educational and professional experience, do you agree with this assessment? Please consider the interests of shareholders.

"An Introduction to Ethics: Framing and Key Themes in Business"

1. Describe an ethical dilemma when you had to lean on your "moral intuition" to make a decision. What was the outcome? Did you trust your intuition? What would you have done differently? Why?

2. The author presents two views on how business and ethics are put together. The first proposes that the two concepts are two distinct disciplines while the second proposes that they are fundamentally connected. Reflect on your experiences and describe your perspective regarding the connection between business and ethics.
3. Rarely do right or wrong answers exist in ethical dilemmas. This massive gray area could lead to apathy when considering ethical issues in business. Given this possibility, why do you believe it is important to study ethics in business? Or, is it? Please support your response.

"The Moral Advantage"
1. Do you agree with the claim that morality is the best pathway to business success, and the surest means of promoting one's own career interests and the interests of those with whom one does business?
2. Support or dispute the statement, "In business, if there is a choice between doing the right thing and making a profit, the moral choice must be to do the right thing." Please consider the interests of shareholders in your response.
3. "Nice guys finish last" is a common expression. Will behaving ethically ultimately advance a career in the long run or will the nice individuals finish last? Please explain your position.

Videos Retrieved from the Internet

"Panel Discussion: Embedding Ethics and Compliance in your Multicultural Organization"

https://www.youtube.com/watch?time_continue=2&v=5_DSUwDtwCg&feature=emb_logo

This video presents a panel of corporate executives discussing the challenges of embedding ethics in organizations.

"Embedding Organizational Ethics in the Way We Do the Work"

https://www.youtube.com/watch?v=yGAA3HJlIos&feature=emb_logo

This video is a presentation on the challenges of embedding ethics in the health care industry.

"Creating Ethical Cultures in Business"

https://www.youtube.com/watch?v=wzicXbnmllc&feature=emb_logo

This video presents ideas to develop the skills necessary to act with courage and ingenuity in the face of challenging situations.

Internet Sites on Embedding Ethics in Organizations

"Three Ways to Embed Ethics and Honesty in Your Organization"

https://www.claconnect.com/resources/articles/three-ways-to-embed-ethics-and-honesty-within-your-organization

This article discusses the importance of culture, accountability, and governance in organizations to improve ethical behavior.

"Embedding Ethics in Business and Higher Education: From Leadership to Management Imperative"

http://www.bhef.com/publications/embedding-ethics-business-and-higher-education-leadership-management-imperative

This article discusses myths, mismanagement, and management strategy relating to organizational ethics.

"The Truth about Ethical Organizations"

https://www.huffingtonpost.com/mark-pastin/the-truth-about-ethical_b_10548990.html

This article outlines factors that improve organization ethics.

"Culture Matters: The Advantage of a Strong Ethical Cultures are Manifold"

https://insights.ethisphere.com/culture-matters/

This paper discusses the importance of measuring ethical behavior.

"How to Build an Ethical Business Culture"

https://www.entrepreneur.com/article/224453

This article outlines steps for building an ethical business culture.

Section II

Ethical Challenges in Today's Multi-Generational Workplace

"The American work ethic is something to be admired. Our workforce, regardless of position, works hard to produce the best product and serve customers to the best of their ability."
Leonard Boswell

IN THIS CHAPTER WE EXPLORE THE challenges of ethical leadership in the multi-generational workplaces you will be entering. For the first time in history, American employers have the potential of five generations working together in the same workplace. The authors discuss how millennials are welcomed into the workplace and the challenges for them, coworkers, and business leaders. What are the generational differences individuals have in defining work values, communications vehicles, and personal work satisfaction? How do business leaders define expectations that are satisfactory to all? These articles are designed to help you better understand today's organizational complexities that leaders are confronting.

By 2020 it is estimated that millennials will comprise half of the U.S. workforce. Jessica McManus Warnell in her book *Engaging Millennials for Ethical Leadership: What Works for Young Professionals and Their Managers*, explores the changing nature of business operations and the significant relevance millennials' talents, skills, abilities, values, and attitudes are having in this ever-changing workplace. She notes that businesses are more connected and communicative, internally and externally, than ever before. These connections can be leveraged for an effective ethical business, where collaboration is the key. Collaboration prompts the consideration of "voice" or ways in which individuals in organizations engage with one another around values, goals, objectives, and activities.

The author discusses generational differences, commonalities, models, and strategies that provide opportunities for exercising responsibility and building consensus based on generational shared values. By focusing on best millennial management practices, she identifies strategies that develop a culture of openness, transparency, and shared purpose that promotes opportunities for expressing values that can be the foundation for ethical organizations.

Finally, Ms. Warnell discusses the role of corporate social responsibility in building intergenerational consecutiveness. She suggests that increasingly sophisticated ethics and compliance programs are creating new norms in individual conduct.

Author Kathryn Woods's article, "Organizational Ambidexterity and the Multi-Generational Workforce," addresses the challenges of organizational ambidexterity in today's organizations trying to succeed in a changing and complex global environment. The organizational workforce is being impacted by falling birthrates, increased life expectancy, demographic shifts, diversity and inclusion, free movement of labor, and shifting values. These shifts present multigenerational workforce challenges and opportunities for leaders. The author reviews literature that suggests that employee values and preferences differ among generational cohorts that challenges the organizational structure. Successful leadership requires implementing new strategies for addressing gaps in a multigenerational workforce to ensure high performance. Through this inquiry the author provides a model for an ambidexterity structure to overcome challenges and capitalize on the dynamic, changing workforce.

Pre-Reading Questions

As you read the chapter articles, reflect on the following:
- What should be millennials' expectations in a five-generation workplace?
- What contribution (talents, skills, and abilities) can millennials provide to reduce the complexities of five generations working together?
- What can millennials learn from senior colleagues? What can they teach senior leaders?

Reading 2.1

Altogether, Now: Engagement and Multigenerational Workplaces

Jessica McManus Warnell

NEXT WE TURN TO EXPLORATION OF the changing nature of business, and the particular relevance of millennial skills and interests to this new space in which engagement and connections are critical. We will explore these characteristics, and consider how they can contribute to productive corporate cultures. Companies are increasingly relying on groups, teams, and multi-team systems to accomplish the complex tasks faced by the modern workplace.[1] Businesses are more connected and communicative, internally and externally, than ever before. These connections can be leveraged toward effective, ethical business, and collaboration is key. Thinking about our connections at work prompts consideration of "voice," or the ways in which we engage with one another around values, goals, objectives, and activities. Importantly, the decision to voice and act on values, both in accordance with personal goals defined individually, and with professional goals such as those defined by our organizations, can be enhanced through training and development.

Why does this consideration of voice matter and have particular resonance with millennial talent? We know that engaged and connected workplaces make for productive and successful companies. Millennial workers are motivated to contribute to the connected workplace, because we also know that millennials express an explicit desire for connections with peers and colleagues. This penchant can enhance economic viability. Research supports the idea of shared leadership, noting that long-term benefits accrue through more balanced, collaborative perspectives in leadership and decision making.[2] "Nearly every person is capable of taking on some leadership responsibility and positively contributing to organizational success. In this regard, knowledge should always trump status .... It is important for the organization to create an environment where every employee is encouraged to provide leadership, not simply those with the highest status or title."[3] These scholars also note the connections between responsible

---

Jessica McManus Warnell, "Altogether, Now: Engagement & Multigenerational Workplaces," *Engaging Millennials for Ethical Leadership: What Works For Young Professionals and Their Managers*, pp. 47-69, 203-206. Copyright © 2015 by Business Expert Press. Reprinted with permission.

leadership, corporate social responsibility (CSR), effective teamwork, and productive organizations: "Shared leadership offers the potential to encourage responsibility at the core of the influence process through the naturally occurring balance that is fostered by spreading leadership throughout a workforce rather than centralizing it in the hands of a few formally designated leaders."[4] Not surprisingly, this approach is quite attractive to millennials, and it has been shown to enhance success across all levels of the organization. Thus, exploring these dynamics can be helpful for young professionals and their managers.

Shared decision making acknowledges that collaborative work is key, and this collaboration can begin between employee and manager. [...] for our purposes here it is important to acknowledge the foundation of the employee–manager relationship for engaged, collaborative, multigenerational cultures. Thus, we can consider another expressed desire of millennials at work—training and development, and regular and open feedback from their superiors. This desire for information exchange extends to matters typically reserved for more senior employees,[5] which, of course, has implications that are interesting for multigenerational cultures. Our task as managers is to influence these dynamics. If we emphasize developing one's skills and voice, in light of research that demonstrates that exchange of diverse ideas and analyses lead to enhanced creativity, opportunities, risk management strategies, and other benefits, we acknowledge that millennials' proclivity toward and comfort with dialogue—encouraged, open, ongoing and two-way—fosters organizational cultures that encourage leveraging our voices toward shared goals.

When we thoughtfully design and implement professional development at work, we can enhance learning and contribution by all employees toward shared goals and outcomes. Managers have a mandate to cultivate employee behavior to align with values and ethical standards of the organization. They can also foster new and further development of key issues within the company as identified by employees, who are increasingly expressing their commitments to ethical workplaces. Fostering a collaborative culture engages all levels of talent, allows for employee alignment with corporate goals, and encourages ownership and commitment toward enhancing the success of the firm.

Commitment to working together toward shared values can begin with considerations of motivation—*why* do we do what we do at work? A fundamental consideration [...] explores why individuals choose to act, or not. This practice "voicing values" can be an invaluable part of professional development. Research indicates that a shared characteristic of those who act with moral courage in the face of confounding circumstances—gathered from situations as perilous as those faced by rescuers providing safety to those under Nazi threat during WWII—is prescripting, or anticipating values challenges and sharing, out loud, how to confront these challenges.[6] Again we see the roles here for professionals, both business people and academics in our business schools. Professional development that involves exploration of case studies, such as those provided in this volume, and "scripting" responses to ethical challenges, can be an effective approach. Determining mechanisms for practicing choice and developing our professional voice is the domain of business schools, and should be that of management as well.

We can consider another millennial phenomenon for clarity. We have all heard the frustration aimed at "helicopter parents" and perhaps lamented the state of "kids today" (as we simultaneously help our progeny complete their college applications with verve and polish). The culture of attention in which millennials were raised—these children of the baby boomers, let us remember who parented them!—is unprecedented. Those experiences of early and consistent intervention and feedback, with their corollary—the self-esteem-building focus where every child gets a trophy, for showing up and giving his or her best—can prove challenging as these young people enter a world rife with competition and little hand-holding.

It is unsurprising that these experiences translate into specific desires at work. Millennials expect not only frequent communication with supervisors, but that the communication be more positive and more affirming than has been the case with those in other generations.[7] Scholars posit that this need for affirmation develops from a constant flow of supportive messages from parents, teachers, and coaches during childhood. Perhaps we can understand, then, why young professionals may be struggling to reconcile the messages from their youth—*Reach for the stars! You can be whatever you want to be (and you'll be great at it)!*—with the current economic conditions and a business community that does not always seem to respond to this approach.

Toward Effective Engagement

Can we channel these tendencies in a positive way, rather than simply lamenting them? Collaborative cultures begin with communication. At even entry- and low-level positions, millennials express a need to be "kept in the loop" of information and expect that supervisors will freely share information such as strategic plans even during the formulation stage by senior management.[8] These tendencies have strong roots, thus, "as teens, [millennials] became comfortable expressing their thoughts and opinions to adults, expecting credibility despite their young age and lack of experiences … . They have also been encouraged by their parents to challenge authority, and to assert themselves, asking for preferential treatment when they believe they can get it."[9]

Therein lies the responsibility of our business schools, and of managers. We would do well to emphasize to young talent that increased engagement must be associated with increased responsibility. Experiential learning through internships and project-based learning are helpful approaches here and many business schools offer these opportunities as a core component of the curriculum. Modeling and providing opportunities for exercising this responsibility is critical for managers. It is worth it—research tells us that investing millennials with more and broader responsibilities can foster feelings of involvement, which in turn fosters organizational attachment and performance.[10]

The goal again becomes encouraging manager openness to millennial strengths, and its necessary corollary, enhancing millennials' appreciation for work relationships and respect for experience. Organizational openness can create a space in which frank communication and problem solving between millennials and their supervisors occurs.[11] Research indicates that consistent communication, regular feedback, and other engagement between supervisor and employee lead to enhanced organizational outcomes. We saw this finding reflected in our own millennial interviews, and as one that may be quite different than that of previous generations: "*I had two different internship experiences ... [during one] I talked to my boss every single day, multiple times a day and I was getting constant feedback on how I was doing .... I always knew if I was doing a good job or what I could do differently. I enjoyed this much more.*"

Developing and encouraging voice at work, which includes effective, constructive engagement around values and perspectives, can channel these characteristics. Further, because of the parenting millennials have often experienced, they clearly value and expect personal achievement. Managers can capitalize on this value toward organizational goals. These need not be resource-intensive. Techniques might include peer recognition of goal achievement and other means to incentivize performance toward shared goals. Acknowledging the role of institution-building in professional leadership development is another opportunity here. A natural place for fostering consensus is around values at work, including considerations of such questions as, *What is our firm's purpose? How can we meet our goals responsibly and sustainably?* Open and participatory communication on these issues can net important advantages for the company.

This task of building consensus and shared engagement is not easy. The oppositional nature of millennials and other age cohorts at work, and of young talent "versus" the establishment, is regularly highlighted in the media, such as this *Businessweek* feature:

> It's the fight of a generation. In this corner, weighing in at 42.5 million people, with a 12.3 percent unemployment rate and $294 billion of combined student loan debt, wearing skinny jeans and headphones: 20 to 29-year-olds. *And* in this corner, tipping the scale at 36.9 million people, with an unemployment rate of 6.6 percent and a median household net worth of $162,000, wearing Crocs and a pair of bifocals: 55 to 64-year-olds. Let's get ready to rumble.[12]

Of course, and as this article's author notes, more realistically millennials and baby boomers are not competing for the same jobs. But considering the relative status of each group can illustrate some of the respective challenges that may engender more *understanding and connection*. The economy matters for both. Young people with lower earning potential in their future than their elder peers, mounting student loan debt, and significantly higher unemployment rates (and the societal challenges we all face) are immediate concerns for millennials, while boomers struggle with relatively more damaging unemployment and shrinking retirement funds—our *Businessweek* author here ends with this less-than-optimistic quote: "Both [millennial and boomer] situations are terrible, but their problems are different."[13]

One student respondent noted his perception of a disconnect and misunderstanding:

> I think that there is a definite distinction between the work ethic of my generation and that of my grandparents. I think that the generalization that my entire generation is comprised of selfish, lazy, & entitled individuals is unfair. I have many peers who are quite the opposite. I think the problem that causes these perceptions is how drastically different the culture that these different generations were born into. My generation seems to be more open minded on social issues. … We were also born into a more stable and very technologically advanced economy. I believe this greatly impacts older generations' view of us millennials because the concept of what constitutes work has greatly changed. … Instead of looking for jobs, many of us are looking for callings. This is an opportunity many members of older generations did not have. In addition, with how quickly technology has evolved in the last 10 to 15 years our entire world has been changed. It is my generation that has grown up with all of the technological advancements and because of this I think it has impacted our way of problem solving in that we instinctively tend to find solutions that involve technology as a way to minimize the necessary work for a result.

Focusing on shared values is more productive for all of us. My contention is that we share many values, and we simply manifest them differently. A study of generations and their values at work[14] found that millennials, generation Xers, and baby boomers all shared the same top-five expectations of their employers:

- challenging work;
- competitive compensation;
- opportunities for advancement, and chances to grow in their jobs;

- fair treatment;
- work–life balance.

This does not mean that cross-generational friction does not occur. Rather, it reminds us of a useful starting point for organizational cohesion and development. All employees can benefit from a culture that encourages proactive decision making and provides opportunity for development and growth. Here we can consider the *Giving Voice to Values* pillar of emphasizing shared values for effective decision making. These values can be a foundation to which we can appeal when trying to address values conflicts. They allow us to consider effective strategies for pursuing shared goals. Articulating and communicating these values, including through technological tools [...], is step one. We can then consider how we model, incentivize, and reinforce them.

Managers can help build these bridges toward engaged multigenerational workforces that collaborate around organizational goals. Recognizing potential issues and proactively addressing them is key. Research on generational team conflict at work[15] identifies four organizationally essential team activities as the roots of most challenges:

- choosing where and when to work;
- communicating among team members;
- getting together;
- finding information or learning new things.

Older colleagues' general conception of work as a "place" versus younger employees' perspective of work as something you do, anywhere, anytime, can be challenging for shared responsibilities. Acknowledging the changing nature of business can be reflected in policies and procedures. Thus, "today most tasks do not require synchronous activities, yet many in older generations—including many senior executives—continue to expect synchronous behavior" despite the realities that the nature of work in most sectors of the economy has changed from the 8 to 5 of previous iterations of work life.[16] In addition, communication can be an issue.

> The crux of most technology-based team misunderstandings is not the technology *per se*—it is how team members interpret each others' intentions based on communication approaches. Younger members are accustomed to rapid responses from peers; they are likely to feel frustrated and, at times, rejected if they don't hear from older colleagues for a day or so. Team members from older generations may not only be uncomfortable with digital communication,

they may even feel offended by a lack of face-to-face or at least voice-to-voice interaction, or left out of the loop.[17]

Additionally, the nature of scheduling can be a concern, with the flexibility of millennials contrasting with the preference for preplanning by older colleagues. Finally, older professionals may often be linear learners with a desire to absorb requisite information via training and manuals before beginning the task at hand, while millennials are largely "on demand" learners that figure things out along the way, reaching out to personal contacts with relevant expertise as needed, with "[millennials] likely to be bored and turned off by a project that begins with a lengthy training phase ... [and older workers] annoyed by [millennials'] frequent questions and requests for input".[18]

One additional insight merits consideration. Research indicates very real differences in the perceptions of management and authority at work, with "baby boomers" and older members of "Generation X" coming of age with a distrust of leaders, and believing that the best work is performed without direct supervision.[19] Millennials, conversely, tend to trust authority figures and look to them for guidance, and this difference poses unique challenges for intergenerational effectiveness at work.

> Forty years ago, young boomers were famous for wanting more personal freedom to direct their lives as they wished, without interference from authority figures in families, schools, or workplaces. In today's workplace, these attitudes have been turned upside-down. It is the younger generation of workers—millennials—who most welcome a closer relationship with supervisors. And it is the older generation of workers—those same boomers—who least welcome a closer relationship.[20]

These differences, as we have discussed, can manifest in many ways. But these characteristics can be channeled to positively impact our organizations. Millennials want consistent feedback and redirection so that they can minimize uncertainty and make sure they are on track for successful achievement of these goals. They want to please the boss and do their job the right way the first time.[21]

Many of the potential pitfalls in intergenerational connection can be mitigated with communication and understanding. Clear expectations on the front end of shared tasks must be explicitly determined. Openness to different ways of thinking is invaluable to intergenerational effectiveness, and allows for voicing ideas, questions, and approaches that can enhance the ethical climate of the organization through greater engagement and transparency. Some of the techniques provided in these chapters can help, for example, starting by explicitly naming shared goals and values, in collaboration with colleagues, and with attention to differences in respectful and open ways. The emerging models of flatter organizational structures rather than the purely hierarchical approach, and greater interest in and potential for interaction with aspirational leaders, facilitates this intergenerational collaboration. Millennials can help us build more collaborative and effective workplaces.

> An interactive activity corporations and universities around the country have used to illustrate issues of collaboration, innovation, and creativity is the "marshmallow challenge"—using simple materials like uncooked spaghetti, participant teams are challenged to build the tallest freestanding structure supporting the marshmallow. Who typically excels at this challenge? Kids—kindergarteners in particular. They prototype and use hands-on, experiential methods of devising their structure—older participants plan and plan, and then plan some more. Interactive, iterative experiences with feedback loops can be invaluable for problem solving at work. Consider one millennial's reflection on his introduction to using computers: *"Our teacher would say 'go ahead and take a few minutes and try things out on the computer, explore the buttons and start looking things up.' …. that curiosity is something that characterizes the way we are today."*[22]

Acknowledging the Benefit of Engaged, Ethical Cultures

Research on corporate best practices for millennial management[23] includes suggestions specific to cultivating teamwork, effective multitasking, and fostering dialogue—all characteristics of millennial workers and the focus of this chapter. These strategies foster an organizational culture of openness, transparency, and shared purpose that promotes opportunities for voicing values and can be foundational for ethical organizations. These include several approaches.

First, attention can be paid to physical space, including lowering walls between workspaces and designing opportunities for connection such as dynamic break rooms. Zappos.com, for example, signals this from the start of each day because workers at every level of the company enter through the same front door, and Zappos provides free lunch to all employees. Second, companies can consider hosting events—off- and on-site—that allow for engagement and connection. When structured around community service opportunities these events can enhance productivity, team capacities, and company engagement while modeling business as community citizen. Third, companies can foster peer interaction through "onboarding" practices that encourage interaction with existing employees, recognition of employees and teams who achieve organizational goals, and enhancing technology to facilitate team connectivity. [...] Recognition can be communicated through these tools or in person, including techniques such as direct communication between senior and junior employee when the junior achieves a milestone—given only when it is earned, and as soon as possible after achievement—and, perhaps, communicated to the organization.

Additionally, companies can allow for consistent accessibility and connection with management. Some companies suggest the act of managers walking around the organization and a literal "open door" policy; others create online portals that function as modern-day suggestion boxes. Here we can consider "highly present role models"[24] as an effective mantra. Other suggestions include "leveling" the value of all workers by providing health insurance and stock options to all, modeled perhaps most prominently by Starbucks; rating 401(k) portfolios for sustainability, which can engage younger and more experienced employees and spur productivity; consideration of approaches such as "reverse mentoring," perhaps in the area of technology, where astute millennials can mentor senior executives on technological tools and trends; and recognition of service anniversary awards.

Experts in the field share the perspective that millennials' inclinations and motivations will change the nature of work for the better. "Innovation thrives when information is unfettered, education is nurtured, people can readily form new groups, and decision-making is inclusive," and to compete for the best young talent, companies must change in fundamental ways.[25] In a move reversing years of tradition, Goldman Sachs recently announced a goal to improve working conditions for its junior bankers by reducing their time spent at work (now advising their employees that an average work week is [only?] 70 to 75 hours, when no such guidelines existed before)—a change prompted in part by the loss of talent to start-ups.[26] Other banks have followed, introducing varying policies with such names as "protected weekends." Early feedback suggests that these new policies have measurable positive effect, and that the effect extends to others in the organization. As one analyst from Goldman noted in an article for *Businessweek*, "All of the new initiatives, such as no work on Saturdays for analysts and associates, have begun to change mindset.... Executives, rather than dwelling on the industry's pressures, speak of the need for a well-rounded life."[27]

Thus, even those organizations in highly regulated or time-sensitive industries can benefit from changes that maximize millennial contribution. Transparency in the recruiting process about the required time spent at work or other factors relating to these issues signal respect for the candidate and will allow for a determination of fit early in the process. Considerations of changes within the organization that align with these work preferences may be transformative for all.

Companies are vulnerable if they do not embrace methods to cultivate young talent, characteristics required for competitiveness in this environment, namely "transparency, free flow of information, and inclusiveness that millennials highly value—and that are also essential for learning and successful innovation." Thus, "rather than complaining [about them], it's time to embrace millennials for what they have to offer, to add experience from older workers to the mix, and to watch innovation explode."[28]

I have learned from the examples of my students as they navigate early career challenges, and this penchant for connectedness and transparency has been a net positive. Students have shared stories of internship challenges that involved uncertainty about the ethical questions including billable hours, expense reporting, client communication, and other very real concerns. For just one example, one student interning at a prestigious investment bank had questions about the appropriateness of a recommendation he and his supervisor had been asked to formulate for the board of directors regarding new investment opportunities. The student first collected data that seemed to confirm his concern, vetted his questions with a trusted friend, and then framed his concerns as questions he raised in a respectful, nonconfrontational manner with his supervisor. The act of raising the questions led his supervisor to view the transaction more closely; he was impressed with the intern's diligence and this student received an employment offer from that firm upon graduation. I am optimistic that he, and the firm, will benefit from his commitment to ethical decision making.

These examples are illustrative for other students. These types of "case studies" are invaluable to me as an instructor, and likewise can be helpful for managers with their young employees. In this way, we are modeling and exploring potential interactions between employee and supervisor, identifying the *Giving Voice to Values* techniques, such as those the student in this episode displayed including collecting data to clarify and support his position, acknowledging his role within the organization as an intern who could frame his concerns by asking questions of his more senior colleague, and embracing a tone of shared learning and purpose. Dialogue among employees and with management thus operationalizes some of the key components of the *Giving Voice to Values* approach, including voice, normality, purpose, and self-knowledge and alignment.

"Take Me to Your Leaders"

We also know that millennials are poised to respond to organizational structures and leaders when explicitly introduced to them. Unlike previous generations, such as "Gen Xers" who largely created new paradigms for work including freelancing and other models, "millennials care about authenticity and institutional values because they are counting on working within organizations to drive change … . [They] seem much more inclined to operate within existing structures. Thus far, they have been able to rely on institutions to provide them with the resources and support they need to solve the tasks set before them, and they are likely to continue to do so."[29] This sensibility bodes extremely well for our businesses. "The members of this generation have a great deal to bring to the organizations within which they operate. Their comfort with technology enables them to not only access information and resources creatively and easily, but also to think and function in a world that, to them, has always been without boundaries … . [T]hey are, as a rule, people- and organization-oriented rather than alienated, thus easing the process of engaging and acculturating them."[30]

We saw this willingness to learn and take queues from leadership throughout our student survey and focus group results. One student shared this anecdote of positive professional development he experienced:

> At [the large firm where I interned last summer] I was the only one within probably twenty or thirty years of my age in my department … . Instinctively when I got there I thought if I had questions, even quick ones, I should email my superiors. After a very short period I realized that they preferred, and it was easier, for me to walk a few minutes to their office and ask them face-to-face. I quickly adapted to how they did things and it ended up being better.

Reflecting the sentiments expressed in our own study, a 2013 Millennial Branding study finds that these workers largely express a positive view of their managers, and appreciate the experience, wisdom, and willingness to mentor that their leaders possess.[31] Managers in the 2013 study expressed some concerns about their millennial employees, including that some have unrealistic compensation expectations, a poor work ethic, and are easily distracted. The research team suggests that the number one thing managers must do to engage millennials is to set expectations clearly and consistently, and to clarify the path toward leadership for the younger employee. Millennials want to know their path, and they want to learn why they are doing a task a certain way.

This potential for engagement may again be under-realized in our companies. According to a large national study, only about half of the millennials feel that the organization for which they work encourages employees to suggest new ways of doing things or rewards them for innovative ideas, and only about half of them agree that their organization does all it can to develop leadership potential.[32]

A senior executive in a top professional services firm in our study described the primary management task as managing expectations. Recognizing this tendency to desire open and consistent feedback, along with the penchant for recognition and advancement, successful managers articulate roles, responsibilities, and what it takes to advance clearly and often. Formal rotation programs, innovative training, and other approaches signal and institutionalize this commitment. Millennials respond to this clarity and will respect the process if they understand it. It also reflects the open, transparent, and collaborative cultures that characterize the most successful of our businesses.

Ethical Engagement at Work

Research on character development in the context of professional life can be considered in the context of multigenerational work cultures. Character, after all, embodies traits and virtues that with practice become good habits. These traits, virtues, and habits are discovered by witnessing and imitating the behavior of others and must be cultivated deliberately. Further, virtues must be examined within a community setting. Thus, in addition to being within the domain of family, education, and other formative experiences, character development clearly belongs at work.

Considerations of our past and future "selves"—what we wanted to become, who we envisioned ourselves to be, and where we will be 5, 10, 20 years out—is positively associated with ethical behavior. An interesting opportunity might be considering whether cultivating those cognitive and emotional queues as a form of self-assessment can help us develop our own moral courage, and help us connect to one another. Can we see something of ourselves in that young new hire? Can we appreciate the concerns of an experienced worker considering his or her legacy after retirement?

Additionally, as we consider young professionals we must acknowledge their training ground—our business schools. Educators play a critical role in this development, and managers may be able to apply their observations at work. Scholarship around the development of leadership character in business schools suggests that character development is essential to moving beyond only acquisition of functional content to developing the capacity to impact today's business challenges.[33] The best of our business schools are thinking carefully and strategically about their role in cultivating tomorrow's leaders in a context in which the stakes are extremely high. Courses, experiential opportunities, and other activities that inform and reinforce ideas of socially responsible business, environmental and social sustainability, the intersection between politics, economics, and peace, the legislative environment, socio-political historical considerations across the globe, economic inequity, and other critical considerations are absolutely necessary. Equipped with this awareness and competency in solution seeking, young professionals are poised for meaningful impact in our organizations and societies.

What can the research tell us about minimizing the potential for unethical behavior, and how to mitigate this risk? It has been suggested that narrow approaches to cultivating negotiation skills at work, a critical competency at all levels of business, have resulted in a generation of leaders who make ethical compromises; by embracing the GVV approach of self-awareness and alignment, young professionals can create positive impact for themselves and their organizations. We must start with acknowledging our values, and attempt to align them with our work. "Business schools and professors need to help students look inward to see the person they become when they negotiate. The way to do this is by showing students how to bring to the negotiating process their full selves from the roles they play in life—account manager, mentor, sibling, adventure traveler—along with the associated values, strengths, creativity, and passion."[34] Embracing our whole selves at work is good for all of us. "The benefits extend beyond the negotiation task. This approach can transform the conversation from 'I win, you lose' into more collaborative discussions about how, through combined efforts, people can explore and create better results for all parties. It also helps people form stronger connections and build better relationships with their negotiating partners, because there will be a feeling of trust and respect."[35] The role of business schools is emphasized here as well; by showing students how to be genuine in strategic dialogue at work, we prepare them for true leadership.

Thus, we return again to engagement within the organization. Connections among employees may also reduce moral transgressions. An engaged organization can be compared to one in which "the lights are shining"—thus, one provocative study shows that physical darkness can conceal identity and encourage unethical behavior. It can induce a psychological feeling of illusory anonymity that disinhibits dishonest and self-interested behavior, regardless of actual anonymity.[36] An extension of this idea suggests that transparency and the lack of feelings of anonymity help "shine a light" and create cultures of mutual responsibility and engagement.

> As we consider the issue of "voice," we can reflect on the emerging challenges facing General Motors in the wake of recalls and failures to communicate problems. Perhaps one of the most damning pieces of this convoluted puzzle was release of internal documents with specific instruction around language to be used by employees discussing the problems. A 68-item list of "banned words" not to be used by employees documenting the safety issues is perhaps as direct an example as possible around the notions of voice at work. This explicit attempt to negatively shape voice may be a reflection of the lack of transparency and willingness to confront and manage challenges that are necessary to successfully display ethical leadership.

How else can we mitigate the risk of unethical behavior at work? James Lang's research[37] on cheating behaviors in the academic setting reminds us that when students believe that their professors are caring and invested in their learning, cheating rates are lower. This dynamic extends to the corporation. Millennials are relational—they perform for (and leave) managers and leaders, they do not perform for (or leave) the company—they "quit the boss, not the job." Investing in your talent, and modeling effective behavior, is mutually beneficial. Peer and direct supervisor interaction is key—the "tone in the middle" matters.

From Engaged Connections to Effective Teams

Open and connected cultures set the stage for collaborative employee impact. Experts in talent management acknowledge a need for careful consideration of "teaming" at work. Effective team participation requires the establishment of relationships. These can be enhanced in new and important ways by embracing millennials values, for example, as one of our corporate respondents indicated, *"this includes willingness to accept diversity and include nontraditional team members."* These connections must be considered thoughtfully or we run the risk of throwing people together in counter-productive ways. Another corporate executive in our study noted, *"there is a sense of collaboration in that [millennial employees] want to be part of the team immediately. However, they often fail to earn their spot as older colleagues have done. And once on the team, they seek leadership positions before establishing a grasp of the basics."*

Additionally, today's new professionals may define relationships differently than experienced workers. Face-to-face interaction may not be a prerequisite in this era of social media. This fluidity of interaction has implications for how teams function at work. Additionally, there is a challenge to effective team structuring, given millennial penchant for individual achievement. Thus, "while the millennials ultimately value working on teams, there is also a perceived need for independence and being able to control the process to get the job done. … [T]his seems to be a misalignment in terms of these values. This generation exhibits a tendency to have the mentality of being able to complete tasks by themselves. … "[38] Yet these tendencies need not be a barrier: "[T]he alignment is in the infrastructure provided for the team and then allowing the individuals to work independently within these parameters. Setting the parameters of the work space and enabling them to operate within this space will allow them to utilize their creativity in order to best accomplish the job."[39]

Both new workers and experienced professionals will benefit from clear dialogue around expectations and contributions, and perhaps reimagining notions of teams and leadership. A useful approach to fostering multigenerational collaboration at work involves presenting guidelines for effective engagement. This method of building bridges among the generations involves conversational learning, which starts with shared agreement around putting the organization first. Conversational learning also includes awareness that we all have biases and "blind spots," and acknowledging an open-mindedness to learning from others, a conscious effort to listen, and an agreement that engagements be characterized by self- and other-respect. These specific "ground rules" can be presented to employees in the context of training, development, peer coaching, and other activities.[40]

> Many of our best companies are incorporating these techniques of explicitly naming these challenges, bringing them to the forefront, and collaborating around solutions. Our corporate executives cited several examples, including presentations regarding generational differences, gamification of training, diversity councils around generational differences, training videos exploring bridging the differences, and group calls with required attendance at all levels of the organization. One executive we surveyed includes not only project updates and responsibilities in company-wide meetings, but recognition of milestones including positive results for clients, new babies, and other important events—this reinforces connections, and fosters appreciation for the challenges and joys of various life stages.

Connected Contributions to Ethical Cultures at Work

Connected employees provide a foundation for shared efforts toward organizational success in a collaborative, ethical manner. Our task as experienced professionals and leaders is to show new businesspeople that it is in their best interest to be ethical and effective at work. Ethical decision making can allow for alignment between our own values and those of our organization. Bill Gates famously appealed to two major drivers of human behavior—self-interest and caring for others—in his call toward "creative capitalism."[41] He acknowledged that the greatest challenges we face, in business and society, demand big solutions. This dynamic operates within our organizations and reflects the nature of ethical business. Meeting financial goals sustainably can only come with simultaneous consideration of the triple bottom line of business—economic, social, and environmental performance. Organizational goals can reflect pursuit of success across these three realms. Young talent, with their penchant for values-based business, can be a crucial part of the process.

Harnessing and channeling the ambition and big ideas of business toward ethical impact is the province of our managers. But these calls for and examples of responsible leadership must not only come from the top. For effective engagement of young talent, this motivation can also be peer-led. Today's emerging leaders are peer-connected and peer-motivated. A recent book with a fascinating look at the power of these social networks[42] reminds us that recognizing and capitalizing on these dynamics are critical to behavior and outcomes. Our connections with other people influence aspects of our lives as diverse as our health and emotions to our political preferences and economic prosperity, and are only becoming more complex and acute in the age of the internet.[43] These phenomena are only heightened for our networked young professionals.

Levering connections toward collaborative team motivation can be an approach toward maximizing effective, ethical organizations. We know that strategic and integrated CSR is critical for today's companies, and that CSR involves, at its root, connections with and impact on others. New studies indicate the specific ways that organizations actually enhance the employee and customer experience by incorporating CSR, and reflect the role of community building and collaborative engagement of employees in CSR strategies. CSR programs help bridge gaps for employees seeking commonalities with senior management, their boss, and their customers, and contribute to positive changes in the dynamics of these relationships by enhancing employee engagement and customer-service performance.[44] Exciting new research finds that work "meaningfulness" is largely perceived by employees as related to perceptions of how their company treats others—thus, not only do employees care about how they themselves are treated by the organization, but they care *more* deeply whether their organization treats third parties (customers, consumers, communities) well.[45] Millennials are primed for both this connection with management and others, and with values-based motivation.

Thus, discussion of ethical impact provides a shared space where employees and their managers can interact, reflecting a key desire of millennial talent for both engaged and socially conscious work. General Electric chairman and CEO Jeff Immelt has remarked that sustainability topics have been the single most galvanizing issues in the areas of innovation, employee motivation, and engagement that he has seen in his company.[46] The late Ray Anderson, groundbreaking sustainable business pioneer at world-leading commercial and residential carpet company Interface, provided an early and much-replicated model for combining sustainability strategies and profitability that transformed his industry.

The notion of voice matters in this consideration of connection as well—"you can tell your CSR story in a compelling way [by communicating activities with current and future employees online, in employee newsletters, and in recruiting materials], encourage people to get involved and champion folks who are involved by highlighting their efforts."[47] This communication—regular, consistent, aspirational, and specific—can be a powerful tool, and one that resonates well with millennial recruits and employees. The benefits of such communication extend beyond employee stakeholders—both large and small firms reap substantial benefits from sharing information on CSR with consumers, investors, and other stakeholders. Research findings indicate that this type of communication reaps significant long-term financial value, and reflect the "causal conclusion that good CSR performance leads to enhanced financial performance."[48]

A piece on "resolutions for aspiring leaders" concludes with advice for emerging leaders from the millennial generation:

> Ask more questions than you answer. With the high velocity of change in the world, it is impossible to have answers to all the important questions. Much more important is a deep curiosity about the world and the ability to frame the right questions in profound ways. The world's toughest problems cannot be solved by you or any one organization. Your role will be to bring the right people together to address the challenging issues you raise. Our research demonstrates that the biggest mistakes result from decisions made by people without deep consideration of thoughtful questions.[49]

The process of enhancing our ethical commitment is ongoing, for all of us. Millennials entering professional life are in a profound place. "The maturation of human morality will, in many ways, resemble the maturation of an individual person. As we come to understand ourselves better—who we are, and why we are the way we are—we will inevitably change ourselves in the process. Some of our beliefs and values will survive this process of self-discovery and reflection, whereas others will not".[50] Sociologist Christian Smith wrote a wonderful book[51] about emerging adults that calls us to understand and explain young millennials within the broader context of American culture and society. Smith cites changing roles, differences in youth socialization, mass consumerism, interlocked institutions, disconnection between older adults and young people, and American individualism as contextual factors that must be acknowledged. Smith argues that we can all flourish only by recognizing the macro-social dimensions of our challenges, by explicitly considering moral reasoning, encouraging civil, functional debate on our most pressing issues, and by fostering intergenerational connections. Managed well, the workplace can be a critical space for this development.

CSR as Competitive Advantage in Attracting and Retaining Top Talent

Research on employee recruitment indicates that an organization's corporate social performance, or the organization's commitment to principles, policies, and practices relating to social responsibilities and relationships with stakeholders, affects attractiveness as an employer, and this dynamic is expected to become even more significant. Corporate social performance indicators can give organizations an immediate competitive advantage by attracting a larger applicant pool.[52] One study finds that "signal-based mechanisms," or signals job seekers receive about the company's social performance are important; thus, perceptions of the company by the potential employees, including anticipated pride from being affiliated with that organization, their perceived value fit with the organization, and their exceptions about how the organization treats its employees are related to perceptions of the company's prosocial performance.

Google, a perennial favorite on the "most desirable companies to work for" lists, has been lauded for its unconventional hiring and management practices. As Tom Friedman reflects in a much-circulated *New York Times* op-ed, Google attracts so much talent it can afford to look beyond most traditional hiring metrics like GPA and test scores. Rather, they can focus on hiring attributes including technical ability and general cognitive ability, defined not as I.Q., but as "learning ability"—the ability to process on the fly, to pull together disparate bits of information—gleaned by structured behavioral interviews that are validated for predictive qualities. Other attributes they pursue include leadership potential, which is defined to include emergent traits such as stepping up to lead and stepping aside to allow someone else to lead, and humility and ownership, including intellectual humility that allows for learning and embracing ideas of others. As Friedman notes, "The world only cares about—and pays off on—what you can do with what you know. … And in an age when innovation is increasingly a group endeavor, it also cares about a lot of soft skills—leadership, humility, collaboration, adaptability and loving to learn and re-learn. This will be true no matter where you go to work."[53] And while Google may be an outlier in its hiring practices, it may also be predictive—its ability to attract top young talent may afford it this approach, yet it may also be because of it—a lesson other companies may adapt for their own organizations.

Notes

1. Snow, C., Miles, R., and Coleman, Jr., H. J. 1992. "Managing 21st Century Network Organizations," *Organizational Dynamics* 20, pp. 5–20.
2. Pearce, C. L., Wassenaar, C. L., and Manz, C. C. 2014. "Is Shared Leadership the Key to Responsible Leadership?" *The Academy of Management Perspectives* 28, no. 3, pp. 275–88.
3. Ibid.
4. Ibid.
5. Myers, K. E., and Sadaghiani, K. 2010. "Millennials in the Workplace: A Communication Perspective on Millennials' Organizational Relationships and Performance," *Journal of Business and Psychology* 25, pp. 225–38.
6. Gentile, M. C. 2008. *Ways of Thinking about Our Values*. www.GivingVoiceToValues.org
7. Gentile, 2008.
8. Gentile, 2008.
9. Myers, K. E., and Sadaghiani, K. 2010. "Millennials in the Workplace: A Communication Perspective on Millennials' Organizational Relationships and Performance," *Journal of Business and Psychology* 25, p. 229.

10. Gentile, 2008.
11. Gentile, 2008.
12. Philips, M. May 22, 2012. "Boomers and Millennials: Who's Got It Worse in the Workplace?" *Bloomberg Businessweek*. http://www.businessweek.com/articles/2012-05-22/boomers-and-millennials-whos-got-it-worsein-the-workplace
13. Ibid.
14. White, M. 2011. *Rethinking Generation Gaps in the Workplace: Focus on Shared Values*. University of North Carolina Kenan-Flagler Business School, UNC Executive Development, http://www.kenan-flagler.unc.edu/executive-development/custom-programs/~/media/C8FC09AEF03743BE91112418FEE286D0.ashx
15. Erickson, T. February 16, 2009. "The Four Biggest Reasons for Genearational Conflict in Teams," *Harvard Business Review*, HBR Blog Network. http://blogs.hbr.org/2009/02/the-four-biggest-reasons-for-i/
16. Ibid.
17. Ibid.
18. Ibid.
19. Howe, N., and Hadler, R. February 2012. "Why Generations Matter: Ten Findings from LifeCourse Research on the Workforce," http://www.lifecourse.com/assets/files/Why%20Generations%20Matter%20LifeCourse%20Associates%20Feb%202012.pdf.
20. Ibid.
21. Ibid.
22. Author-Led Student Focus Group. 2014. Quotations throughout the book presented in callout boxes are derived from a focus group with 22 senior undergraduate business students, with anonymous attribution by permission, conducted February 2014.
23. Eisner, S. 2012. "Best Practices for Managing Generation Y," *Managing Human Resources from the Millennial Generation*. Charlotte, NC: Information Age, pp. 251–78.
24. Ibid.
25. Agan, T. "Embracing the Millennials' Mind-Set at Work," *New York Times*, November 9, 2013.
26. Ibid.
27. Kitroeff, N. August 19, 2014. "Life is Actually Getting Easier for Goldman Sachs Interns," *Bloomberg Businessweek*.
28. Agan, 2013.
29. Hershatter, A., and Epstein, M. 2010. "Millennials and the World of Work: An Organization and Management Perspective." *Journal of Business and Psychology* 25, pp. 211–223.
30. Ibid.
31. Millennial B. "Millennial Branding and American Express Release New Study on Gen Y Workplace Expectations." http://millennialbranding.com/2013/09/gen-workplace-expectations-study/
32. Deloitte, 2014. *The Deloitte Millennial Survey*.
33. Crosson, M., Mazutis, D., Seijts, G., and Gandz, J. 2013. "Developing Leadership Character in Business Programs," *Academy of Management Learning & Education* 12, no. 2. http://amle.aom.org/content/early/2012/07/26/amle.2011.0024A.abstract.

34. Kopelman, S. May 15, 2014. "Corporate Ethics Slide Because of Bad Negotiations," *BloombergBusinessweek*. http://www.businessweek.com/articles/2014-05-15/narrow-approaches-to-teaching-negotiation-have-resulted-in-a-generation-of-leaders-who-make-ethical-compromise
35. Ibid.
36. Zhong, C. B., Bohns, V. K., and Gino, F. 2010. "A Good Lamp Is the Best Police: Darkness Increases Self-interested Behavior and Dishonesty," *Psychological Science 21*, no. 3, pp. 311–4.
37. Lang, J. 2013. *Cheating Lessons: Learning from Academic Dishonesty*. Cambridge, MA: Harvard University Press.
38. Bias, S. K., and Phillips, D. L. 2012. "Implications of Values of the Millennial Generation on HR Infrastructure," *Managing Human Resources from the Millennial Generation*. Charlotte, NC: Information Age, pp. 301–21.
39. Ibid.
40. Sims, R. R. 2012. "Building Bridges Between the Millennials and Other Generations", *Managing Human Resources from the Millennial Generation*. Charlotte, NC: Information Age, pp. 421–44.
41. Kiviat, B. and Gates, B. "Making Capitalism More Creative," *Time* Magazine. July 31, 2008.
42. Christakis, N., and Fowler, J. 2001. *Connected: The Surprising Power of Our Social Networks and How They Shape Our Lives—How Your Friends' Friends' Friends Affect Everything You Feel, Think, and Do*. New York, NY: Back Bay Books.
43. Ibid.
44. Patton, C. June 6, 2014. "Study: CSR Encourages Better Customer Service," http://www.hreonline.com/HRE/view/story.jhtml?id=534357176.
45. Glavas, A., and Kelley, K. April 2014. "The Effects of Perceived Corporate Social Responsibliity on Employee Attitudes," *Business Ethics Quarterly 24*, no. 2.
46. Immelt, J. 2009. "Driving Innovation and Economic Renewal in a Global Context," *Keynote Presentation, Net Impact Conference*. Ithaca, New York.
47. Patton, 2014. "Study: CSR Encourages Better Customer Service."
48. Yu, Kun, Du, Shuili, and Bhattacharya, C. B. 2014. "Everybody's Talking But is Anybody Listening? Stock Market Reactions to Corporate Social Responsibility Communications," Harvard Business School Working Paper.
49. Coleman, J., and George, B. December 30, 2011. "Five Resolutions for Aspiring Leaders," *Harvard Business Review*, Harvard Working Knowledge.
50. Greene, J. D. 2003. "From Neural 'Is' to Moral 'Ought': What are the Moral Implications of Neuroscientific Moral Psychology?" *Nature Reviews Neuroscience 4*, pp. 847–50.
51. Smith, C. 2011. *Lost in Transition: The Dark Side of Emerging Adulthood*. New York, NY: Oxford University Press.
52. Jones, D. A., Willness, C. R., and Madey, S. 2014. "Why Are Job Seekers Attracted by Corporate Social Performance? Experimental and Field Tests of Three Signal-Based Mechanisms," *Academy of Management Journal 57*, no 2, pp. 383–404.
53. Friedman, T. L. "How To Get a Job at Google," *New York Times*, February 22, 2014.

Reading 2.2

Organizational Ambidexterity and the Multi-Generational Workforce

Kathryn Woods

Abstract: Organizational ambidexterity, or the ability to succeed both in core business and future planning and innovation, is an important concept for businesses trying to survive in the modern market. The composition of today's workforce is rapidly shifting as Millennials are quickly outnumbering Baby Boomers in the workplace. This shift presents its own subsets of challenges and opportunities for organizations. Existing research has provided evidence that employee values and preferences differ among the generational cohorts currently represented in the workforce. These topics are explored, and an updated model for an ambidextrous structure is recommended for organizations that wish to increase their ambidexterity by overcoming the challenges and capitalizing on the strengths found in a diverse, multi-generational workforce.

Introduction

As Birkinshaw and Gibson (2004) reported, economic instability experienced in the early 2000's solidified the idea that adaptability is paramount for an organization to succeed. However, moving quickly toward new opportunities and adjusting to unpredictable economic shifts are often not enough to carry an organization through a period of sustained success. Organizations must also focus on alignment, or developing a "clear sense of how value is being created in the short term and how activities should be coordinated and streamlined to deliver that value" (p. 47). Companies who master both important strategic initiatives—also known as adaptability and alignment, or exploitation and exploration—are often referred to as ambidextrous (Duncan, 1976). These researchers warn leaders that focusing too narrowly on adaptability will cause an organization to lose today's business at the expense of tomorrow's business. Conversely, focusing too narrowly on alignment will help business succeed today, but make it susceptible to inevitable industry changes.

The traditional "Ambidextrous Structure" that is widely accepted in research maintains that businesses should employ two completely separate units, one that focuses on core business, and one that focuses only on innovation. These units are encouraged to maintain their own separate identity, budget, culture, etc., and do not interact directly. In this model, the head of each unit reports to a common general or executive-level manager (O'Reilly & Tushman, 2004). Leaders in ambidextrous organizations must consider many different factors when planning how to balance their organization's efforts to exploit their core business and explore potential opportunities. When reviewing the necessary components that allow an organization to maximize both core business and innovation, Scott (2014) found that, "the ability to compete in current and new markets begins with the strategies and priorities that are responsible for the very nature of innovation capabilities" (p. 44). Aligning organizational strategies with innovative priorities is of paramount importance for businesses that desire to maintain success with core business while also innovating new products or services that go beyond the incremental innovations occurring in the core business unit.

Other researchers have highlighted the importance of examining the changing landscape of the workforce in a time when a new generation is gaining a majority representation in the workplace. The workforce has shifted from a composition of roughly half Baby Boomers in 2005 to about a third in 2015 (Fry, 2015). Millennials, a generation that outnumbers members of Generation X in population by nearly twelve million, have entered the workforce and surpassed the percentage of Baby Boomers and Gen Xers represented in the workplace in just under a decade's time (Pew Research Center, 2015). As new research about generational strengths and preferences emerges, business leaders are adapting to this generational shift in the workforce by updating policies on flexible work hours, changing the expectations for providing and receiving feedback, and implementing reciprocal mentorship programs (Bannon, Ford & Meltzer, 2011; Meister & Willyerd, 2010; Chaudhuri & Ghosh, 2012).

New research suggests that the ambidexterity of organizations—their ability to effectively innovate while still maintaining focus on their core business—is being impacted by the changing landscape of the generational mix represented in the workplace (Blackburn, 2011; Moon, 2014), although little direction in the literature exists to strongly connect this relationship. This author proposes that the development of an updated ambidextrous organization structure for businesses would contribute to the knowledge base of business strategy scholars and professionals for this topic. Constructing a model highlighting the need to encourage knowledge transfer while a generation that dominated the workforce ten years ago is rapidly replaced by one who dominates the others in tech skills and desire for constant feedback (Chaudhuri & Ghosh, 2012; Gibson, Greenwood & Murphy, 2009; Patterson, 2005; Stevens, 2010; Thompson & Gregory, 2012; Yu & Miller, 2005) could be a good initial step for many organizations in the move toward becoming a more innovative enterprise.

The aim of this paper is to broadly describe current considerations and suggestions regarding the basic structure for ambidextrous organizations as well as to contend that the recent shift in the generational representation of the workforce should be considered as a new model can be explored to help organizations assuage some of the challenges created by this generational shift. This article adds to the literature stream by focusing on two primary research questions:

1. What are the current considerations regarding business structure for ambidextrous organizations?
2. What are the emerging opportunities and challenges for ambidextrous organizations considering the shifting makeup of the multi-generational workforce?

Literature Review

Organizational Ambidexterity

Tushman, Smith, and Binns (2011) examined executives' tendencies to over-emphasize the now, or the alignment side of ambidexterity, especially when pressured to cut costs. These researchers found that some CEO's deferred the decisions about exploratory projects designed to foster the adaptability side of the equation to the department heads, without prescribing any kind of ideal ratio for spending on current versus exploratory projects. In other cases, they found that decisions to reduce spending on bringing innovative ideas to life were often made when an organization's top leaders did not fully understand side projects or new ventures, and therefore dismissed them as a threat to the company's core values or identity.

These researchers also concluded that a proper mix can be achieved when a CEO commits to several practices. First, engaging their senior team around a forward-looking strategic aspiration can lend a broader identity to an organization, and gives units permission to engage in opposing strategies. (For example, a wireless carrier could position itself as a communications organization instead of a cell phone company; an auto maker could position itself as a transportation organization instead of a car manufacturer. This broader definition of the core business allows for greater creativity and a wider scope.) Second, CEO's should be "holding the tension" between the demands of innovation units and core business at the top of the organization. The researchers contend that when conflicts about funding old and new businesses are resolved at lower levels, innovation usually loses out since it is more difficult to coordinate initiatives from the bottom up. Finally, CEO's are encouraged to embrace inconsistency by maintaining multiple and often conflicting strategic agendas. Innovation units should be held to different standards than existing units, and each unit should maintain independent schedules, cultures, etc. for maximum benefit (Tushman et al., 2011).

In their large-scale study of employees at multinational companies, Birkinshaw and Gibson (2004) found a strong, positive correlation between business performance and organizational ambidexterity. So, what fosters organizational ambidexterity? In the same study, these researchers also found a strong, positive correlation between a perceived supportive organizational context (regarding performance management and social support) and organizational ambidexterity. When ambidexterity and organizational context together were analyzed as predictors of performance, only ambidexterity had a significant influence. Thus, the influence of organizational context on performance only occurs through the creation of ambidexterity. In other words, a supportive organizational context enables individual employees' ambidexterity, which leads to high performance. The findings of this study also indicated that ambidextrous employees possess some common qualities including taking initiative, being alert to opportunities beyond the constraints of their own jobs, seeking out opportunities for collaboration, multitasking, and maintaining many different responsibilities and roles within their organization.

Wang, Li, and Mobley (2011) found that managers seeking to promote ambidextrous work teams should not only focus on selecting creative team members, but also members who are sensitive to the rules and regulations of the current business operation and those who are focused on the details of carrying out innovation. They found that in some cases, creative types must be balanced by more organized minds in order for a project to reach its full potential.

A number of factors will affect the potential ambidexterity of organizations, including industry climate, available resources, strategic plans, and company culture. Organizations that are thriving in core business may ultimately fail (in a project, or sometimes as a business) if improper resources or planning are put toward innovation, just as companies can struggle if too much is invested in the future and not enough in the present. Ideally, all business executives will see the value of working toward placing the maximum possible emphasis on both areas, and no business will minimize efforts in both areas (Krakovsky, 2013).

One example of an organization that ultimately folded altogether due to a lack of ambidexterity is Blockbuster Video. In 2004, this movie-rental giant operated more than 9,000 stores nationally. In just over a decade, that number shrunk to about fifty stores. The organization was focused on their core business of in-store video rentals, and realizing multimillion dollar profits in doing so, but invested almost nothing into innovation, or exploration (Taylor, 2013). Many attribute the company's demise to the introduction of more forward thinking rent-by-mail turned video streaming service Netflix (Chowdhury, 2015; Satell, 2014).

Netflix got its start by providing a service in which customers could rent DVD's selected online through the mail. Customers could keep the movies as long as they liked, without worrying about the late fees incurred for missing the due date. This service became popular quickly, and patrons preferred the lack of late fees over Blockbuster's expensive charges for late returns. Listening to customers and investing in innovation sparked the next phase for the company—video streaming. As Netflix gained traction in their streaming service in 2000, the company's CEO offered Blockbuster an opportunity to purchase the company for about fifty million dollars. Blockbuster declined, seeing the new venture as an unwanted risk, and this decision is still notable today, as Netflix is valued at over twenty billion dollars, and is viewed as one of the most ambidextrous companies in business today, maintaining a proper focus on both core and future business (Bushey, 2014; Kellmurray, n.d; Krakovsky, 2013).

In contrast to the previous example, in some scenarios, companies experience failure because they succumb to the pressure to innovate at the expense of the core business, even when the core business is thriving (Gottfredson & Aspinall, 2005). One of the most well-known failed efforts from an otherwise successfully company is that of "New Coke". In 1985, while maintaining the number one spot in the soft-drink business, Coca-Cola announced that they were changing their more than one hundred year old formula to have a sweeter taste, much like Diet Coke. This shift was reportedly made to try to stave off the increasing market share of their closest competitor, Pepsi Cola. Only a small percentage of consumers reported that they liked the new formula better than the old one, and loyal customers wasted no time obtaining signed petitions and even organizing protests to bring back their beloved Coca-Cola Classic. After only a few short months on the market, Coca-Cola agreed to once again offer their original formula to consumers, and the "New Coke" product faded completely away soon after (Haoues, 2015; Ross, 2005).

The Ambidextrous Structure

Since the concept of organizational ambidexterity has been popularized both in theory and practice, researchers and practitioners alike have looked to develop a formalized structure or framework that supports the two essential elements required to be ambidextrous—a focus on core business, and a focus on innovation. When structuring a business for ambidexterity, corporate leaders must consider which employees, departments, functional areas, or business units will be responsible for core business processes, and which will be responsible for exploratory or innovative business processes.

O'Reilly and Tushman (2004) observed real business situations, and identified some common activities from organizations who have proven themselves able to excel in the present while simultaneously planning for the future as ambidextrous organizations. They found that in successful ambidextrous organizations, communicating a clear vision from the top was a key to success. They observed successful ambidextrous organizations maintaining separate units for core business and innovation development, both reporting to an integrated senior team. Based on this, difficult decisions were often made in terms of staffing when a company increased their efforts to become ambidextrous. If a company's senior leaders were not committed to the process, a CEO had to be willing to let those who might hold the team back move on from the company. When this business model was implemented, executives were encouraged to communicate accomplishments that occurred due to the new approach, and hold workshops on exactly how jobs were changing when applicable. These researchers concluded that,

> one of the most important lessons is that ambidextrous organizations need ambidextrous senior teams and managers—executives who have the ability to understand and be sensitive to the needs of very different kinds of businesses. Combining the attributes of rigorous cost cutters and free-thinking entrepreneurs while maintaining the objectivity required to make difficult trade-offs, such managers are a rare but essential breed (O'Reilly & Tushman, 2004, p. 5).

These researchers (O'Reilly & Tushman, 2004) created a widely accepted business model for organizations seeking to increase their ambidexterity, called the "Ambidextrous Structure" (see Figure 2.2.1). They found that organizations who integrated responsibilities related to innovation into the existing units, as part of cross-functional teams, and/or as unsupported teams (teams that exist outside of the managerial hierarchy) had much less success with breakthrough projects than organizations who utilized independent units (each maintaining their own processes, structures, and cultures) that were still integrated into the existing managerial hierarchy. This model has been used as a template in many industries by organizations attempting to excel in their core business while continuing to ensure market adaptability in the future through innovation.

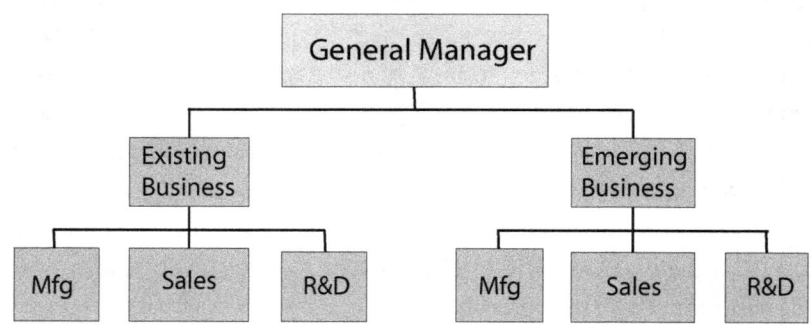

FIGURE 2.2.1 Ambidextrous Organization Structure. Reprinted from "The Ambidextrous Organizations," by C. A. O'Reilly and M. L. Tushman, 2004. Copyright 2004 by Harvard Business School Publishing Corporation.

Another large-scale study on the impact of employing various models designed to promote ambidexterity shows that new product development is significantly affected by this structure. Visser et al. (2010) found that firms that apply a functional structure for the incremental new product development process perform significantly better in terms of innovation performance than firms that apply a cross-functional structure. This can be interpreted to mean that a separate business unit dedicated to innovation can achieve greater success in new product innovation than cross-functional teams made up of employees with many other responsibilities, treating the innovation process like a project.

Vinekar, Slinkman, Craig and Nerur (2006) also supported the notion that dual structures are the most beneficial to organizations desiring to strike a proper balance between existing and emerging business functions. Their study found that the separate structures were often necessary due to the conflicting technical demands, management styles, reward systems, and cultures needed for either area to operate effectively. These researchers also highlight the importance of the executive management's ability to identify successful and failed efforts that come from each unit, and to consider modifying the structure of the individual units as needed based on trends found in that information.

Other researchers have determined that businesses remaining flexible in the way they approach structuring for ambidexterity will be able to reduce resistance to change, and therefore spend more time and energy planning for opportunities. (Bock, Opsahl, George & Gann, 2011; Boumgarden, Nickerson & Zenger, 2012). This can be interpreted to mean that business models accepted for this type of structuring will have more potential for usefulness if created at a high level, as adjustments will be needed in practice based on a number of individualized variables such as industry climate, available resources, strategic plans, and company culture. Similarly, Simsek (2009) reported that the success of the implementation of an Ambidextrous Structure depends partly on variables such as a firm's place within its network and position in the market. Firms with a more established presence may be better suited to split into two separate business units without fear of overextending their resources.

Creating a Culture of Innovation

Aside from available research and a widely-accepted model that work together to provide a framework for organizations to be structured in the ideal way to exploit core business and explore the potential for innovation, another body of research exists regarding creating a culture of innovation. Several researchers have studied variables within organizations, including qualities of an executive leader or group of leaders, corporate values, and communication strategies that may contribute to the successful efforts of the business unit charged with leading the way in innovation.

Choudary (2014) found that innovation is nurtured in companies that focus on several specific practices. First, innovative companies were found to maintain a happy and motivated staff by providing exceptional benefits and compensation, regular professional development opportunities, and maintaining an environment in which socialization is encouraged. Second, the customer focus in these companies was based on doing something good for society, in addition to making their customers happy. Third, the leadership committed to innovations by encouraging and rewarding risk takers, making quick decisions, and providing vision for the company. Finally, the executive leaders created and maintained a sense of urgency and fear in the workplace by openly communicating the importance of innovation to continuing employment and ultimately the company's existence.

Some researchers contend that a culture of innovation starts with employees. Moon (2014) found that organizational cultures that foster creativity and passion and value their employees will be innovation leaders. Martensen and Dahlgaard (1999) found that in order to build a successful culture of innovation, employees must be encouraged to learn, and leaders must commit to studying how outputs are improving. Other researchers highlighted the importance of employees being free to collaborate with groups both inside and outside the organization to encourage new ideas and fresh perspectives (Jamrog, Vickers & Bear, 2006). "Innovation happens in the context of relationships. They are internal and external. These relationships are with superiors, subordinates, and colleagues. They are between organizations, customers, and suppliers" (Moon, 2014, p. 26).

Other researchers focused more on how business processes affect the culture of innovation. Jamrog, Vickers, and Bear (2006) found that companies who desire to create and sustain a culture of innovation must maintain focus on current and future customers, since these are the stakeholders that will eventually decide the fate of the company with their spending. To encourage innovation for new products and services, it has also been reported that organizations must encourage employees to understand the life-cycle impacts of existing products, build a network of potential innovation partners that extends beyond the current supply chain and sector, and gather consumer insight to be able to add value to new products and services (Coad & Pritchard, 2013).

Many studies have shown that work teams were more innovative when task conflict was present during the decision-making process (Dreu, 2006; Martins & Terblanche, 2003; Oster, 2009; Tesluk, Farr & Klein, 1997). This conflict was especially productive when mediated by collaborative problem solving, and that well-managed conflict and debate about product or task ideas increased productivity in innovative work environments. Allowing team members to express their preferences and support their suggestions with evidence that supported their choices allowed the others on the team to appreciate different ideas and perspectives, thus leading to a more creative environment capable of producing innovative ideas that were truly created by the group, rather than a dominant individual within the group. Similarly, Jamrog, Vickers, and Bear (2006) also placed a heavy value on hiring a diverse group of employees, as they found that their differences naturally led to healthy conflict that produced more varied and creative ideas.

Jong and Hartog (2007) found that leaders who created a culture of innovation among their employees asked for their employees' opinions and advice more often than managers who did not. They also ensured that employees were recognized for innovative initiatives and efforts, supported open and transparent communication processes both internally (with peers and management) and externally (with customers, suppliers, etc.), created opportunities for knowledge sharing and diffusion, and assigned challenging tasks to employees. These researchers concluded that "creating a positive and safe atmosphere that encourages openness and risk taking seems to encourage idea generation and application" (p. 58). Hurley and Hult (1998) and Somech (2006) also found that innovative cultures must support participative decision-making.

Tesluk, Farr, and Klein (1997) and Martins and Terblanche (2003) both found that close observation frustrates employees tasked with creating innovative ideas. Similarly, Jong and Hartog (2007) found that a culture of innovation is built on task autonomy, or the ability of workers who are tasked with creating innovative ideas to be able to choose the way they complete tasks, and feel supported in their choices.

The Multi-Generational Workforce

While there is some debate regarding the beginning and end dates for birth years assigned to each generation, Pew Research Center (Comparing Millennials, 2015) defined the members of the Millennials in the workforce as those born between 1981 and 1997 (age 18–34 in 2015). The members of Generation X, or Gen Xers, were born between 1965 and 1980 (age 35–50 in 2015), and members of the Baby Boomers generation were born between 1946 and 1964 (age 51–70 in 2015).

In 2005, Baby Boomers made up 49 percent of the U.S. workforce, while members of Generation X comprised about 31 percent (Fry, 2015). The same report makes known that for the first time, in 2015, more than one-third of American workers were Millennials, surpassing Generation X to become the most populous group in the active labor force. (Just one year prior, in 2014, the number of working Millennials surpassed the number of working Baby Boomers.) The numbers in 2015 showed a nearly even distribution of the three most represented generations in the workforce with the Baby Boomers representing 29 percent of the work force, Gen Xers representing 34 percent, and the Millennials just over 34 percent.

Researchers continue to study and draw conclusions about multiple generations in the workplace as information continues to be collected. A common statistic that has been reported in the popular media is that members of the Millennial generation will make up as much as 75 percent of the work force by the year 2025 (Matchar, 2012; Cook, 2014; Deloitte Millennial Survey, 2014; Winograd & Hais, 2014). More conservative, substantiated estimates come in between 44 and 50 percent (Zumbrun, 2014; Gorman, 2015). No matter what percentage of the workforce Millennials might comprise a decade from now, researchers and employers do seem to agree that the workplace is changing and will continue to change based on the fluctuation in generational representation in the overall workforce. Fry (2015) also offered a bit of insight on the future of the growth of Millennials in the workforce by highlighting the disproportionately large share of U.S. immigrants who fall into this age range, stating that in the past five years, more than fifty percent of newly arrived immigrant workers have been Millennials.

While the workforce has always been made up of multiple generations, the concept of shared values and workplace preferences as grouped by generation is a relatively new concept, and has become increasingly popular as an area of research. As the number of workers representing each generation in the work force continues to change, organizations are reacting to the differences in values of the shifting populations in various ways.

Younger Millennials are the first generation to grow up with technology at their fingertips, and to have access to the internet from birth. The generation is perceived as hopeful, inclusive, tech-savvy, ambitious, casual, globally aware, and easily bored, and as employees they tend to value feedback, open communication, diversity, change, and work that is meaningful to their greater community. (The popular media has also stereotyped the members of this generation as self-centered, lazy, entitled, too reliant on technology, and fickle.) Gen Xers have been dubbed as skeptical, self-reliant, risk-taking, independent job-hoppers who [value] work-life balance, while Baby Boomers are perceived as driven, loyal, self-absorbed, work-centered, optimistic, team-oriented, ambitious, and placing a heavy value on relationship-building (Gibson, Greenwood & Murphy, 2009; Patterson, 2005). As the balance of generational representation continues to shift in the workplace, the body of research documenting generational attitudes and preferences continues to grow, occasionally de-bunking these stereotypes. Some specific preferences of each group have been revealed through this research.

Several studies have highlighted some generational differences in job satisfaction factors. Gen Xers are often credited as the first group to openly place a high importance on work-life balance. Twenge (2010) found that Gen X and especially Millennials rated work as less central to their lives, valued leisure more, and expressed a weaker work ethic than Baby Boomers. Beutell and Wittig-Berman (2008) reported that managers and human resource professionals need to consider generational differences in work-family program design and monitor patterns of program usage for each group, as Generation X members are particularly concerned about work/life balance. Cennamo and Gardner (2008) and Gibson et al. (2009) both found that Gen X and Millennials valued freedom in their schedules more than Baby Boomers. Other researchers concluded that Gen X started the movement toward work-life balance, but Millennials accelerated it (Thompson & Gregory, 2012). Studies show that when considering their level of job satisfaction, only Millennials factored in whether their employers actively seek opportunities for corporate social responsibility and operate with respect for the environment (Winograd & Hais, 2014). Hewlett, Sherbin, and Sumbert (2009) and Gibson et al. (2009) reported that only Millennials rank having a network of friends at work as very important with regards to job satisfaction. Thompson and Gregory (2012) found that relationships with immediate managers may be the key to fully leveraging, motivating, and retaining Millennials. This information on generational preferences in job satisfaction could be particularly useful for executive leaders who desire higher levels of organizational ambidexterity, as they consider the results of studies previously mentioned that highlight the link between increased employee satisfaction and increased potential for successful innovation (Choudary, 2014; Moon, 2014).

Research on factors affecting employee motivation also revealed a few differences between the groups. Extrinsic work values such as salary were highest in Gen X, and were less important to Millennials, and even less to Baby Boomers (Twenge, 2010). Hewlett et al. (2009) reported that both Millennials and Baby Boomers shared the perspective that salary is less important than other considerations such as challenging assignments, a range of new experiences, and explicit performance evaluation and recognition. Twenge also found that Gen X, and especially Millennials were consistently higher in the recognition of individualistic traits than Baby Boomers. Ng, Schweitzer, and Lyons (2010) found that Millennials placed the highest importance on opportunities for job advancement. These research findings could also be beneficial for organizations seeking to improve their culture of innovation, as supported by the results of several aforementioned studies that indicated the importance of providing challenging assignments and employee recognition as ways to encourage innovation (Choudary, 2014; Jong & Hartog, 2007).

Thompson and Gregory (2012) noted the differences between generations in preferred leadership styles. Millennials desired feedback and accomplishment, lending themselves to respond in a positive way to transformational leadership or coaching. Gen X's value on autonomy and job satisfaction over promotion influenced their desire to work with a collaborative leader (Yu & Miller, 2005). According to Arsenault (2004) Baby Boomers preferred a directive style. These differences in generational preferences regarding leadership style can be linked back to the aforementioned studies suggesting that innovation was fostered most when a participative leadership style was employed for diverse work groups (Hurley & Hult, 1998; Jong & Hartog, 2007; Somech, 2006).

Researchers found that while Gen X will struggle to avoid conflict, Millennials will be bothered very little by it. They also report that working in teams is a top motivator for employees in the Millennial generation, and they look for accessibility in their co-workers, even in their high-level bosses (Hewlett et al., 2009; Gibson et al., 2009). Knowledge of these preferences could prove to be useful for managers seeking to foster a culture of innovation, as several researchers found in studies mentioned previously that conflict is an essential element of a culture of innovation, and that it promoted collaborative decision-making by creative teams (Dreu, 2006; Jamrog, Vickers & Bear, 2006; Oster, 2009; Martin & Terblanche, 2003; Tesluk, Farr & Klein, 1997). Research mentioned in the previous section also noted the importance of open communication to achieve success in innovation (Jong & Hartog, 2007; Moon, 2014).

Generational cohorts also display differences in work process preferences. Hershatter and Epstein (2010) reported that significantly more Millennials than Gen Xers prefer to work in organizations with centralized decision-making, clearly defined responsibilities, and formalized processes and rules. Gibson et al. (2009) reported that Millennials place significantly more importance on being challenged in the workplace than Gen Xers or Baby Boomers.

As reported in the Deloitte Millennial Survey,

> Millennials reported that they want to work for organizations that support innovation. In fact, 78 percent of Millennials were strongly influenced by how innovative a company was when deciding if they wanted to work there, but most say their current employer does not encourage them to think creatively. They believe the biggest barriers of innovation were management attitude (63 percent), operational structures and procedures (61 percent), and employee skills, attitudes, and diversity (39 percent) (2014, p.3).

In any industry, a diverse workforce breeds opportunities in addition to the challenges. Generational cohorts afford many of these opportunities to leaders willing to thoughtfully balance the need for adaptability with the need for alignment based on the strengths of their workforce as a whole. As noted in this section, executives armed with knowledge of the essential elements of a culture of innovation as well as the preferences and strengths of generational cohorts may be better equipped to implement a successful plan designed to increase organizational ambidexterity.

Knowledge Transfer

Researchers have documented employer concerns that as Baby Boomers begin to retire, executive leaders need to take proactive steps to ensure that their knowledge and experience does not retire with them (Calo, 2008; McNichols, 2010). The Deloitte Millennial Survey (2014) highlighted Millennials' viewpoints that innovation is frequently hampered by managers who are unwilling to collaborate with other groups, and a lack of formal processes to encourage innovation. Downing (2006) found that more than thirty percent of members of each generation represented in the workforce admitted to maintaining negative assumptions and stereotypes about other generations. Research indicates that these issues could be effectively addressed and a culture of innovation could be fostered in organizations by employing a type of formalized knowledge transfer known as reverse or reciprocal mentoring.

Hewlett et al. (2009) highlighted the success of Time Warner's reverse mentoring program, designed to pair Millennials with Baby Boomers one-on-one to transfer knowledge and skills in a way that benefits both members of the pair. Tech-savvy Millennials are able to assist Boomers with the latest digital media, trends, and technologies. In turn, Boomers are able to pass on their knowledge of the industry, history of client relations, status of works in progress, and insights related to career advancement. Other research suggested formal and informal classroom-style knowledge transfer or the formation of learning communities, in which employees are grouped into teams according to their area of interest/expertise can be effective (Stevens, 2010).

Chaudhuri and Ghosh (2011) identified many benefits for both parties—Baby Boomers and Gen Xers—in reverse mentoring relationships. In addition to gaining new insights in technology, reverse mentoring relationships can help Boomers develop sensitization to issues of workplace diversity, subject matter advances, work–life balance, and global perspective, all of which can contribute to increasing their levels of engagement at work. Potential benefits for Millennials include information access, appreciation and professional respect, personal fulfillment and satisfaction, power development, improved morale, and reduced turnover. Boehle (2009) also noted that the process can improve working relationships and increase engagement for both parties as well as spark new projects, processes, and products that benefit the organization.

Moon (2014) contends that Millennials arrive into the workplace primed to be innovators due to their passion, creativity, and the deep meaning they find in value creation. While these qualities can sometimes cause friction with more experienced employees or established business units, this researcher suggests that this friction can transform into productive innovation by establishing a reciprocal mentoring program that encourages strengthened relationships, fosters trust, and changes perceptions. Moon also found that the development of stronger working relationships achieved through reciprocal mentoring encouraged engagement from both the experienced and new employee, and often led to the creation of innovative new projects.

Gursoy, Maier, and Chi (2008) reported that Baby Boomers respect authority and hierarchy, while the Gen X-ers rebel against authority. The Millennial Generation tends to show more trust in centralized authority. While Boomers and Gen Xers value autonomy, Millennials like teamwork, showing a strong will to get things done with a great spirit. Myers and Sadaghiani (2010) found that Millennials are likely to have broader perspectives about the world marketplace and "ways that communication and information technology can be used to enhance organizational performance and maximize productivity" (p. 235). Similiarly, Blackburn (2011) contends that Millennial employees are innovators who diffuse new technologies into organizations. These findings on differences in generational preferences support the notion that Millennials and Baby Boomers have much to gain from each other.

Birkinshaw and Gibson (2004) asserted that organizational context enabled individual employees' ambidexterity that over time led to high performance. Working toward a culture of organizational ambidexterity requires constant monitoring, re-evaluation, planning, innovating, and changing directions when needed. At the present time, when the percentage of Baby Boomers represented in the workforce is rapidly declining, and the percentage of Millennials represented in the workforce is rapidly increasing, a formal or informal knowledge transfer plan is considered a necessity for organizations that want to avoid losing valuable information each time they issue a retirement package.

Discussion

Combining existing knowledge about the necessity of ambidexterity in organizations with the increasing necessity of accommodating multiple generations in the workplace could help organizational leaders apply theory to practice in a thoughtful, deliberate manner. Leaders face challenges in managing generational cohorts who maintain conflicting values. Millennials want more feedback, and members of Gen X and the Baby Boomer generation have historically valued operating under less oversight rather than more. Taking note of Millennials desire for more feedback and recognition could build a bridge that allows all employees to feel valued (Thompson & Gregory, 2012).

O'Reilly and Tushman's (2004) "Ambidextrous Structure" was accepted in a time when Millennials were only just entering the workforce. Since that time, we have seen massive changes in technology, communication, and the balance of different generations in the workforce. This author contends that organizational leaders should consider what we know about the shifting dynamics of a multi-generational workforce to update the traditional structure of an ambidextrous organization.

The notion to update this widely-accepted model is also supported by research from Mootee (2012), who contends that organizations with rigid, stand-alone management structures that do not support the flow of information between the core business unit and the innovation unit are poorly connected and less agile than their competitors who encourage an organizational design that allows both units to be able to react to external changes by working together. This researcher suggested that businesses "consider a new organizational design that can both manage stability and handle change" (p. 4). This researcher also directed organizations striving for ambidexterity to perform a critical self-analysis to determine their own capabilities when considering their skills, culture, processes, and behavior. This thoughtful process allows organizations to control the scope of their business, while allowing creative ideas to surface and freely flow from the core business unit to the innovation unit.

Fernholz, Hughes, and Dingwall (2014) completed an in-depth case study on a technology business that employed a traditional Ambidextrous Structure. The firm maintained separate business units to focus on core business and innovation independently. These researchers found that blending the contexts of core business and innovation exploration activities could be more effective than the traditional model, especially in technology-based businesses. These researchers also concluded that businesses could determine whether the traditional Ambidextrous Structure could be a useful tool in managerial practice only on a case-by-case basis rather than applying the structure as a trusted model for all types of business.

Scott (2014) also suggested that firms introduce coordination as an element of ambidexterity, especially when funds are at a minimum for various business processes such as marketing. This researcher found that frequent communication between business units built to exploit the core business and units designed for innovation can achieve a greater synergy when resources are at least partially shared, and regular cross-unit meetings are held across like departments to ensure that both sides are aware of new trends, data, customer feedback, marketing efforts, intelligence on competition, and changes in resource allocation.

He and Wong (2004) also supported the traditional view that exploitation and exploration activities should be maintained in separate business units, highlighting the idea that exploration activities should be allowed more freedom to fail without negative consequences. They contended that keeping the units separate reduced the negative effects that the failure of a new idea or product had on the traditional core business unit. However, they also advocated for interaction between like functional areas from each unit, noting that this regular interaction was positively correlated with sales growth. This interaction was sometimes in the form of a weekly meeting, or sometimes simply a regularly scheduled exchange of a summary of efforts and planned efforts. Maintaining open lines of communication led to positive implications for the firm's bottom line.

As the workforce continues to shift in demographics, generational mix, and employee values, businesses must be ambidextrous about what it means to be ambidextrous. A business model is meant to guide people in a direction that will help them succeed, but if the mix of people are changing, it stands to reason that models must shift, or be examined to see how they can adapt to the updated landscape. Just as a heightened awareness of cultural diversity is valued in the workplace, a heightened awareness of generational values and preferences can help managers gain a more complete perspective on decision-making processes, employee assignments, and business structure. While all individuals will not share their generation's preferences, becoming aware of patterns in this data can help companies make decisions that affect the future of their organization.

Based on the review of literature and considerations provided in studies of the shifting mix of generations represented in the workforce, this author recommends an updated approach to O'Reilly and Tushman's suggested structure for ambidextrous organizations. Challenges faced by businesses due to the Boomer generation retiring and the Millennial generation occupying the lion's share of the workforce in the near future can be converted to opportunities for knowledge transfer by implementing an important update to the structure. The proven need for a transfer of knowledge between generations (Calo, 2008; Hewlett et al., 2009; McNichols, 2010; Stevens, 2010) combined with the Millennials' desires to receive constant feedback (Gibson et al., 2009; Patterson, 2005; Thompson & Gregory, 2012) and maintain constant, open communication with their peers and executives (Deloitte Millennial Survey, 2014; Gibson et al., 2009; Hewlett et al., 2009; Thompson & Gregory, 2012) should encourage business leaders to set up a system that facilitates this exchange within and between the leaders of the existing business and emerging business units, as illustrated below in Figure 2.2.2.

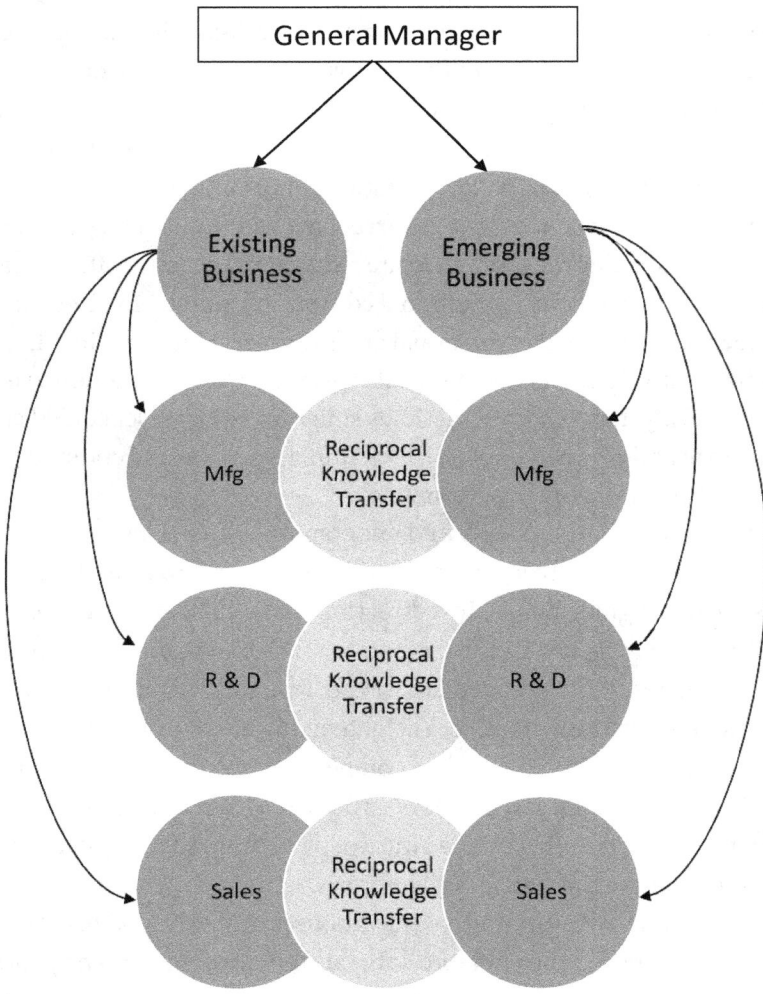

FIGURE 2.2.2 Updated Ambidextrous Organization Structure.

74 ▪ Business Ethics for Future Leaders

The original structure called for completely separate units regarding existing business and emerging business, both of which maintained their own culture, employees, manufacturing, sales, and research and development efforts. Information was only passed from one unit to the other based on communications with corporate management. In the updated model, all parties are better served by encouraging regular, structured communication (and reciprocal knowledge transfer and/or reciprocal mentoring relationships) between the employees within like functional areas of the business units, rather than expecting these departments to rely on the executive leader to act as a bridge between the two. The improved flow of communication has the potential to satisfy both generational disparities in work processes as well as knowledge transfer requirements as Baby Boomers age out of the workforce. Additionally, this structure addresses updated practices in communication without fully shifting to the cross-functional team model.

Implications

Since this study has developed concepts at a high level, academic researchers can further develop these ideas into industry-specific empirical investigations to determine the extent to which the updates to the traditional Ambidextrous Structure could affect business processes and outcomes in different fields. Reciprocal mentoring relationships could be further studied by department or functional area as well as type of industry.

From a practitioner's perspective, the figures presented in this paper could be compared to determine which structure seems to hold the most potential value for their specific business or industry. Managers may find that certain departments or functions in their area work best as stand-alone entities, but others can reap benefits from staying in constant contact. A starting point to determine which departments or functional areas may be able to reap the most benefits by opening the lines of communication could be found by examining where resources seem to be sparse on either side, or whether a department or functional area employs mostly members of one generation, as opposed to a more diverse mix. For example, if the sales department of the core business is comprised of mostly individuals who are within five years of retirement, companies may consider implementing a reciprocal mentorship with less experienced employees in the sales department of the innovation unit.

References

Arsenault, P. M. (2004). Validating generational differences: A legitimate diversity and leadership issue. *Leadership and Organization Development Journal, 25*(2), 124–141.

Bannon, S., Ford, K., & Meltzer, L. (2011). Understanding millennials in the workplace. *The CPA Journal, 81*(11), 61–65.

Beutell, N. J. & Wittig-Berman, U. (2008). Work-family conflict and work-family synergy for generation X, baby boomers, and matures: Generational differences, predictors, and satisfaction outcomes, *Journal of Managerial Psychology, 23*(5), 507–523.

Birkinshaw, J., & Gibson, C. (2004). Building ambidexterity into an organization. *MIT Sloan Management Review, 45,* 47–55.

Blackburn, H. (2011). Millennials and the adoption of new technologies in libraries through the diffusion of innovations process. *Library Hi Tech, 29*(4), 663–677. doi:http://dx.doi.org.ezproxy.lib.apsu.edu/10.1108/07378831111189769

Bock, A. J., Opsahl, T., George, G., & Gann, D. M. (2011, October). The Effects of Culture and Structure on Strategic Flexibility During Business Model Innovation. *Journal of Management Innovation, 49*(2), 279–305.

Boehle, S. (2009). Millennial mentors. *Training, 46*(6), 34–36.

Boumgarden, P., Nickerson, J. & Zenger, T. (2012). Sailing into the wind: Exploring the relationships among ambidexterity, vacillation, and organizational performance. *Strategic Management Journal, 33*(6), 587–610.

Bushey, R. (2014, January 31). Netflix CEO Confesses He Tried to Sell the Company to Blockbuster … But Blockbuster Wasn't Interested. *Business Insider Tech.* Retrieved from http://www.businessinsider.com/blockbuster-missed-buying-netflix-2014-1

Calo, T. (2008). Talent management in the era of the aging workforce: The critical role of knowledge transfer. *Public Personnel Management, 37*(4), 403–416.

Cennamo, L. & Gardner, D. (2008). Generational differences in work values, outcomes and person-organisation values fit. *Journal of Managerial Psychology, 23*(8), 891–906.

Chaudhuri, S. & Ghosh, R. (2012). Reverse mentoring: A social exchange tool for keeping the Boomers engaged and Millennials committed. *Human Resource Development Review, 11*(1), 55–76.

Choudhary, A. (2014). Four Critical Traits of Innovative Organizations. *Journal of Organizational Culture, Communication and Conflict, 18*(2), 45–58.

Chowdhury, T. (2015, January 30). Failure to Innovate—Why Did Blockbuster Fail? *Verb Brands Thoughts.* Retrieved from http://verbbrands.com/failure-to-innovate-why-did-blockbuster-fail

Coad, N., & Pritchard, P. (2013). *Leading Sustainable Innovation.* Oxford: DoSustainability.

Cook, N. (2012, May 29). How Millennials will change the world of work. *National Journal.* Retrieved from http://www.nationaljournal.com/next-economy/solutions-bank/how-millennials-will-change-world-work?mref=scroll

Deloitte. The Deloitte Millennial Survey. Retrieved from https://www2.deloitte.com/content/dam/Deloitte/global/Documents/About-Deloitte/gx-dttl-2014-millennial-surveyreport.pdf

Downing, K. (2006). Next generation: What leaders need to know about the Millennials. *Leadership in Action, 26*(3), 6.

Dreu, C. K. W. (2006). When too little or too much hurts: Evidence for a curvilinear relationship between task conflict and innovation in teams. *Journal of Management, 32*(1), 83–107.

Duncan, R.B. 1976. The Ambidextrous Organization: Designing Dual Structures for Innovation. In R. Kilman and L. Pondy (Eds.), *The Management of Organizational Design*: 167–188. New York, NY: North Holland.

Fernholz, O., Hughes, & Dingwall, R. (2014). Innovational Ambidexterity: Addressing Gaps in Theoretical and Empirical Interpretations. *Helice, 3*(1). Retrieved from https://www.triplehelixassociation.org/helice/volume-3-2014/helice-issue-1/innovation-ambidexterity-addressing-gaps-theoretical-empirical-interpretations

Fry, R. (2015, May 11). Millennials surpass Gen Xers as the largest generation in U.S. labor force. *Fact Tank: News in the Numbers.* Retrieved from http://www.pewresearch.org/fact-tank/2015/05/11/millennials-surpass-gen-

Gibson, J. W., Greenwood, R., & Murphy, E. F. (2009) Generational differences in the workplace: Personal values, behaviors, and popular beliefs. *Journal of Diversity Management 4*(3), 1–7.

Gorman, S. (2015, June 15). Warner says millennials will have 75 percent of jobs by 2025. *Politifact.* Retrieved from http://www.politifact.com/virginia/statements/2015/jun/15/mark-warner/warner-says-millennials-will-have-75 percent-jobs-/

Gottfredson, M. & Aspinall, K. (2005, November). Innovation Versus Complexity: What is Too Much of a Good Thing? *Harvard Business Review,* Retrieved from https://hbr.org/2005/11/innovation-versus-complexitywhat-is-too-much-of-a-good-thing

Gursoy, D., Maier, T. A., & Chi, C. G. (2008). Generational differences: An examination of work values and generational gaps in the hospitality workforce. *International Journal of Hospitality Management, 27*(3), 448–458.

Haoues, R. (2015, April 23). 30 Years Ago Today, Coca-Cola Made Its Worst Mistake. *CBS News.* Retrieved from http://www.cbsnews.com/news/30-years-ago-today-coca-cola-new-coke-failure/

He, Z. L., & Wong, P. K. (2004). Exploration vs. exploitation: an empirical test of the ambidexterity hypothesis. *Organization Science, 15*(4), 481–494.

Hershatter, A., & Epstein, M. (2010). Millennials and the World of Work: An Organization and Management Perspective. *Journal of Business & Psychology, 25*(2), 211–223.

Hewlett, S.A., Sherbin, L, & Sumberg, K. (2009, July-August). How Gen Y and Boomers will reshape your agenda. *Harvard Business Review.* Retrieved from https://hbr.org/2009/07/how-gen-y-boomers-will-reshape-youragenda

Hurley, R. F. & Hult, G. T. M. (1998). Innovation, market orientation, and organizational learning: An integration and empirical examination. *Journal of Marketing, 62*(3), 42–54.

Jamrog, J., Vickers, M., & Bear, D. (2006). Human Resource Planning, 29(3), 9–19.

Jong, J. P. & Hartog, D. N. (2007). How leaders influence employees' innovative behaviour, *European Journal of Innovation Management, 10*(1), 41–64.

Kellmurray, B. (n.d.). Learning from Blockbuster's Failure to Adapt. *Above the Fold Magazine*. Retrieved from http://abovethefoldmag.com/?q=article/learning-blockbuster%E2%80%99s-failure-adapt

Krakovsky, M. (2013, May 31). Charles O'Reilly: Why Some Companies Seem to Last Forever. *Insights by Stanford Business*. Retrieved from https://www.gsb.stanford.edu/insights/charles-oreilly-why-some- companies-seemlast-forever

Martensen, A. & Dahlgaard, J. J. (1999). Integrating business excellence and innovation management: Developing vision, blueprint, and strategy for innovation in creative and learning organizations. *Total Quality Management 10*(4/5), 627–635.

Martins, E. C. & Terblanche, F. (2003). Building Organisational Culture that Stimulates Creativity and Innovation, *European Journal of Innovation Management 6*(1), 64–74.

Matchar, E. (2012, August 16). How those spoiled millennials will make the workplace better for everyone. *The Washington Post.*

McNichols, D. (2010). Optimal knowledge transfer methods: a Generation X perspective, *Journal of Knowledge Management, 14*(1), 24–37.

Meister, J. C. & Willyerd, K. (2010, May). Mentoring Millennials. *Harvard Business Review*. Retrieved from https://hbr.org/2010/05/mentoring-millennials

Moon, T. (2014). Mentoring the Next Generation for Innovation in Today's Organization. *Journal of Strategic Leadership*, 5(1), 23–35. Retrieved from http://www.regent.edu/acad/global/publications/jsl/vol5iss1/fullvol5iss1.pdf

Mootee, I. (2012). Organizational Ambidexterity. *Ivey Business Journal, 76*(6), 1–4.

Myers, K. K., & Sadaghiani, K. (2010). Millennials in the Workplace: A Communication Perspective on Millennials' Organizational Relationships and Performance. *Journal of Business & Psychology,* 25(2), 225–238.

Ng, E. W., Schweitzer, L., & Lyons, S. T. (2010). New Generation, Great Expectations: A Field Study of the Millennial Generation. *Journal of Business & Psychology, 25*(2), 281–292.

O'Reilly III, C. A. & Tushman, M. L. (2004, April). The Ambidextrous Organizations. *Harvard Business Review*. Retrieved from https://hbr.org/2004/04/the-ambidextrous-organization/

Oster, G. (2009). Emergent innovation: A new strategic paradigm. *Journal of Strategic Leadership,* 2(1), 40–56.

Patterson, C. (2005, January). Generational diversity: Implications for consultation and teamwork. Paper presented at the meeting of the Council of Directors of School Psychology Programs on generational differences, Deerfield Beach, FL.

Pew Research Center (2015, March 19). Comparing Millennials to Other Generations. Retrieved from http://www.pewsocialtrends.org/2015/03/19/comparing-millennials-to-other-generations/

Pew Research Center (2015, September 3). The Whys and Hows of Generations Research. Retrieved from http://www.people-press.org/2015/09/03/the-whys-and-hows-of-generations-research/

Ross, M. (2005, April 22). It Seemed Like a Good Idea at the Time. *NBC News.* Retrieved from http://www.nbcnews.com/id/7209828/ns/us_news/t/it-seemed-good-idea-time/#.VuMIUPkrLIU

Satell, G. (2014, September 5). A Look Back at Why Blockbuster Really Failed and Why It Didn't Have To. *Forbes Tech*. Retrieved from http://www.forbes.com/sites/gregsatell/2014/09/05/a-look-back-at-why-blockbusterreally-failed-and-why-it-didnt-have-to/#6c7c1084261a

Scott, N. (2014, July). Ambidextrous Strategies and Innovation Priorities: Priming the Pump for Continual Innovation. *Technology Innovation Management Review*. Retrieved from http://timreview.ca/article/812

Somech, A. (2006). The Effects of Leadership Style and Team Process on Performance and Innovation in Functionally Heterogeneous Teams. *Journal of Management, 32*(1), 132–157.

Stevens, R. (2010, July). Managing human capital: How to use knowledge management to transfer knowledge to today's multi-generational workforce. *International Business Research. 3*(3). Retrieved from http://www.ccsenet.org/journal/index.php/ibr/article/view/6507/5123

Taylor, K. (2013, November 15). The Fall of a Franchise: Blockbuster and 5 Other Chains that Went Bust. *Entrepreneur*. Retrieved from http://www.entrepreneur.com/slideshow/229944

Tesluk, P. E., Farr, J. L. and Klein, S. R. (1997). Influences of organizational culture and climate on individual creativity. *The Journal of Creative Behavior, 31*(1), 27–41.

Thompson, C. & Gregory, J. B. (2012). Managing Millennials: A framework for improving attraction, motivation, and retention. *The Psychologist-Manager Journal, 15*(4), 237–246.

Tushman, M. L., Smith, W. K., & Binns, A. (2011, June). The Ambidextrous CEO. *Harvard Business Review*. Retrieved from https://hbr.org/2011/06/the-ambidextrous-ceo

Twenge, J. M. (2010). A Review of the Empirical Evidence on Generational Differences in Work Attitudes. *Journal of Business & Psychology*, 25(2), 201–210.

Vinekar, V., Slinkman, C. W. & Nerur, S. (2006). Can Agile and Traditional Systems Development Approaches Coexist? An Ambidextrous View. *Information Systems Management, 23*(3), 31–42.

Visser, M., Weerd-Nederhof, P., Faems, D., Song, M., Looy, B. & Visscher, K. (2010). Structural ambidexterity in NPD processes: A firm-level assessment of the impact of differentiated structures on innovation performance. *Technovation, 30*(5), 291–299.

Wang, Y., Li, M., & Mobley, W. H. (2011). *Advances in Global Leadership*. Bingley: Emerald.

Winograd, M. & Hais, M. (2014, May). How Millennials Could Upend Wall Street and Corporate America. *The Initiative on 21st Century Capitalism, 17*. Retrieved from http://www.brookings.edu/research/papers/2014/05/millenials-upend-wall-street-corporate-americawinograd-hais

Yu, H. C. & Miller, P. (2005). Leadership Style—The X Generation and Baby Boomers compared in different cultural contexts. *Leadership and Organizational Development Journal, 26*(1), 35–50.

Zumbrun, J. (2014, November 27). How to tell if a 'fact' about millennials isn't actually a fact. *The Wall Street Journal*. Retrieved from http://blogs.wsj.com/economics/2014/11/27/how-to-tell-if-a-fact-about-millennialsisnt-actually-a-fact/

Post-Reading Questions

1. Describe the differences in values and preferences that you see between generational cohorts in your workplace. Discuss how these differences impact your workplace, work processes, or work relationships. Please support and connect your experiences with the evidence in the article.
2. Discuss the differences between adaptability and alignment in the workplace. Describe the impact of the multigenerational workplace on each of these concepts. How do you believe that the shifting generational mix in the workplace impacts organizations' ability to thrive both in the maintenance of core business and innovation? Please explain your answer.

Videos Retrieved from the Internet

"Millennials in the Workforce, A Generation of Weakness"

https://www.youtube.com/watch?v=QXWNCh0Iluo

This video discusses how failed parenting strategies, technology, impatience, and environment have created the world of millennials.

"Simon Sinek on Millennials in the Workplace"

https://www.youtube.com/watch?v=YrT8lJNa9Z8

This video discusses the factors in understanding how to motivate millennials.

"Hiring Millennials in the Workplace"

https://www.youtube.com/watch?v=_Os7Nl9EwSU

This video discusses how to find the millennials who are compatible with your organization.

"PSA: Millennials in the Workplace"

https://www.youtube.com/watch?v=13JpzNZNJhM&feature=emb_logo

This video uses comedy to discuss the challenges of millennials in the workplace.

Internet Sites on Millennials

"And This Is Why Millennials Get Such a Bad Rap"

https://www.themuse.com/advice/and-this-is-why-millennials-get-such-a-bad-rap

This essay discusses the stereotypes that millennials are entitled, narcissistic, spoiled, and lazy.

"What Happens When Millennials Run the Workplace?"

https://www.nytimes.com/2016/03/20/fashion/millennials-mic-workplace.html?_r=0

This *New York Times* article explores the professional lives of millennials.

"I'm a millennial and my generation sucks"

https://nypost.com/2016/07/04/im-a-millennial-and-my-generation-sucks/

This *New York Post* editorial reviews the downside of millennial challenges.

"7 Ways Millennials Are Changing the Workplace"

https://www.nbcnews.com/better/business/7-ways-millennials-are-changing-workplace-better-ncna761021

This article discusses the positive contributions millennials are making in the workplace.

"Millennials in The Workplace: They Don't Need Trophies but They Want Reinforcement"

https://www.forbes.com/sites/jefffromm/2015/11/06/millennials-in-the-workplace-they-dont-need-trophies-but-they-want-reinforcement/#4d33ca6b53f6

This editorial discusses four positive needs of millennials in the workplace.

"5 Ways Millennials Will Transform the Workplace in 2018"

https://www.forbes.com/sites/larryalton/2017/12/28/5-ways-millennials-will-transform-the-workplace-in-2018/#72a-63ec6558d

This editorial discusses five ways millennials are changing values in the workplace.

Section III

Mind-sets for Ethical Leaders

"Leadership and learning are indispensable to each other."
John F. Kennedy

ORGANIZATIONAL ETHICAL DILEMMAS ARE UNIQUE FOR business leaders because they are complex. Leaders mind-sets have been conditioned to quickly reduce this complexity in pursuit of efficiency to obtain organizations' financial goals. In the process, leaders developed unique leadership styles. These styles set the tone of the organization. The readings in the chapter address these leadership styles: the good, the bad, and the ugly. They provide a framework for what type of leader you wish to become.

In the reading, "One Bad Apple: The Role of Destructive Executives in Organizations," by Alexa A. Perryman, David Sikora, and Gerald Ferris, the authors examine the personal characteristics and organization conditions that are responsible for the creation of a destructive leader. The authors note that Americans have a romantic notion of leadership. This notion, accompanied with attributional egoism on the part of leaders, allows executives to take credit for organizational successes regardless of the amount of influence they had on the outcome. History is filled with good and bad leaders. Infamous leaders may be fewer in numbers, but their behaviors and actions set them apart from other leaders, and they provide a cautionary road sign for future leaders.

The authors argue that everyone has a dark side. Their concept of a dark side is not about possessing or having a tendency to certain characteristics; rather, it is about certain characteristics overtaking leaders. They suggest that leaders with narcissism, exaggerated self-confidence, or Machiavellianism characteristics fit under the umbrella of destructive leaders. They suggest that leaders with these overlapping constructs are linked by an underlying need for a highly positive self-assessment that if left unchallenged would have disastrous results. Additionally, they examine the contextual conditions that help foster a dark side in leaders. On the positive side, they identify three skill sets necessary for leaders to help keep them on the positive side of leadership. These skills sets are political astuteness, empathy, and humility. Internal self-monitoring and external regulations also support the positive side of leadership. They conclude with an examination of the ways individuals and organizations can help prevent the dark side from taking over.

Tammy Cowart, Ann Gilley, Sherry Avery, Afton Barber, and Jerry W. Gilley in their chapter from the book *Executive Ethics II: Ethical Dilemmas and Challenges for the C Suite*, ask, "What characteristics influence employee perceptions of ethics in their leaders and managers?" They address this question by noting that guidance concerning specific characteristics that influence an individual's perceptions of ethics proves useful for both their leader and their company. However, they argue that the ethical challenge is inherently personal in nature. An individual's ethical standards evolve through family, education, religious training, personal relationships, and lifelong experiences. As these experiences are different for everyone, they lead to various standards and perceptions of ethics. Despite these individual differences and complexities, they argue that it is important for companies to develop programs that encourage leaders to act ethically. Three items measure positive leadership behaviors: trust, promoting work-life balance, and treating employees as unique individuals are discussed. The three items that measured negative behaviors, a hostile work environment, lack of management skills, and promoting ineffective leaders are also discussed.

Pre-Reading Questions

- What are the character traits of an outstanding leader you know?
- What are the character traits of an unsuccessful leader you know?
- What are the character traits you need to develop to be an outstanding leader?

Reading 3.1

One Bad Apple: The Role of Destructive Executives in Organizations

Alexa A. Perryman, David Sikora, and Gerald R. Ferris

Introduction

When it comes to examining leadership, most individuals like to focus on the positive. It's far more pleasant and inspiring to discuss the actions of Abraham Lincoln than Adolf Hitler or Costco's champion of corporate responsibility chief executive officer (CEO) James Sinegal than Global Crossing's former Chairman Gary Winnick, whom *Fortune* named the Emperor of Greed in 2002. However, looking on the bright side has the potential to result in seeing an incomplete picture. A romantic view of leadership, coupled with attributional egoism on the part of the leader, allows executives to take credit for successes regardless of the amount of influence, if any, they had on successful outcomes (Brown, 1997; Meindl, Ehrlich, & Dukerich, 1985). This is not to say that executives cannot influence organizations, and do so in positive fashion, or that good leaders do not exist. Instead, we point out that history is filled with both good and bad leaders. Although infamous leaders may be fewer in number, their actions and behaviors set them apart and can serve as a cautionary tale for future leaders.

Everyone has a dark side. Arguably, executives have more opportunities for their dark side to become publicly apparent, given the stresses and demands of managing a firm. In general, there are few leadership characteristics that are inherently negative. This "dark side" of leadership is not about possessing or having a tendency toward certain characteristics—it is about certain characteristics overtaking leaders. Those who are in positions to destroy value most likely reached the top by demonstrating the ability to create value. For example, leaders with narcissistic tendencies do not sit back and try to understand their firm's role in the future; they see the big picture and they shape it though transformative actions and charismatic personalities. Eradicating all characteristics with the potential for a dark side would result in a new era

Alexa A. Perryman, David Sikora, and Gerald R. Ferris, "One Bad Apple: The Role of Destructive Executives in Organizations," *The 'Dark' Side of Management*, ed. Linda L. Neider and Chester Schriesheim, pp. 27-48. Copyright © 2010 by Information Age Publishing. Reprinted with permission.

of leaders that are uninspiring, lacking in grand vision, and unwilling to break free from the mold of business as usual. Instead, by discussing the dark side, we hope to bring to the surface how characteristics that can bring about exceptional performance also can be highly damaging if they are not managed in a constructive fashion.

In this paper, we begin by discussing the characteristics that have the most potential to be used in a destructive fashion. Most of the research on the dark side of leadership has taken a characteristic-by-characteristic approach to examining the potential for problems. We suggest that corporate leaders with characteristics such as narcissism, hubris, Machiavellianism, and the like can fit under the umbrella heading of destructive executives.

More specifically, we suggest that these separate, but often overlapping, constructs are linked by an underlying need for a highly positive self-assessment that, if unchecked, can lead to disaster. In turn, we also examine the contextual conditions that help foster the dark side of leadership, such ineffective corporate governance mechanisms. At extreme levels, the dark side of leadership can be translated to the organization itself. We conclude with an examination of ways in which both individuals and organizations can help to prevent the dark side of leadership from taking over.

The Dark Side of Leadership

We begin with a focus on the individual, the CEO. Few organizations would champion a leader fraught with self-loathing, lacking self-confidence, who has an inability to get things done. However, at the opposite end of the spectrum, it is the extreme of traits such as narcissism, hubris, and a Machiavellian view of the world that can lead to destructive executives.

Narcissism

The concept of narcissism has its roots in Greek mythology. Depending on the version of the myth, the rationale for Narcissus staring into a clear pool of water varies, however, the outcome is the same. He was mesmerized by the reflection in the water. Today, narcissism is used to denote excessive self-esteem, self-love, or self-involvement. Central to the modern version of narcissism is that the resulting positive self-assessments are ego-defense mechanisms necessary to preserve self-esteem (Banaji & Prentence, 1994; Greenwald, 1980). However, a distinction must be made between normal or healthy narcissism and dysfunctional or pathological narcissism. All individuals arguably must have some level of narcissism, as the concept deals with positive views of self, self-esteem, and fantasy. It is at high levels that narcissism interferes with an individual's ability to function, form meaningful relationships, and lose empathy (Brown, 1997).

With regard to leadership, what can start as a vision for the future can turn into a concentrated focus on acquiring more power in order to be able to build an external world that supports ever more grandiose visions (Glad, 2002). As such, narcissistic leadership is driven by unyielding arrogance, self-absorption, and a personal egotistical need for power and admiration (Kets de Vries & Miller, 1997). Narcissists also draw on feelings of superiority to overcome a personal sense of inferiority, thus making them more likely to react toward their subordinates with extreme hypersensitivity and anger (Horowitz & Arthur, 1988). As a result, narcissistic leaders can make for abusive managers.

Abusive managers, although subjective in nature, are managers whose subordinates' perceive then to engage in sustained displays of hostile verbal and nonverbal behaviors (Tepper, 2000). These behaviors can range from angry outbursts and publicly ridiculing subordinates to withholding needed information and the silent treatment to taking credit for subordinates' successes and scapegoating (Keashly, 1998; Keashly, Trott, & MacLean, 1994). The driver behind such abusive behaviors stems from a combination of factors at both the manager and employee levels. At the employee level, factors such as personality (e.g., negative affectivity, conscientiousness, self-esteem, etc.), employee characteristics (e.g., appearing weak, vulnerable, or proactive, etc.), and their perceptions of the context (e.g., job mobility and organizational power) (Tepper, 2007). For executives, abusiveness is fostered by a combination of organizational injustice perceptions, whether they are procedural or interactional, and, in addition to narcissism, personality traits, such as moral disengagement and neuroticism. The combination of narcissism and abusive management practices leads to managers not only with grossly unrealistic senses of entitlement, but also ones who are likely to actively use their skills in deception, manipulation, and intimidation for self-promotion (Glad, 2002).

Aside from the potential for abuse, narcissistic CEOs may be drawn to the limelight and seek to be viewed as celebrities. Although celebrity begins with positive media attention (Hayward, Rindova, & Pollock, 2004), many CEOs, similar to their entertainment counterparts, have fallen from grace. Celebrity CEOs may seek higher pay, while performance for their firms fades back to consistent levels before the media attention began or worsens (Wade et al., 2006). This is not to say that CEO celebrity is universally negative for CEOs and their respective firms. Celebrity CEOs can send favorable signals (e.g., legitimacy, positive reputation, and increased discretion) to the financial, consumer, and labor marketplaces (Fombrun, 1996; Wade et al., 2008). However, if not kept in check, celebrity also can lead to increased hubris (Hayward & Hambrick, 1997), and investments in personal projects of questionable value to the firm (Malmendier & Tate, 2005).

Hubris

One measure of how successful an individual will be is to look at how that individual reacts to failure (Frankl, 1962). Aristotle suggested that all humans, despite the best of intentions, are predisposed to failure based on personal character flaws (i.e., hamartia) and excessive pride (i.e., hubris). By definition, hubris implies a failure to recognize one's own limitations. From its Greek roots, hubris is associated with regarding oneself as equal to the gods. From its Greek history to modern days, hubris has been a reoccurring theme in leadership.

Leadership as a concept entails being in a position of power and authority. Whereas power and authority can allow those in leadership roles the discretion and credibility to accomplish great things, it also can promote extreme pride and arrogance. The more successes leaders achieve the more likely they are to be revered, as well as revere themselves, as more than the common man. As a result, hubris can be viewed as a derivative of narcissism (Kets de Vries, 1990).

The relationship between leaders and followers is not always rational, particularly when the leader is charismatic or possesses other transformational qualities. Followers look to leaders for direction, but also inspiration. Followers can serve as figurate mirrors that reassure and romanticize leaders (Kohut, 1977). Whereas mirroring and idealizing can lead to group cohesion and a unified direction in the short-term, it is also highly likely to lead to a skewed view of reality in the long-term.

At the executive level, founders and high-powered CEOs are the most likely candidates to fall into the trap of hubris. As with many destructive qualities, there is a fine line between benefit and detriment. In this case, the question becomes one of insightful vision or hubris. As a group, founders are entrepreneurs with a vision of the future. In their search for new opportunities, they face uncertainty and must see value in markets that do not yet exist. As such, innovativeness, risk-taking, and proactiveness are hallmarks of entrepreneurs (Miller, 1983). This suggests that entrepreneurial founders are chosen not only for their ability to find opportunities in the face of uncertainty, but also for their self-confidence and persistence (Hayward, Shepherd, & Griffin, 2006). As a whole, this puts founders at a greater risk for hubris as self-confidence and pride are likely to increase with the success of entrepreneurial ventures.

Founders or not, high-powered CEOs also can be guilty of hubris. In addition to a false sense of self, hubris can lead to a misrepresentation of the firm's place in an industry or the business landscape as a whole. In the case of Enron, hubris led to, among other things, an overly broad vision for the company—as was evidenced by changing the company's vision statement from the world's best oil and gas company to the world's best company. Additionally, until negative feedback from external groups, such as shareholders and the business press, is received, CEOs infected with excessive hubris are likely to overpay or be unable to make corrections quickly enough in merger and acquisition dealings (Aktas, de Bodt, & Roll, in press; Roll, 1986).

Machiavellianism

Generally, Machiavellianism is seen as a belief that manipulative and persuasive behaviors may be used to accomplish personal objectives. As a result, individuals high in Machiavellianism believe in using guile and deceit to accomplish personal objectives (Gable & Topol, 1991).

Such individuals also believe it is perfectly acceptable to treat people as a means toward a desired end (Lewin & Stephens, 1994). Put simply, a stereotypical Machiavellian leader will employ aggressive, manipulative, exploitative, and devious moves in order to achieve personal and organizational objectives (Calhoun, 1969).

High-Machs also tend to be very concerned with relative organizational position. Consequently, this suggests that CEOs high in this trait will favor reward systems based on status, with widely different pay between levels and highly visible perquisites such as staff, company cars, and executive dining rooms (Lewin & Stephens, 1994). The need for control that characterizes Machiavellian individuals also suggests that such CEOs do not tolerate diversity of opinion. Instead, they prefer subordinates to be submissive, conforming, and obedient. As a result, they are more likely to exhibit highly directive leadership styles with little focus on interpersonal concerns, such as managing staff issues or showing consideration for followers' feelings (Dahling, Whitaker, & Levy, 2009). In fact, they often are concerned more with their own feelings of control rather than with objective organizational outcomes (Lewin & Stephens, 1994).

Machiavellian traits impact job and organizational behavior in a number of ways. Sakalaki, Richardson, and Thepaut (2007) demonstrated that high-Machs were more likely to maximize their own economic benefits rather than trusting and cooperating with potential economic partners. Similarly, Gunnthorsdottir, McCabe, and Smith (2002) found that, in a trust game in which both participants could profit, high-Machs overwhelmingly chose to take maximum personal benefits rather than reciprocate the trust shown by other participants.

Despite these behaviors, there is another side to Machiavellian individuals. They should not be consistently viewed as frequent liars or unethical. Although this view can pose a threat to ethical behavior, particularly if it stands in the way of personal rewards (Dahling et al., 2009), it is possible for Machiavellian individuals to achieve their ends through ethical means, such as alliance formation (Gable & Topol, 1991).

Along these lines, there is mixed evidence regarding the performance impact of Machiavellianism. Chonko (1982) investigated the relationship between job performance and this trait in purchasing managers, with findings suggesting that managers high in Machiavellianism were perceived to have higher job performance than those low in the trait. In contrast, Gable and Topol (1991) found no significant differences in job performance and Machiavellian orientation in retail managers.

Overall, Machiavellian CEOs present a complex paradox. Their strengths can include aggressive and opportunistic actions to maximize economic outcomes. Unfortunately, these behaviors can come at the expense of manipulating or exploiting those around them. As a result, these CEOs can undermine organizational trust and create a climate of unethical behavior, which can become socialized, reinforced, and eventually ingrained into corporate culture (Anand, Ashforth, & Joshi, 2004).

At the extreme, narcissism, hubris and Machiavellianism reflect the dark side of leadership. Individuals and organizations need to be aware of these traits, and should not accept extremes of these behaviors as part of "normal" leadership. Whereas these characteristics tend to be viewed as individual issues, organizations can, and often do, play a role in facilitating these harmful attributes.

The Organization's Role in the Dark Side of Leadership

It is easy to point to the CEO, and suggest that one individual can singlehandedly change the fate of an organization, in this case for the worse. However, CEOs themselves are not the only force contributing to the dark side of leadership. In this section, we examine the role the organization plays both in fostering and facilitating destructive executives.

The Role of the Board of Directors

The board of directors has long been a focal point of debate for combating potential abuses of power in CEOs. To date, agency theory dominates much of the literature on boards. Agency theory deals with relationships where one party, the principal, delegates decision making-authority to a specialist, the agent. Agents are assumed to be self-interested and possess goals that are divergent from principals (Eisenhardt, 1989). Applying agency theory to the executive suite suggests that without proper incentives and monitoring CEOs will focus on their own wealth maximization and job security at the expense of shareholders' best interests (Shleifer & Vishny, 1989). In turn, the task of providing these incentives and monitoring falls to the board.

A primary debate over the role of the board concerns whether the board is an effective control mechanism or merely a rubber stamp that can be used as a tool by management (Westphal & Zajac, 1995). One source of this debate is the fact that CEOs have the ability to direct the selection process of board members (Mace, 1971; Pfeffer, 1972). Entrenched CEOs may use the board to pursue self-interested actions via control or manipulation of board members (Wade, O'Reilly, & Chandratat, 1990). One way to influence the board is to handpick members. Research suggests that CEOs tend to favor new board members who are similar to themselves (e.g., particularly in terms of demographics) and, in turn, share like-minded philosophies on strategy and administration (Kanter, 1977; Pfeffer, 1981; Westphal & Zajac, 1995).

Another source of debate over the functionality of boards relates to the composition of the board. Specifically, both research and legal guidelines (e.g., Sarbanes-Oxley) largely have focused on the role of outside directors (Certo et al., 2007; Johnson, Daily, & Ellstrand,

1996). In theory, inside directors are more dependent on the CEO, and can easily be dismissed from the board for questioning the CEO's leadership, whereas outside directors are more likely to operate in the best interest of stakeholders, as they are less dependent on the CEO (Pitcher, Chriem, & Kisfavli, 2002). As a result, director independence is thought to lead to decision-making that is free of self-interest. Although outsider-dominated boards have been shown to be more inline with shareholder interests (e.g., less likely to offer golden parachutes or re-price underwater options), the degree to which all outside directors are truly free of self-interest has been called into question.

Outside directors are nominated members, and thus largely dependent on the CEO for their seat (Walsh & Seward, 1990). Aside from having a personal relationship with a CEO, many directors generate one-third of their total income from their compensation package as a director (Certo et al., 2007). The greater directors' salaries are, the more likely it is that they will seek reelection. In turn, a successful board appointment and reelection are likely to lead to other, and potentially more lucrative, board appointments (Bebchuck & Fried, 2004). Moreover, directors determine not only CEOs' compensation, but also their own compensation packages (Dalton & Daily, 2001). Aside from specific stock-based elements, true independent oversight does not occur with regards to either compensation. This suggests that directors, external or not, are likely to face ethical dilemmas similar to CEOs in that they too can benefit from approving decisions that may reduce shareholder wealth. As such, although boards are viewed as a means to protect shareholders, they can play a part in fostering destructive behaviors by allowing executive power to go unchecked.

The Role of CEO Power

Power, put simply, is the ability to influence others (Yukl, 1998). The CEO position has been viewed as the most visible and pertinent strategic manager responsible for guiding both the formulation and implementation of business strategies (Thompson & Strickland, 1992). Organizations contribute to CEO power via the amount of equity ownership CEOs hold in the firm, the extension of CEO tenure beyond their usefulness, and the naming of the CEO to the role of board chair.

Beginning with ownership, a curvilinear relationship has been suggested between ownership and firm performance (McConnell & Servaes, 1990). At low levels of ownership, CEOs run the risk of being less invested and concerned with the success of the organization. In turn, CEOs may exhibit a high tolerance for risks that are not in alignment with shareholder concerns. At the other end of the spectrum, high levels of ownership can lead to CEOs confusing their personal interests with those of the organization and, at extreme levels, exhibit low tolerance for risk.

Tenure also is viewed as an important component is gaining power. During their early years in power, CEOs are under scrutiny from both internal and external parties. Over time,

CEOs build relationships with key constituents, and establish records of successful performance if they are to maintain in the position. In addition to credibility, with increased tenure comes job security, as their network of relationships is likely to make them less susceptible to removal. However, extended tenure can increase the likelihood that CEOs will cling to past successes and views of the competitive landscape, resulting in CEOs becoming "stale in the saddle" (Miller, 1991). Moreover, entrenched managers are more likely to pursue self-interested actions, such as manipulation and control of board members (Wade et al., 1990).

Additionally, duality can be a means for increasing CEO power. If the board is viewed as a means for evaluating CEOs' performance, and the CEO, in the role of chair, is the primary source of information to the board, the ability for the board to accurately and without bias assess the CEO is low at best. However, duality may not be dysfunctional in all instances. Duality can provide a focal point for accountability and faster strategic response times (Finkelstein & D'Aveni, 1994), and can be functional when the board is dominated by non-affiliated outsiders, or when the CEO is low in power (Combs et al., 2007; Finkelstein & D'Aveni, 1994).

The Organization Itself

It has been argued that firms have been anthropomorphized into popular culture to the point where they not only have marketable personas, but also take on lives and personalities as distinct as individuals (Duchon & Burns, 2008; Rindova, Pollock, & Hayward, 2006). Further, this anthropomorphism suggests that firms can transcend their leaders. Firms can attain celebrity status, via achieving positive evaluations from journalists and the media, from two broad courses of action. In the first course of action, firms may be admired for their deviance through low behavioral conformity, while maintaining positive public evaluations (Rindova et al., 2006). This is referred to as deviance admiration (Heckert & Heckert, 2002). Firms taking this path are likely to be labeled as rebels and, consequently, must be ever vigilant of changing environmental conditions.

In the second course of action, firms can pursue positive deviance through high behavioral conformity by over-conforming to positively evaluated norms (Rindova et al., 2006). This is referred to as positive deviance (Heckert & Heckert, 2002). Not only do these firms run the risk of being labeled as rebellious, but also they increase the likelihood of being viewed as market leaders (Rindova et al., 2006). Firm celebrity generally is viewed as having a positive connotation. However, like celebrities at the individual level, it is conceivable that there can be too much of a good thing. Under this logic, organizations can become myopically focused on protecting an identity to the point that the organization itself becomes narcissistic at an unhealthy level (Duchon & Burns, 2008).

Organizations can become narcissistic based on high organization self-esteem (e.g., when an organization denies reality, self-aggrandizes, and embraces a sense of entitlement) or low organizational self-esteem (e.g., when anxiety, alienation, and a pervasive fear of failure take hold) (Duchon & Burns, 2008). In connotation with celebrity, narcissism based on high self-esteem is of concern. Enron often is viewed as a classic example of a firm once viewed as a celebrity (Rindova et al., 2006). In the beginning Enron was a rebel, a change agent for the way energy was bought, sold, and moved. However, Enron became the poster child for greed and unethical behavior. Celebrity depends on the minds of the audience, in this case the general business public. If cases such as Enron become commonplace, where celebrity leads to infamy, it is possible that the general business public will become increasingly weary of star performing firms.

As illustrated above, both individuals and organizations can contribute to the dark side of leadership. High levels of narcissism, hubris, and Machiavellianism detract from the strengths and abilities of CEOs, whereas ineffective governance and organizational narcissism can lead to the downfall of the organization itself. As a whole, this suggests that both CEOs and their organizations can contribute to the problem of the dark side of leadership. In the subsequent sections, we examine ways to impede the darker side of leadership from taking over.

Characteristics CEOs Should Foster to Combat Their Dark Sides

What can be done to prevent these negative leadership characteristics from overwhelming CEOs' positive traits? At the individual-level, three attributes appear to offer an effective remedy. The first positive attribute is political skill, which can help leaders to more effectively influence those around them, while enhancing their ability to attain personal and/or organizational goals. Despite a sometimes negative reputation, political skill can play an important role in the difference between a positive, widely supported outcome and a public-relations nightmare.

The next attribute suggested is empathy. Applied at the executive level, empathy involves taking into account a variety of viewpoints when making important decisions or setting corporate policy. As a result, it can increase organizational support and participation. Lastly, we suggest CEOs seek to develop a sense of humility, which reflects the ability to objectively and accurately assess oneself. This characteristic helps CEOs to maintain a balanced perspective and increases organizational learning. Taken together, these attributes can help balance the dark side of leadership.

Political Skill

Organizations are inherently political arenas (Mintzberg, 1985). As a result, in addition to intelligence, hard work, and effective job performance, additional political factors such as social astuteness, positioning, and savvy play important roles in career success (Luthans,

Hodgetts, & Rosenkrantz, 1988; Mintzberg, 1985). Ferris et al. (2005, p. 127) defined political skill as "the ability to effectively understand others at work, and to use such knowledge to influence others to act in ways that enhance one's personal and/or organizational objectives." Within this definition, there are four key political skill dimensions: social astuteness, interpersonal influence, networking ability, and apparent sincerity (Ferris et al., 2007).

Together, these skills help individuals more effectively navigate the complexities of organizational life. For example, managerial effectiveness may be greatly determined by an individual's ability to effectively deal with an organization's political context (Ferris, Fedor, & King, 1994). This suggests that political behavior is driven by a combination of factors, such as self-monitoring, locus of control, Machiavellianism, the need for power, and risk propensity (Ferris et al., 1994; Porter, Allen, & Angle, 1981).

With these traits in mind, politically-skilled leaders appear to be distinguished by three key factors. First, individuals high in political skill comprehend social cues and accurately attribute others' behavioral motivations. Second, it allows for influence and control over people and situations with relatively little effort. Third, it aids in effectively building the networks and social capital necessary to both elevate their status within the organization, and provide scarce resources to their followers (Treadway et al., 2004). Together, these factors provide politically-skilled leaders the ability to cast their actions in a more acceptable, genuine, and sincere manner (Ferris et al., 2005).

Political skill also can play an important role in job success and leader effectiveness (Douglas & Ammeter, 2004). Inline with this view are findings suggesting that effective managers are distinguished more by effective political skill than by their cognitive abilities (Spencer & Spencer, 1993); that job performance is highest when individuals possess high levels of both general mental ability and social skill (Ferris, Witt, & Hochwarter, 2001); and that the primary reason for managers' career derailments is a lack of interpersonal or social skills (Van Velsor & Leslie, 1995). Moreover, politically-skilled leaders have been shown to improve the organizational experience of their employees by building perceived organizational support (Treadway et al., 2004).

Political skill also can be a key component of leader reputation and perceived trustworthiness, which affect the extent to which formal stakeholder accountability mechanisms are imposed upon leaders (Hall et al., 2004). Lastly, effective political skill has the potential to reduce the negative consequences of engaging in "political" behavior at work (Treadway et al., 2005). Together, these findings illustrate the effectiveness of political skill in shaping CEO performance, and highlight the construct's potential to serve as a means to balance potentially destructive CEO behaviors.

It is noteworthy that political skill can be seen in both a positive and negative manner. On the negative side, politics often are perceived as manipulative and self-serving (Ferris & Kacmar,

1992; Romm & Drory, 1988), and several studies found organizational politics to be negatively related to job satisfaction (Bozeman et al., 1996; Ferris & Kacmar, 1992) and positively related to employee turnover intentions (Bozeman et al., 1996; Cropanzano et al., 1997). Thus, it is important to recognize that taken to extremes, even positive attributes can loose some of their benefit.

Empathy

At the executive level, empathy involves thoughtfully considering a variety of employee, customer, and stakeholder feelings in the process of making intelligent decisions (Hicks & Dess, 2008; Lei & Greer, 2003). More specifically, empathetic CEOs take into account the desires of their subordinates when making decisions (Rotemburg & Saloner, 1993). Empathetic CEOs approach critical decisions from a different viewpoint than non-empathetic leaders. Generally, empathetic leaders tend to be more participatory in style, whereas more selfish CEOs tend to be more autocratic. Empathetic CEOs also tend to display more care for employee and customer views, and are more likely to both solicit their views and consider their preferences on important issues (Rotemburg & Saloner, 1993).

A common thread in works on empathy is understanding and considering the views of others when making decisions and setting policy. Given business' growing use of teams, increased globalization, and a greater importance of high-quality talent retention, empathy is particularly vital in today's changing business landscape (Hicks & Dess, 2008). Although research that directly links empathy to business performance is limited, Rotemburg and Saloner (1993) illustrated five key conclusions about the business impact of leader empathy:

1. Leaders who empathize with their employees adopt a more participatory style.
2. More empathic CEOs will ask their managers questions about a broader range of issues than more selfish ones. As a result, a more empathic CEO is likely to delegate more decision making to his or her managers.
3. More empathic CEOs can be profitable when the environment is rich in potential ideas.
4. When the firm has the potential for exploiting innovative ideas, shareholders gain from appointing empathetic leaders.
5. Holding everything else constant, firms in innovative business sectors should benefit from having empathetic CEOs.

Humility

Humility is sometimes associated with shyness, lack of ambition, passivity, and/or lack of confidence. However, rather than a potential weakness, humility can be a critical business strength. Humility can offer strategic value for firms by providing organizational leaders with a more realistic perspective of themselves, their firm, their competition, and the overall business environment (Vera & Rodriguez-Lopez, 2004).

Humility is best understood as a positive human trait that is both stable and enduring (Peterson & Seligman, 2004). Humility does not involve self-disparagement or negativity. Rather, it involves a willingness to objectively look at oneself. As a result, humility is defined as a personal orientation based on a willingness to see oneself accurately, and to put it in proper perspective. More specifically, it involves self-awareness, openness, and transcendence (Morris, Brotheridge, & Urbanski, 2005).

Self-awareness is the ability to understand one's strengths and weaknesses. Consistently and objectively appraising one's abilities and limitations builds a more realistic sense of self. Similarly, openness also implies an awareness of personal limitations along with the willingness to learn from others. Lastly, transcendence can be thought of as an acceptance of something greater than oneself. This acceptance increases the appreciation of others, and the recognition that others have positive worth.

Humility is valuable to firms because it enhances the ability to understand and respond to external threats and opportunities, and it helps executives avoid complacency and overconfidence. Humility also plays a key role in organizational learning, providing high-quality customer service, and in developing organizational resilience (Vera & Rodriguez-Lopez, 2004). Furthermore, humility can play an important role in effective leadership. Collins (2001a,b) provided strong support for the value of humility in leadership. He found that consistently high-performing organizations shared several important characteristics, one of which was that many great companies were led by individuals who possessed a blend of humility and strong personal will. Collins (2001a,b) asserted that these leaders were still ambitious, but that their primary focus was organizational, rather than personal, success.

Collins (2001a) also described a number of benefits realized by organizations led by leaders of this nature: (1) sustained performance over long periods (e.g., decades); (2) being viewed a "benchmark" performer in and industry; (3) sustainable superior performance after the leader's tenure; and (4) avoidance of public scandal or embarrassments, such as "cooking the books." In support of this view, a similar link was found between CEO humility and business performance (Griffith, 2002). Support for this connection was shown via the personal characteristics of CEOs from *Chief Executive's* 2002 Top 25 Market Value Added (MVA) Companies, with success attributed to CEOs' personal humility, dependability, and consistency.

Humility also helps organizations learn and prosper in a number of ways, such as openness to new ideas, eagerness to learn from others, acknowledgment of limitations and mistakes, pragmatic acceptance of failure, ability to ask for advice and effective employee development (Vera & Rodriguez-Lopez, 2004). Instead of seeing the world only one way (their own), or wanting the organization to remain dependent on them, humble CEOs embrace organizational learning and actively build their firm's human capital as a competitive advantage. In this way, humility can help an organization overcome the limits and confines of arrogant or ego-driven leadership behaviors.

In summary, political skill, empathy, and humility are positive attributes that offer CEOs ways to offset the darker side of CEO leadership. Specifically, these attributes help individuals build positive reputations and increase trustworthiness while avoiding complacency and overconfidence. From an organizational standpoint, these attributes also may bring about additional benefits, such as enhanced firm performance. Although CEOs should take personal responsibility for demonstrating these attributes, organizations and external parties should seek to play an active role in monitoring and holding CEOs accountable for positive and effective leadership behaviors.

Combating the Dark Side of Leadership: External and Organizational Measures

Ideally, self-awareness and self-monitoring would be suggested for all individuals, rather than just CEOs. However, sometimes we all just need a little help along the way. Arguably, it is easier to combat our dark sides when others are watching us or when guidelines, particularly those with consequences, exist to help direct behavior. Under this reasoning, we look at ways external parties and organizations can shape leader behaviors.

The Role of External Monitoring Mechanisms

Without diminishing the role corporate watchdog groups and the media can play in corporate monitoring, it is legal changes in recent years that have received the most attention. A major governing body of corporate behavior is the Securities and Exchange Commission (SEC). The SEC has numerous acts and rules relating to board of director selection, executive compensation disclosure, and other similarly focused items concerning corporate dealings. Despite the steps taken by the SEC, many consider Congress' approval of the Sarbanes-Oxley Act of 2002 (SOX) as one of the most dramatic changes to the corporate landscape, particularly corporate governance, since the 1930s.

In evidence of this view, SOX was named the top legal milestone of the last 10 years (Myers, 2005). SOX's enactment occurred largely as a response to mismanagement, misrepresentation, and managerial excess by companies such as Enron, Tyco, WorldCom, and others. Many advocates of SOX viewed a lack of board proactivity, monitoring, and overall concern as a primary driver behind these recent corporate scandals. In addition to moving jurisdiction from the state to the federal level, SOX represents a push toward transparency, disclosure, and, most notably, independence. New laws and regulations such as these can operate as coercive influences to bring about desired behaviors, in this case ethical behaviors (Valenti, 2007). Moreover, such changes can establish a "broad cultural framework that influences organizations both mimetically and normatively (Suchman & Eldman, 1997, p. 920)."

The Organization as a Monitor of Itself

As suggested by SOX, many of the corporate failures, corruption, and overall mismanagement that has occurred in recent years was attributed to corporate governance failures and, more specifically, ineffective boards of directors. Consequently, it would be all too easy to view the sole role of boards as a gatekeeper to keep executive power in check. However, this narrow view of the role of boards does not account for the resources board members bring to an organization, or the role of advice and counsel (and, in turn, encourage positive behaviors). Although monitoring is an extremely important function of boards, directors also bring resources to the firm (Pfeffer & Salancik, 1978). The challenge of successful and effective boards thus becomes how to juggle these potentially competing roles while adding value to the organization.

Taking together resource dependency, which assumes that management decisions are influenced by internal and external agents, who control critical resources (Pfeffer & Salancik, 1978), and stewardship theory, which views individuals' behavior as having the potential to be pro-organizational, cooperative, and collectivistic (Donaldson & Davis, 1991), boards serve as more than a tool to evaluate management. By viewing directors in terms of their capital (Hillman & Dalziel, 2003), director selection and director diversity (e.g., female board members) are critical components to both organization success and curbing the potential dark sides of leadership.

At a more macro level, organizations should seek to form an environment and culture that fosters not only ethical behavior, as outlined by SOX and the SEC, but also credible and open processes that allow for collaboration, mutual discussions, and information sharing (Ford, 2006). By understanding the needs and resources of all organizational stakeholders, organizations are likely to be more flexible and responsive, as well as be able to head off actions that are self-serving to only one party.

A more unorthodox approach that can lead to organizational openness can be taken from the field of literature. In literature, the role of the fool was that of an individual who, typically through humor, reminded the king of the reality of situations and the transience of power (Kets de Vries, 1990). Arguably, the majority of US organizations today are not true democracies despite corporate governance initiatives. Most organizations' strategies, tactics, and processes are decided by a select few.

Although an inherently risky occupation, an "organizational fool" may be a needed function to counteract the risk of shortsightedness inherent in working closely within a firm

(Kets de Vries, 1990). The risk associated with being the individual (a.k.a. fool) that points out the potential follies of a firm and its management grows if such a person is an insider to the company. Consequently, an external member of the board, such as the board chair or a lead independent director, may be best suited to this role. Through the use of humor and playing dumb, an external member can help a CEO see what is truly possible, what is wishful thinking, and what is best for all stakeholders in an organization.

Lastly, in the same spirit that organizations can be narcissistic, it has been suggested that organizations also can be empathic. Here, empathy is described as the process of learning and growing with customers in order to understand and satisfy their needs via tacit knowledge, sense-making, and articulation skills (Lei & Greer, 2003). In this view, the competitive strength of an empathetic organization is the accumulated customer knowledge that employees possess. Consequently, management practices that promote individual initiative, deep product knowledge, personal interaction with customers, and problem-solving skills are key to the success of empathetic organizations. Empathetic organizations also emphasize employee empowerment, openness, trust, and caring (Lei & Greer, 2003). Collectively, these traits help shape an organizational culture that can limit the impact of negative leadership behaviors.

Although none of these measures are likely to be quick fixes, over time they can lay the foundation for lasting solutions. Such measures, particularly those internal to the organization, can build an organizational culture that curbs the dark side of leadership while not stifling beneficial tendencies, such as believing and actively pursuing a better vision for both the organization and its customers. In the end, it is likely that all stakeholders will need to play a part in fostering the best in leaders.

Conclusion

On their journey to the top, CEOs typically demonstrate a pattern of strong results and a set of behaviors that help consistently deliver positive outcomes. These behaviors include creating value, visualizing opportunities other do not, and shaping the future to fit their long-term vision. However, in some circumstances, leaders lose the critical balance between these positive behaviors and the negative characteristics that lead to the dark side of leadership. When this balance is lost, the dark side of leadership frequently is the result. This dark side hurts not only employees and organizations, but also the leaders themselves. Although our list of dark side characteristics, means of facilitating the dark side, and the means of prevention are not all-inclusive, we hope this discussion can shed some light on extreme behaviors in order to begin restoring the critical equilibrium needed for sustained, effective leadership.

References

Anand, V., Ashforth, B. E., & Joshi, M. (2004). Business as usual: The acceptance and perpetuation of corruption in organizations. *Academy of Management Executive, 18,* 39–55.

Aktas, N., de Bodt, E., & Roll, R. (in press). Learning, hubris and corporate serial acquisitions. *Journal of Corporate Finance.*

Banaji, M. R., & Prentice, D. A. (1994). The self in social contexts. *Annual Review of Psychology, 45,* 297–332.

Bebchuck, L., & Fried, J. (2004). *Pay without performance: The unfulfilled promise of executive compensation.* Cambridge, MA: Harvard University Press.

Bozeman, D. P., Perrewé, P. L., Hochwarter, W. A., Kacmar, K. M., & Brymer, R. A. (1996). Opportunity or threat? An examination of differential reactions to perceptions of organizational politics. In M. Schnake (Ed.), *Proceedings of the Southern Management Association,* Southern Management Association, Atlanta, GA.

Brown, A. D. (1997). Narcissism, identity, and legitimacy. *Academy of Management Review, 22*(3), 643–686.

Calhoun, R. P. (1969). Niccoli Machiavelli and the twentieth century administrator. *Academy of Management Journal, 12,* 205–212.

Certo, S. T., Dalton, C. M., Dalton, D. R., & Lester, R. H. (2007). Boards of directors' self interest: Expanding for pay in corporate acquisitions? *Journal of Business Ethics, 77,* 219–230.

Chonko, L. B. (1982). Machiavellianism: Sex differences in the profession of purchasing management. *Psychological Reports, 51,* 645–646.

Collins, J. (2001a). *Good to great: Why some companies make the leap and others don't.* New York: Harper Business.

Collins, J. (2001b). Level 5 leadership: The triumph of humility and fierce resolve. *Harvard Business Review, 79*(1), 67–77.

Combs, J. G., Ketchen, D. J., Perryman, A. A., & Donahue, M. S. (2007). The moderating effect of CEO power on the board composition-firm performance relationship. *Journal of Management Studies, 44*(8), 1299–1323.

Cropanzano, R., Howes, J. C., Grandey, A. A., & Toth, P. (1997). The relationship of organizational politics and support to work behaviors, attitudes, and stress. *Journal of Organizational Behavior, 18,* 159–180.

Dahling, J. J., Whitaker, B. G., & Levy, P. E. (2009). The development and validation of a new machiavellianism scale. *Journal of Management, 35,* 219–255.

Daily, C. M., & Dalton, D. R. (2003). Are director equity policies exclusionary? *Business Ethics Quarterly, 13,* 415–432.

Dalton, D. R., & Daily, C. M. (2001). Director stock compensation: An invitation to a conspicuous conflict of interests? *Business Ethics Quarterly, 11*(1), 89–108.

Donaldson, L., & Davis, J. H. (1991). Stewardship theory or agency theory: CEO governance and shareholder returns. *Australian Journal of Management, 16,* 49–64.

Douglas, C., & Ammeter, A. P. (2004). An examination of leader political skill and its effect on ratings of leader effectiveness. *The Leadership Quarterly, 15,* 537–550.

Duchon, D., & Burns, M. (2008). Organizational narcissism. *Organizational Dynamics, 37*(4), 354–364.

Eisenhardt, K. M. (1989). Agency theory: An assessment and review. *Academy of Management Review, 14,* 57–74.

Ferris, G. R., & Kacmar, K. M. (1992). Perceptions of organizational politics. *Journal of Management, 18,* 93–116.

Ferris, G. R., Fedor, D. B., & King, T. R. (1994). A political conceptualization of managerial behavior. *Human Resource Management Review, 4,* 1–34.

Ferris, G. R., Treadway, D. C., Kolodinsky, R. W., Hochwarter, W. A., Kacmar, C. J., Douglas, C., & Frink, D. D. (2005). Development and validation of the political skill inventory. *Journal of Management, 31,* 126–152.

Ferris, G. R., Treadway, D. C., Perrewé, P. L., Brouer, R. L., Douglas, C., & Lux, S. (2007). Political skill in organizations. *Journal of Management, 33,* 290–320.

Ferris, G. R., Witt, L. A., & Hochwarter, W. A. (2001). Interaction of social skill and general mental ability on job performance and salary. *Journal of Applied Psychology, 86*(6), 1075–1082.

Finkelstein, S., & D'Aveni, R. A. (1994). CEO duality as a double-edged sword: How boards balance entrenchment avoidance and unity of command. *Academy of Management Journal, 37,* 1079–1108.

Fombrun, C. (1996). *Reputation: Realizing value from the corporate image.* Boston, MA: Harvard Business School Press.

Ford, R. (2006). Why we fail: How hubris, hamartia, and anagnosis shape organizational behavior. *Human Resource Development Quarterly, 17*(4), 481–489.

Frankl, V. (1962). *Man's search for meaning.* Boston, MA: Beacon Press.

Gable, M., & Topol, M. T. (1991). Machiavellian managers: Do they perform better? *Journal of Business and Psychology, 5*(3), 355–356.

Glad, B. (2002). Why tyrants go too far: Malignant narcissism and absolute power. *Political Psychology, 23,* 1–37.

Greenwald, A. G. (1980). The totalitarian ego: Fabrication and revision of personal history. *American Psychologist, 35*(7), 603–618.

Griffith, V. (2002). Steady as they go. *Chief Executive, 184,* 24–33.

Gunnthorsdottir, A., McCabe, K., & Smith, V. (2002). Using the Machiavellianism instrument to predict trustworthiness in a bargaining game. *Journal of Economic Psychology, 23*(1), 49–66.

Hall, A. T., Blass, F. R., Ferris, G. R., & Massengale, R. (2004). Leader reputation and accountability in organizations: Implications for dysfunctional leader behavior. *The Leadership Quarterly, 15,* 515–536.

Hayward, M. L. A., & Hambrick, D. C. (1997). Explaining the premiums paid for large acquisitions: Evidence of CEO hubris. *Administrative Science Quarterly, 42,* 103–127.

Hayward, M. L. A, Rindova, V. P., & Pollack, T. G. (2004). Believing one's own press: The causes and consequences of CEO celebrity. *Strategic Management Journal, 25,* 637–653.

Hayward, M. L. A., Shepherd, D. A., & Griffin, D. (2006). A hubris theory of entrepreneurship. *Management Science, 52*(2), 160–172.

Heckert, A., & Heckert, D. (2002). A new typology of deviance: Integrating normative and reactivist definitions of deviance. *Deviant Behavior: An Interdisciplinary Journal, 23,* 449–479.

Hicks, R., & Dess, G.D. (2008). A question of leadership: Are there any potential downsides to emotional intelligence for executives, and if so, what are they? *Leadership in Action, 28*(5), 18–24.

Hillman, A. J., & Dalziel, T. (2003). Boards of directors and firm performance: Integrating agency and resource dependence perspectives. *Academy of Management Review, 28,* 383–396.

Horowitz, M. J., & Arthur, R. J. (1988). Narcissistic rage in leaders: The intersection of individual dynamics and group processes. *The International Journal of Social Psychiatry, 34,* 135–141.

Johnson, J. L., Daily, C. M., & Ellstrand, A. E. (1996). Boards of directors: A review and research agenda. *Journal of Management, 22,* 409–438.

Kanter, R. M. (1977). *Men and women of the corporation.* New York: Basic Books.

Keashly, L. (1998). Emotional abuse in the workplace: Conceptual and empirical issues. *Journal of Emotional Abuse, 1,* 85–117.

Keashly, L., Trott, V., & MacLean, L. M. (1994). Abusive behavior in the workplace: A preliminary investigation. *Violence and Victims, 9,* 341–357.

Kets de Vries, M. F. R. (1990). The organizational fool: Balancing a leader's hubris. *Human Relations, 43*(8), 751–770.

Kets de Vries, M., & Miller, D. (1985). Narcissism and leadership: An object relations perspective. *Human Relations, 38*(6), 583–601.

Kets de Vries, M. F. R., & Miller, D. (1997). Narcissism and leadership: An object relations perspective. In R. P. Vecchio (Ed.), *Leadership: Understanding the dynamics of power and influence in organizations* (pp. 194–214). Notre Dame, IN: University of Notre Dame Press.

Kohut, H. (1977). *The restoration of the self.* New York: International Universities Press.

Lei, D., & Greer, C. R. (2003). The empathetic organization. *Organizational Dynamics, 32*(2), 142–164.

Lewin, A. Y., & Stephens, C. U. (1994). CEO attitudes as determinants of organization design: An integrated model. *Organization Studies, 15*(2), 183–212.

Luthans, F., Hodgetts, R. M., & Rosenkrantz, S. A. (1988). *Real managers.* Cambridge, MA: Ballinger.

Mace, M. L. (1971). *Directors: Myth and reality.* Boston: Harvard Business School Press.

Malmendier, U., & Tate, G. (2005). Does overconfidence affect corporate investment? CEO overconfidence measures revisited. *European Financial Management, 11,* 649–659.

McConnell, J. J., & Servaes, H. (1990). Additional evidence on equity ownership and corporate value. *Journal of Financial Economics, 27,* 595–612.

Meindl, J. R., Ehrlich, S. B., & Dukerich, J. M. (1985). The romance of leadership. *Administrative Science Quarterly, 30,* 78–102.

Miller, D. (1983). The correlates of entrepreneurship in three types of firms. *Management Science, 29,* 770–791.

Miller, D. (1991). Stale in the saddle: CEO tenure and the match between organization and environment. *Management Science, 32,* 1389–1409.

Mintzberg, H. (1985). The organization as a political arena. *Journal of Management Studies, 22,* 133–154.

Morris, J. A., Brotheridge, C. M., & Urbanski, J. C. (2005). Bringing humility to leadership: Antecedents and consequences of leader humility. *Human Relations, 58,* 1323–1350.

Myers, R. (2005). The top 10 legal milestones of the last 10 years. *Corporate Board Member, 8,* 48–62.

Peterson, C., & Seligman, M. (2004). *Character strengths and virtues: A handbook and classification.* New York: Oxford University Press.

Pfeffer, J. (1972). Size and composition of corporate boards. *Administrative Science Quarterly, 17,* 218–228.

Pfeffer, J. (1981). *Power in organization.* Marshfield, MA: Pitman.

Pfeffer, J., & Salancik, G. R. (1978). *The external control of organizations: A resource dependence perspective.* New York: HarperCollins.

Pitcher, P., Chreim, S., & Kisfavli, V. (2002). CEO succession research: Methodological bridges over troubled waters. *Strategic Management Journal, 21,* 625–648.

Porter, L. W., Allen, R. W., & Angle, H. L. (1981). The politics of upward influence in organizations. In L. L. Cummings, & B. M. Staw (Eds.), *Research in organizational behavior* (Vol. 3, pp. 109–149). Greenwich, CT: JAI Press.

Rindova, V. P., Pollock, T. G., & Hayward, M. L. A. (2006). Celebrity firms: The social construction of market popularity. *Academy of Management Review, 31,* 50–71.

Roll, R. (1986). The hubris hypothesis of corporate takeovers. *Journal of Business, 59*(2), 197–216.

Romm, T., & Drory, A. (1988). Political behavior in organizations—a cross-cultural comparison. *International Journal of Value Based Management, 1,* 165–179.

Rotemberg, J. J., & Saloner, G. (1993). Leadership style and incentives. *Management Science, 39*(11), 1299–1318.

Sakalaki, M., Richardson, C., & Thepaut, Y. (2007). Machiavellianism and economic opportunism. *Journal of Applied Social Psychology, 37,* 1181–1190.

Schuman, M. C., & Edelman, L. B. (1997). Legal rational myths: The new institutionalism and the law and society tradition. *Law and Social Inquiry, 27,* 903–941.

Shleifer, A., & Vishny, R. W. (1989). Management entrenchment: The case of manager-specific investments. *Journal of Financial Economics, 25,* 123–129.

Spencer, L. M., & Spencer, S. M. (1993). *Competence at work: Models for superior performance.* New York: John Wiley.

Tepper, B. J. (2000). Consequences of abusive supervision. *Academy of Management Journal, 43*(2), 178–190.

Tepper, B. J. (2007). Abusive supervision in work organizations: Review, synthesis, and research agenda. *Journal of Management, 33,* 261–289.

Thompson, J., & Strickland, A. J. (1992). *Strategic management: Concepts and cases.* Homewood, IL: Irwin.

Treadway, D. C., Hochwarter, W. A., Ferris, G. R., Kacmar, C. J., Douglas, C., Ammeter, A. P., & Buckley, M. R. (2004). Leader political skill and employee reactions. *The Leadership Quarterly, 15,* 493–513.

Treadway, D. C., Hochwarter, W. A., Kacmar, C. J., & Ferris, G. R. (2005). Political will, political skill, and political behavior. *Journal of Organizational Behavior, 26,* 229–245.

Valenti, A. (2007). The Sarbanes-Oxley Act of 2002: Has is brought about changes in the boards of large U.S. corporations? *Journal of Business Ethics, 81,* 401–412.

Van Velsor, E., & Leslie, J. B. (1995). Why executives derail: Perspectives across time and cultures. *Academy of Management Executive, 9,* 62–72.

Vera, D., & Rodriguez-Lopez, A. (2004). Strategic values: Humility as a source of competitive advantage. *Organizational Dynamics, 33*(4), 393–408.

Wade, J., O'Reilly, C., & Chandratat, I. (1990). Golden parachutes: CEOs and the exercise of social influence. *Administrative Science Quarterly, 35,* 587–603.

Wade, J. B., Porac, J. F., Pollock, T. G., & Graffin, S. D. (2006). The burden of celebrity: The impact of CEO certification contests on CEO pay and performance. *Academy of Management Journal, 49,* 643–660.

Wade, J. B., Porac, J. F., Pollock, T. G., & Graffin, S. D. (2008). Star CEOs: Benefit or burden? *Organizational Dynamics, 37*(2), 203–210.

Walsh, J. P., & Seward, J. K. (1990). On the efficiency of internal and external corporate control mechanisms. *Academy of Management Review, 15,* 421–458.

Westphal, J. D., & Fredrickson, J. W. (2001). Who directs strategic change? Director experience, the selection of new CEOs and change in corporate strategy. *Strategic Management Journal, 22,* 1113–1137.

Westphal, J. D., & Zajac, E. J. (1995). Who shall govern? CEO/board power, demographic similarity, and new director selection. *Administrative Science Quarterly, 40*(1), 60–83.

Yukl, G. (1994). *Leadership in organizations* (3rd edition). Englewood Cliffs, NJ: Prentice Hall.

Yukl, G. (1998). *Leadership in organizations* (4th edition). Englewood Cliffs, NJ: Prentice Hall.

Reading 3.2

Ethical Leaders: Trust, Work-Life Abundance, and Treating Individuals as Unique

Tammy Cowart, Ann Gilley, Sherry Avery, Afton Barber, and Jerry W. Gilley

THE ETHICS RESOURCE CENTER REPORTS THAT two major drivers of ethical culture are senior executives and supervisors (Ethics Resource Center, 2012). According to the Ethics Resource Center's 2011 National Business Ethics Survey, employee perceptions of both groups has declined, with one third of employees reporting that their managers do not display ethical behavior, the highest percentage ever reported. In addition, confidence in senior leadership was at a historic low.

Schein (1985, p. 2) stated that the "only thing of real importance that leaders do is to create and manage culture." Prior research demonstrates that leaders influence company culture by focusing the organization's way of thinking and taking action (Gilley, Anderson, & Gilley, 2008). However, when leaders and managers also employ an ethical focus, the result can improve the overall long-term performance of the company (Caldwell, Hayes, Karri, & Bernal, 2008; Longenecker, 1985).

What characteristics influence employee perceptions of ethics in their leaders and managers? Guidance concerning specific characteristics that influence employee perceptions of ethics would prove useful for both companies and their managers. However, the challenge here is that ethics is inherently personal in nature. One's ethical lens develops through family, education, relationships, and life experiences, leading to different standards and approaches to ethics (Gilley et al., 2008). Despite these differences and complexities, it is important for companies to develop programs that encourage leaders and managers to act ethically.

This study explores leadership and management practices that influence employees' perceptions that their managers are ethical. Respondents were asked to specify, in their opinion, how frequently firm managers were considered ethical. The three items that measured positive management behaviors included trust, promoting work–life balance, and treating employees as unique individuals. The three items that measured negative behaviors included creating a hostile work environment, lack of management skills, and promoting ineffective managers. Results and implications are discussed below.

Background

Leaders are challenged more than ever to think and plan strategically, act decisively, enhance performance, work collaboratively, focus on customers, and develop the organization and its people (Holt, 2011). Leadership has been found to be of particular importance to organizations in crisis situations (Weick, 1995).

For decades, researchers have sought to identify the behaviors, skills, and styles demonstrated by effective leaders capable of meeting these myriad demands (Bass & Avolio, 1994; Gilley, McMillan, & Gilley, 2009; Ligon, Wallace, & Osburn, 2011). More recently, much of the research and literature has shifted from trait theory to behavioral theory, which focuses on what the leader says and does (Miner, 2003). Despite this shift, Hemsley (2001) reminds us that a leader's behavior is based on his or her skills and traits. Today, research continues to seek a better understanding of effective leader behaviors (Steers, Mowday, & Shapiro, 2004) and their predictors (Ferraro, Pfeffer, & Sutton, 2005).

Leadership has been viewed as a social phenomenon based on interactive relationships between leaders and followers (Griffin & Stacey, 2005) and as a shared influence process that flows from the interactions of diverse individuals (Van Ameijde, Nelson, Billsberry, & Van Meurs, 2009). The emphasis on interpersonal and social skills finds support in the literature on effective leaders that posits a transformational as opposed to transactional approach (Harris, Day, Hopkins, Hadfield, Hargreaves, & Chapman, 2003). The four interpersonal aspects of transformational leadership are idealized influence, inspirational motivation, intellectual stimulation, and individualized consideration (Bass, 1985, 1998; Bass & Avolio, 1993). According to Astin and Astin (2000, p. 49), these concur in their view of transformational leadership as "self-aware, authentic, and empathetic, and because it develops trust through listening, collaborating, and shaping a common purpose."

Although linkages have been found between transformational leadership and greater satisfaction with and trust in leaders (Keller, 1995), Martin (1999) found that the most important element for leadership, in general, is the ability to engender trust. Additional behaviors and skills critical for effective leadership are ethics (Neubert, Carlson, Kacmar, Roberts, & Chonko, 2009; Walumba, Mayer, Wang, Wang, Workman, & Christensen, 2011), the ability to build relationships and enhance collaboration (Martin, 2005), and treating individuals as unique (Gilley, Heames, & Gilley, 2012), among others.

Ethical Leadership

Ethics, a subject discussed for centuries (Toor & Ofori, 2009), has been anecdotally defined as "doing the right thing when no one else is watching" (Leopold, n.d.). In a business context, ethics generally refers to the social and moral obligations of business. Thus, leaders and managers must pay attention to the obligations and expectations society places on business.

It has been fairly well established that managers and leaders influence ethical culture (Bass & Steidlmeier, 1999; Ciulla, 1995; Trevino, Brown, & Hartman, 2003; Trevino, Hartman, & Brown, 2000). In terms of ethics, ethical leadership has been defined as the "demonstration of normatively appropriate conduct through personal actions and interpersonal relationships, and the promotion of such conduct to followers through two-way communication, reinforcement, and decision-making" (Brown, Trevino, & Harrison, 2005, p. 120).

Establishing a positive ethical culture can lead to improvements in the entire culture of an organization (Brown et al., 2005), such as extra effort, reporting problems, and other employee outcomes. Previous studies have linked ethical leadership to higher job satisfaction and job commitment (Neubert et al., 2009), better performance (Walumba et al., 2011), and lower levels of deviance (Mayer, Kuenzi, Greenbaum, Bardes, & Salvador, 2009). Thus, the characteristics and behaviors of those who would have such an influence over an organization are important (Jordan, Brown, Trevino, & Finkelstein, 2013). Jordan et al. (2013) focused on what made followers, or employees, perceive that executives were ethical. Their findings have shown that managers who are "caring, honest, and principled individuals" are ethical, as well as those who are fair and trustworthy, reward ethical behavior, punish unethical behavior, and communicate the importance of ethics to followers (Brown et al., 2005; Trevino et al., 2003; Trevino et al., 2000; Yukl, Mahsud, Hassan, & Prussia, 2013). Among these attributes, trust has the strongest correlation to job satisfaction and organizational commitment (Dirks & Ferrin, 2002). As trust seems to be an important theme in ethical leadership, we review the literature on trust below.

Discussion

Trust

Trust is a vital element in all of our relationships—personal, professional, and community. While there are numerous definitions of trust in the literature, most focus on the idea of constancy (Bennis, 1989) and positive expectations of the intentions or behaviors of others (Hodson, 2004; Mayer, Davis, & Schoorman, 1995; Nooteboom, 1997; Rousseau, 1998). Trustworthiness has been defined as an attribute of exchange partners in which an exchange partner who will not exploit another's vulnerabilities is worthy of trust (Barney & Hansen, 1994). Merriam Webster Dictionary defines trust as "assured reliance on the character, ability, strength, or truth of someone or something" and includes trustworthiness in its definition as well (Trust, n.d.). In the business ethics realm, some minimal level of trust is critical for employees and managers to effectively interact with each other (Bandsuch, 2008). Unfortunately however, society generally regards business leaders as untrustworthy (Child, 2004).

Developing trust is important for managers. From the manager's perspective, trustworthiness is a trait that is most often associated with ethical leadership (Trevino et al., 2000). To establish trust, leaders must clearly and fully communicate, institutionalize, and embody the company's values. According to Mayer et al. (1995), managers' and employees' perceptions of each other's trustworthiness will affect their risk-taking behavior, which will ultimately influence trust. Konovsky and Pugh (1994) wrote that employees who believe that their manager has acted or will act with care and consideration will spend more time on required job performance tasks. Employees are more likely to trust management if the manager's behavior conforms to prevailing norms of fairness, integrity, and respect for employees' rights and interests, such as predictability and justice (Caldwell et al., 2008; Hodson, 2004; Kickul, Gundry, & Posig, 2005). Bandsuch (2008) identifies the following factors as significant influences upon trust: competency, openness, concern for stakeholders, shared goals, reliability, frequency of interactions, rewards, and sanctions.

Wright (2005) contends that trust allows managers and employees to enhance their relationships with each other. Accordingly, they can build a positive, comfortable, and nonthreatening communication climate—one that encourages employees to discuss organizational issues, problems, and other ideas openly and honestly, without fear of reprisal. It has been theorized that such an environment establishes conditions that will expedite trust-based synergistic relationship processes that are

> the interdependence of individuals working toward a common goal, which simultaneously provides for growth and development opportunities for both participants as well as the organization. Such relationships yield five benefits: enhancing and building managers' and employees' self-esteem, enhancing productivity, enhancing and building organizational communications, enhancing and building organizational understanding, and enhancing and building organizational commitment. (Gilley & Boughton, 1996, p. 72)

Accordingly, trust-based synergistic relationships are healthy relationships between mangers and their employees, which yield five benefits:

1. Enhancing and building self-esteem
2. Improving productivity
3. Improving and building organizational communications
4. Enhancing and building organizational understanding
5. Facilitating and building organizational commitment (Gilley & Gilley, 2006)

Furthermore, Gilley and Boughton (1996) identified a nine-step process for building positive, healthy, trust-based synergistic relationships. The steps are:

1. Freedom from fear refers to creating work environments that are safe, respectful, and conducive to acceptance.
2. One-on-one communication actively sharing information with others.
3. Interaction is more than communication because it implies a personal engagement with employees where members take the time to discuss issues and problems.
4. Acceptance requires respect for employees as a unique individual with differing characteristics, personalities, life experiences, and professional paths.
5. Personal involvement requires employees to spend significant time with each other.
6. Trust implies open, honest, and direct and truthful communication.
7. Honestly sharing more and more private information with others, which increases the level of personal intimacy.
8. Self-esteeming is the mutual and reciprocal respect and confidence present when two parties work collaboratively to achieve desired results.
9. Professional development is the key output of a synergistic relationship where employees directly and honestly discuss ways of improving their colleagues' competencies and skills designed to improve performance impact (Gilley, Boughton, & Maycunich, 1999; Katzenbach & Smith, 2003)

When these nine are present, the manager–employee relationships are honest and trust-based, and employees are completely accountable for performance results, which is customary in highly effective organizations (Klein et al., 2009). When employees are respectful, caring, and cooperative, it can also enhance business results (Whichard & Kees, 2006). Thus, it is extremely difficult to produce the performance results desired by an organization without managers and employees establishing positive trust-based synergistic relationships (Gilley & Gilley, 2006). In fact, the ultimate outcome of a positive trust-based relationship with employees is known as rapport, which is the unconditional positive regard between managers and employees and is further defined as a deep concern for the well-being of others

(Whichard & Kees, 2006). Rapport is established through your sincere interest in and acceptance of others (Kirkman, Jones, & Shapiro, 2000).

Organizational Culture

Organizational culture is indeed the important artifacts, rules, values, principles, and assumptions that guide organizational behavior. According to Schein (1992), organizational culture can be defined as

> a pattern of basic assumptions invented, discovered, or developed by a given group as it learns to cope with the problems of external adaptation and internal integration that all works well enough to be considered valid and therefore to be taught to new members as the correct way to perceive, think, and feel in relation to those problems. (p. 9)

Schein's definition illustrates that culture involves assumptions, adaptations, perceptions, and learning. More simply, Gilley and Maycunich (2000) refer to organizational culture as "the way we do things around here" (p. 108). Organizational culture is, indeed, a complex topic strongly influenced by history, customs, and practices. Moreover, organizational culture is what employees perceive to be the pattern of belief, values, and expectations that guide behavior and practice within the organization. Quite simply, culture determines the type of institution the organization becomes.

Effective organizations manifest the optimal organizational culture. According to Burke (1992), optimal organizational culture exhibits the following characteristics:

1. growth and development of organizational members is just as important as making profits or staying within budget
2. equal opportunity and fairness for people within an organization is commonplace, the rule rather than the exception
3. managers exercise their authority more participatively than unilaterally or arbitrarily; authority is associated more with knowledge and competence than role or status
4. cooperative behavior is rewarded more than competitive behavior
5. organizational members are kept informed or at least have access to information, especially concerning matters directly impacting their jobs or them personally
6. members feel a sense of ownership of the organization's mission and objectives
7. conflict is dealt with openly and systematically rather than ignored, avoided, or handled in a typical win–lose fashion
8. rewards are based on a system of quality, fairness, and equitable merit

9. organization members are given much more autonomy and freedom to do their respective jobs as possible, enduring both a high degree of individual motivation and accomplishment of the organization's strategic goals and objectives (pp. 196–197)

When these characteristics are present, a positive culture can be established.

Treating People as Unique Individuals

Recent research on individual differences lends support to our findings on the importance of treating employees as unique. Research by Wong, Gardiner, Lang, and Coulon (2008) emphasized "the importance of focusing on individual differences" (p. 878). This theme was supported by participants in a study by Gilley et al. (2012), who indicated that unique treatment of the individual "was a critical ingredient and primary remedy to managerial ineffectiveness" (p. 74). The rise of influence in the workplace of generations X, Y, GenMe, and Millennials lends further support to the need for emphasis on individualism and recognition of employee uniqueness (Twenge, 2010). Moreover, leaders are perceived as ethical when they consider the individual needs of employees (Zhu, May, & Avolio, 2004). Organizations who seek to hire or retain these talented employees will need to attend to policies and practices that support the evolving needs of new generations of workers.

Work–Life Balance

Work–life balance is an increasingly studied topic, particularly in light of generational differences (Chao, 2005; Twenge & Campbell, 2008; Wong et al., 2008). Twenge (2010), for example, found that GenY/GenMe employees gravitate to companies that focus on work–life balance issues. This is salient to our study as well, as a significant percentage of the respondents in our study were under the age of 35.

Findings of our study suggest that the manager is a key factor in promoting work–life balance. Scholars have noted that managerial support, understanding, and communication are critical to employees' achievement of work/family balance (Anderson et al., 2002; Batt & Valcour, 2003; Clark, 2002; Eversole, Venneberg, & Crowder, 2012). A manager's positive behaviors, such as flexibility and sensitivity, have a positive impact on establishing work–life balance. Eversole et al. (2012) claim "an insensitive and inflexible manager increases tension, decreases productivity, and has the single most negative influence on work-life" (p. 615). The managerial support factor defined as "the extent to which managers were supportive and sensitive to employees' family responsibilities" influences work–life balance (Thompson, Beauvais, & Lyness, 1999, p. 401).

"While researchers have posited that 'contextual factors' such as work-life policies and managerial support are important, there is not substantial empirical research that examines employees' perceptions regarding the extent to which a context is supportive of work–life issues and the implications this has for work–life policy utilization (Allen, 2001)" (Greenberg & Landry, 2011, p. 1164).

Conclusion

Our study implies that leaders and managers who create trust-based relationships, respect work–life balance, and treat their employees as unique individuals are perceived as more ethical than those who do not. Additionally, when individuals who do not possess appropriate management skills are placed in leadership/managerial positions, they are perceived as unethical. Our results point to positive constructs managers can use to enhance their ethical behavior.

Employees from generations X, Y, GenMe, and Millennials are more interested in issues such as work–life balance and being treated uniquely. Creating programs that support work–life balance will validate the unique individual needs of employees. These efforts promote an environment of trust between manager and employee, laying the foundation for an ethical culture. Conversely, our results point to negative behaviors that erode perceptions of ethics. Leaders and managers who lack appropriate management skills or are ineffective may unwittingly create a hostile work environment, which negatively affects perceptions of ethics. Intentional efforts to emphasize these simple but critical positive elements may help create a work environment in which ethical behavior is the norm.

References

Allen, T. D. (2001). Family-supportive work environments: The role of organizational perceptions. *Journal of Vocational Behavior, 58*, 414–435. doi:10.1006/jvbe.2000.1774

Anderson, J. C., & Gerbing, D. W. (1988). Structural equation modeling in practice: A review and recommended two-step approach, *Psychological Bulletin, 103*(3), 411–423.

Anderson, S. E., Coffey, B. S., & Byerly, R. T. (2002). Formal organizational initiatives and informal workplace practices: Links to work-family conflict and job related outcomes. *Journal of Management, 28*, 787–811.

Astin, W. A., & Astin, H. S. (2000). *Leadership reconsidered: Engaging higher education in social change.* Battle Creek, MI: Kellogg Foundation.

Bandsuch, M. P. (2008). Rebuilding stakeholder trust in business: An examination of principle-centered leadership and organizational transparency in corporate governance. *Business and Society Review*, 99–127.

Barney, J. B., & Hansen, M. H. (1994). Trustworthiness as a source of competitive advantage. *Strategic Management Journal*, 175–190.

Bass, B. M. (1985). *Leadership and performance beyond expectations.* New York, NY: Free Press.

Bass, B. M. (1998). *Transformational leadership: Industry, military, and educational impact.* Mahwah, NJ: Erlbaum.

Bass, B. M., & Avolio, B. J. (1993). Transformational leadership: A response to critiques. In M. M. Chermers & R. Anyman (Eds.), *Leadership theory and research: Perspectives and directions* (pp. 49–80). New York, NY: Free Press.

Bass, B. M., & Avolio, B. J. (1994). Transformational leadership and organizational culture. *International Journal of Public Administration, 17,* 541–554.

Bass, B. M., & Steidlmeier, P. (1999). Ethics, character, and authentic transformational leadership behavior. *Leadership Quarterly, 10*(2), 181–217.

Batt, R., & Valcour, P. M. (2003). Human resource practices as predictors of work—family outcomes and employee turnover. *Industrial Relations, 42,* 189–220.

Bennis, W. (1989). *Why leaders can't lead.* San Francisco, CA: Jossey-Bass.

Brown, M. E., Trevino, L. K., & Harrison, D. A. (2005). Ethical leadership: A social learning theory perspective for construct development. *Organizational Behavior and Human Decision Processes, 97,* 117–134.

Burke, W. W. (1992). *Organizational development: A process of learning and changing.* Reading, MA: Addison-Wesley.

Caldwell, C., Hayes, L. A., Karri, R., & Bernal, P. (2008). Ethical stewardship—Implications for leadership and trust. *Journal of Business Ethics, 78,* 153–164.

Chao, L. (2005). For Gen Xers, it's work to live: Allowing employees to strike balance between job and life can lead to better retention rates. *The Wall Street Journal,* Eastern edition, November 29, B6.

Child, J. A. (2004). Repairing the breach of trust in corporate governance. *Corporate Governance: An International Review,* 143–152.

Ciulla, J. B. (1995). Leadership ethics: Mapping the territory. *Business Ethics Quarterly, 5*(1), 5–28.

Clark, S. C. (2002). Communicating across the work/home border. *Community, Work and Family, 5,* 23–49.

Dirks, K., & Ferrin, D. (2002). Trust in leadership: Meta-analytic findings and implications for research and practice. *Journal of Applied Psychology, 87*(4), 611–628.

Eversole, B. A. W., Venneberg, D. L., & Crowder, C. L. (2012). Creating a flexible organizational culture to attract and retain talented workers across generations. *Advances in Developing Human Resources, 14*(4), 607–625.

Ethics Resource Center. (2012). 2011 National Business Ethics Survey. Retrieved from www.ethics.org/nbes

Ferraro, F., Pfeffer, J., & Sutton, R. I. (2005). Economic language and assumptions: How theories can become self-fulfilling. *Academy of Management Review, 30*(1), 8–24.

Fornell, C., & Larcker, D. (1981). Structural equation models with unobserved variables and measurement errors: Algebra and statistics. *Journal of Marketing Research, 18*(1), 39–50.

Gilley, J. W., Anderson, S., & Gilley, A. (2008). Human resources management as a champion for corporate ethics: Moving ethical integration and acculturation in the HR function and profession. In S. Quatro & R. Sims (Eds.), *Executive ethics: Ethical dilemmas and challenges for the C-suite.* (pp. 191–213). Armonk, NY: M. E. Sharpe.

Gilley, J. W., & Boughton, N. W. (1996). *Stop managing, start coaching: How performance coaching can enhance commitment and improve productivity.* New York, NY: McGraw-Hill.

Gilley, J. W., Boughton, N. W., & Maycunich, A. (1999). *The performance challenge: Developing management systems to make employees your greatest asset.* Cambridge, MA: Perseus.

Gilley, J. W., & Gilley A. (2006). *Manager as politician.* Hartford, CT: Praeger.

Gilley, A., Heames, J., & Gilley, J. W. (2012). Leaders and change: Attend to uniqueness of individuals. *Journal of Applied Management and Entrepreurship, 17*(1), 69–84.

Gilley, J. W., & Maycunich, A. (2000). *Beyond the learning organization: Creating a culture of continuous and development through state-of-the-art-human resource practices.* Cambridge, MA: Perseus Books.

Gilley, A., McMillan, H. S., & Gilley, J. W. (2009). Organizational change and characteristics of leadership effectiveness. *Journal of Leadership and Organizational Studies, 16*(1), 38–47.

Greenberg, D., & Landry, E. M. (2011). Negotiating a flexible work arrangement: How women navigate the influence of power and organizational context. *Journal of Organizational Behavior, 32*(8), 1163–1188. doi:10.1002/job.750

Griffin, D., & Stacey, R. (2005). *Complexity and the experience of leading organizations.* New York, NY: Routledge.

Hair, J. F., Black, W. C., Babin, B. J., Anderson, R. E., & Tatham, R. L. (2006), *Multivariate data analysis,* Upper Saddle River, NJ: Pearson/Prentice Hall.

Harris, A., Day, C., Hopkins, D., Hadfield, M., Hargreaves, A., & Chapman, C. (2003). *Effective leadership for school improvement.* New York, NY: Routledge-Bass.

Hemsley, A. (2001). Willpower vs. skill power: Defeating self-doubts and restoring self-confidence are essential to achieving greater success and happiness. *Research, 24,* 26–30.

Hodson, R. (2004). Organizational trustworthiness: Findings from the population of organizational ethnographies. *Organization Science, 15*(4), 432–445.

Hogan, R., Curphy, G. J., & Hogan, M. (1994). What we know about leadership: Effectiveness and personality. *American Psychologist, 49,* 493–504.

Holt, S. (2011). *Creating effective leadership development programs: A quantitative case study.* (Unpublished octoral dissertation). University of Nevada, Las Vegas.

Hu, L. T. & Bentler, P. M. (1999). Cutoff criteria for fit indexes in covariance structure analysis: Conventional criteria versus new alternatives. *Structural Equation Modeling: A Multidisciplinary Journal, 6,* 1–55.

Jordan, J., Brown, M. E., Trevino, L. K., & Finkelstein, S. (2013). Someone to look up to: Executive-follower ethical reasoning and perceptions of ethical leadership. *Journal of Management, 39,* 660–683.

Katzenbach, J. R., & Smith, D. K. (2003). *The wisdom of teams: Creating the high-performance organization* (3rd ed.). New York, NY: HarperCollins Publishers.

Keller, R. (1995). Transformational leaders make a difference. *Research-Technology Management, 38,* 41–44.

Kickul, J., Gundry, L., & Posig, M. (2005). Does trust matter? The relationship between equity sensitivity and perceived organizational justice. *Journal of Business Ethics, 56,* 205–218.

Kirkman, B. L., Jones, R. G., & Shapiro, D. L. (2000). Why do employees resist teams? Examining the "resistance barrier" to work team effectiveness. *International Journal of Conflict Management, 11,* 74–92.

Klein, C., DiazGranados, D., Salas, E., Le, H., Burke, C. S., Lyons, R., & Goodwin, G. F. (2009). Does team building work? *Small Group Research, 40*(2), 181–222.

Konovsky, M. & Pugh S. (1994). Citizenship behavior and social exchange. *Academy of Management Journal, 37*(3), 656–669.

Leopold, A. (n.d.). http://www.goodreads.com/quotes/355449-ethical-behavior

Ligon, G. S., Wallace, J. H., & Osburn, H. K. (2011). Experiential development and mentoring processes for leaders for innovation. *Advances in Developing Human Resources, 13*(3), 297–317.

Longenecker, J. G. (1985). Management priorities and management ethics. *Journal of Business Ethics, 4,* 65–70.

Martin, A. (2005). *The changing nature of leadership.* Retrieved from http://www.ccl.org

Martin, M. M. (1999). Trust leadership. *Journal of Leadership and Organizational Studies, 5*(3), 42–49.

Mayer, R. C., Davis, J. H., & Schoorman, F. D. (1995). An integrative model of organizational trust. *Academy of Management Review, 20*(3), 709–734.

Mayer, D. M., Kuenzi, M., Greenbaum, R., Bardes, M., & Salvador, R. (2009). How low does ethical leadership flow? Test of a trickle-down model. *Organizational Behavior and Human Decision Processes, 108,* 1–13.

Miner, J. B. (2003). The rated importance, scientific validity, and practical usefulness of organizational behavior theories. *Academy of Management Learning and Higher Education, 2*(3), 250–268.

Neubert, M. J., Carlson, D. S., Kacmar, K. M., Roberts, J. A., & Chonko, L. B. (2009). The virtuous influence of ethical leadership behavior: Evidence from the field. *Journal of Business Ethics, 90,* 157–170.

Nooteboom, B. B. (1997). Effects of trust and governance on relational risk. *Academy of Management Journal,* 308–338.

Rousseau, D. S. (1998). Introduction to special topic forum: Not so different after all: A cross-discipline view of trust. *Academy of Management Review,* 393–404.

Schein, E. (1985). *Organisational culture and leadership.* San Francisco, CA: Jossey-Bass.

Schein, E. H. (1992). *Organizational culture and leadership.* San Francisco, CA: Jossey-Bass.

Steers, R. M., Mowday, R. T., & Shapiro, D. L. (2004). The future of work motivation theory. *Academy of Management Review, 29*(3), 379–387.

Thompson, C. A., Beauvais, L. L., & Lyness, K. S. (1999). When work–family benefits are not enough: The influence of work–family culture on benefit utilization, organizational attachment, and work–family conflict. *Journal of Vocational Behavior, 54*, 392–415.

Toor, S. & Ofori G. (2009). Ethical leadership: Examining the relationships with full range leadership model, employee outcomes, and organizational culture. *Journal of Business Ethics, 90*, 533–547.

Trevino, L., Brown, M., & Hartman, L. (2003). A qualitative investigation of perceived executive ethical leadership: Perceptions from inside and outside the executive suite. *Human Relations, 56*(1), 5–37.

Trevino, L., Hartman, L., & Brown, M. (2000). Moral person and moral manager: How executives develop a reputation for ethical leadership. *California Management Review*, 128–142.

Trust. (n.d.). *Merriam-Webster* [online]. Retrieved from http://www.merriam-webster.com/dictionary/trust

Twenge, J. M. (2010). A review of the empirical evidence on generational differences in work attitudes. *Journal of Business Psychology, 25*, 201–210.

Twenge, J. M., & Campbell, S. M. (2008). Generational differences in psychological traits and their impact on the workplace. *Journal of Managerial Psychology, 23*, 862–877.

Van Ameijde, J. D. J., Nelson, P. C., Billsberry, J., & Van Meurs, N. (2009). Improving leadership in higher education institutions. A distributed perspective. *Higher Education, 58*(6), n.p., doi:10.1007/s10734-009-9224-y.

Walumba, F. O., Mayer, D. M., Wang, P., Wang, H., Workman, K., & Christensen, A. L. (2011). Linking ethical leadership to employee performance: The roles of leader–member exchange, self-efficacy, and organizational identification. *Organizational Behavior and Human Decision Processes, 115*, 204–213.

Weick, K. E. (1995). *Sensemaking in organizations*. Thousand Oaks, CA: Sage.

Whichard, J., & Kees, N. L. (2006). *Manager as facilitator*. Hartford, CT: Praeger.

Wong, M., Gardiner, E., Lang, W., & Coulon, L. (2008). Generational differences in personality and motivation: Do they exist and what are the implications for the workplace? *Journal of Managerial Psychology, 23*, 878–890.

Wright, J. (2005). Workplace coaching: what's it all about? *Work, 24*(3), 325–328.

Yukl, G., Mahsud, R., Hassan, S., & Prussia, G. (2013). An improved measure of ethical leadership. *Journal of Leadership & Organizational Studies, 20*(1), 38–48.

Zhu, W., May, D. R., & Avolio, B. J. (2004). The impact of ethical leadership behavior on employee outcomes: The roles of psychological empowerment and authenticity. *Journal of Leadership and Organizational & Organizational Studies, 11*(1), 16–26.

Applied Ethics Case

Founded in Rome, Italy, in 2009, Arete Ghadha International (AGI), a family-owned company, established itself as a major competitor in the Chevon markets of southeastern Europe. Based on this southeastern European competitive advantage, AGI made the decision to enter the Russian Federation markets with moderately priced, high-quality meat products. AGI priced its products to reach professional, middle-income families. Hannu Leostrin, a 27-year-old native of St. Petersburg, Russia, who was educated at Moscow State University, was hired as vice president of operations for the Russia operations. Hannu was viewed as an ideal fit for AGI's target markets. He was a relaxed, introverted individual. During his leadership training sessions in Rome, that were taught by Martina Gasbarrini, president/CEO of AGI, he was attentive and self-assured.

Hannu's training program focused on the importance of achieving the AGI financial goals for his territory. Martina, daughter of the founder, had been promoted to the president/CEO position from the chief financial officer position 18 months earlier. She was well respected and was viewed as being efficient, driven, and precise in her interactions with her leadership team. She demanded a lot from herself and her senior team. She was an intense individual.

Immediately following the leadership training program, Hannu was sent to St. Petersburg to assume responsibility for his territory. Three months after Hannu arrived in St. Petersburg, Martina began to be concerned that something was not quite right. The problem was not Hannu's position. He seemed to be engaged in the public relations aspect of opening the office and hiring staff. However, his sales and advertising activities were lacking. He had often dreamed of reaching out to help his people. His perception of his performance was fine. However, Martina felt that the communications and interactions were not satisfactory and not as effective as they needed to be. Hannu's follow-up to Martina's directives were lacking in detail and not as timely as Martina wanted.

In an effort to enhance and further develop their relationship, Martina made an unannounced visit to Russia to discuss with Hannu the details that were to be in the marketing, advertising, and sales plans. Explicit discussions were held on a multitude of details needed in the plan. Martina reminded Hannu the plan needed to be developed as soon as possible because its implementation promised to be both difficult and time consuming in a new market. Martina explained that AGI needed a return on their investment. Hannu responded by listening very intently, demonstrating enthusiasm, commenting extensively, and indicating he understood what was expected of him.

After 45 days there were no changes in the situation. As a result, Martina fired Hannu and brought in an international business consultant.

1. As the international business consultant, how would you define Martina's and Hannu's leadership styles?
2. What leadership changes would you recommend based on the readings in this chapter?
3. How should your proposed leadership changes be implemented?

Post-Reading Questions

1. Discuss the ethical implications of leaders and managers who lack appropriate management skills and inadvertently create a hostile work environment.
2. Reflecting on your professional experience, have you experienced the effects of the "dark side of leadership" translated into the organization? Describe the context, the dark leadership characteristic, and the impact on the organization.
3. The authors' argument is that narcissistic leaders are unyielding, arrogant, and self-absorbed; possess an egotistical need for power and admiration; and make abusive managers. However, Steve Jobs, a legendary leader, was described as a narcissist. Is narcissism a trait of a "dark-side" leader? Please support your response.

Videos Retrieved from Internet

"The Mindset of a Leader: Bridging the Management—Leadership Gap"
https://www.youtube.com/watch?v=owjtGaf8XII

This video is a comprehensive presentation on leadership with emphasis on emotional intelligence.

"The Power of Leader Mindsets"

https://www.youtube.com/watch?v=qr6FKbmoxLA

This video addresses the importance of mind-sets in developing leaders.

"Leadership: Reinvent the Mindset"

https://www.youtube.com/watch?v=ycwjiUZxNVM

This short video is a discussion between two individuals on what is leadership.

"Best TED Talk on Leadership"

https://www.youtube.com/watch?v=TPA5-uFquGI

This video explores finding one's leadership abilities through personal examples.

"Thirty of the Best TED Talks on Leadership"

https://www.inspiringleadershipnow.com/best-ted-talks-on-leadership/

This video is a comprehensive discussion on leadership through thirty presentations.

"Four Principles for Creating a Leadership Mindset"

https://www.youtube.com/watch?v=6cZ6FEKcIB0

This video introduces four principles to model, teach, and reinforce to create a leadership mind-set.

Internet Sites on Leadership

"Strong Leadership Starts with Your Mindset"

https://www.psychologytoday.com/us/blog/the-power-prime/201406/strong-leadership-starts-your-mindset

This article discusses four mind-sets that are important to understand for becoming a leader. A short exercise is included.

"To Be a Brilliant Leader, Mindset Is Everything (Infographic)"

https://www.entrepreneur.com/article/238858

This article provides ten tips for developing successful leadership skills.

"The Mindset of a Leader"

https://sloanreview.mit.edu/article/the-mindsets-of-a-leader/

This article summarizes the results of a 4.5-year study of 12 executives in six major companies examining successful mind-sets.

"13 Signs that a Leadership Mindset is Inside You: Though You Do Not Know"

https://www.lifehack.org/articles/productivity/13-signs-that-leadership-mindset-inside-you-though-you-dont-know.html

This article examines 13 leadership traits that individuals possess, although they are unaware of them.

"4 Mindsets that Drive Dysfunctional Leadership"

https://www.td.org/insights/4-mindsets-that-drive-dysfunctional-leadership

This article lists and discusses four dysfunctional mind-sets leaders may have.

Section IV

Ethical Challenges Relating to Cyber Security/Internet

"We are now living on Internet time. It's a new territory, and the cyber equivalent of the Oklahoma land rush is on."
Andy Grove

ROGER SILVERSTONE IN HIS ARTICLE, "Proper Distance" engages the reader with a range of theories and positions on community and identity, on reciprocity and responsibility, and on the way in which the media and Internet may be seen to enable or disable what he refers to as the moral life. His focus is on the moral life and the conditions of its possibility in electronic space. The basis for his definition of a moral life is based in part on the French philosopher Emmanuel Levinas and his work grounded in transcendence and critique.

Silverstone argues that the moral life is dependent on our capacity to define and sustain a proper distance in the relationships we have between ourselves, others, and our media technology. He suggests that the Internet is providing new, more intense, and more genuine forms of social relationships.

He defines proper distance in a discussion that incorporates human relationships, technology, and cyberspace. He concludes that for those involved in cyberspace, their ethics must be able to address problems and act responsibly.

Author Robert Scheer's reading is taken from his book *They Know Everything About You: How Data-Collecting Corporations and Snooping Government Agencies Are Destroying Democracy*. He discusses the changing challenges confronting personal privacy as it relates to the internet commerce industry. He asks the question: "What is the role of privacy in the twenty-first century?" To leaders in the internet commerce industry, whose business model exploits the minutiae of their customers' lives, the idea of personal privacy is being lost. Scheer uses Facebook as an example of an organization with changing values regarding the collection and selling of personal data. Today, the perception of companies engaged in internet commerce, which profits from the exploitation of privacy, is that the traditional definition of privacy is an "anachronism."

Scheer concludes his work by discussing Chief Justice John Roberts' interpretation of privacy and government abuses of personal privacy.

After reading the case study, reflect on the post-reading questions.

Pre-Reading Questions

- Should there be ethical standards for internet/cyber companies?
- What should be the acceptable ethical standards for cyber employees?
- What ethical standards should international internet/cyber companies advocate?

Reading 4.1

Proper Distance: Toward an Ethics for Cyberspace

Roger Silverstone; ed., Gunnar Liestøl, Andrew Morrison, and Terje Rasmussen

> *It is only in approaching the Other that I attend to myself. ... In discourse I expose myself to the questioning of the Other, and this urgency of the response—acuteness of the present—engenders me for responsibility; as responsible I am brought to my final reality.*
>
> Emmanuel Levinas, *Totality and Infinity*

THIS IS A CHAPTER ON MEDIA ethics. And as such it is neither easy nor fashionable. It attempts a critical engagement with a range of theories and positions that touch on community and identity, on reciprocity and responsibility, and above all on the way in which media, and especially the new medium of the Internet, might be seen to enable or disable what I will call the moral life. The ethics I intend are not specific. I will not be arguing about particular individual, institutional, or professional ethics in defined circumstances. I will not be making recommendations on how people should behave either online or offline. I will not be drafting an ethical code. I will not be discussing netiquette.

In this sense maybe the word "ethical" should be substituted for "ethics," and in this sense too the ethical elides with the moral, with what I have already called the moral life. It is this, the moral life, and the conditions of its possibility in electronic space, that provides my focus in what follows.

This is also a chapter on metaphysics, since it draws on what I have understood from the work of French philosopher Emmanuel Levinas, who resolutely refuses a singular ontology as a basis for understanding the human condition in favor of an (admittedly often somewhat equally unhistorical and unsociological) approach grounded in transcendence and critique. I would contend,

Roger Silverstone, "Proper Distance: Toward an Ethics for Cyberspace," *Digital Media Revisited: Theoretical and Conceptual Innovations in Digital Domains*, ed. Gunnar Liestøl, Andrew Morrison, and Terje Rasmussen, pp. 469-479. Copyright © 2004 by MIT Press. Reprinted with permission.

however, that metaphysics, in my case as in Levinas's, provides a basis for measuring history, society, and technology—and for calling all of them to account.

My own concern, therefore, is also critique: to interrogate both the claims for, and the consequences of, the increasingly intense and interactive mediation of social relations by information and communication technologies. I will argue that the possibility of a moral life is dependent upon our capacity to define and sustain a proper distance in the relationships we have between ourselves and others and that our media technologies can be seen to affect that. I will suggest that claims that the Internet is capable of providing new, more intense, more genuine forms of social relationships are based on unexamined notions of what social relationships are or could be.

In one obvious sense it would be perfectly reasonable to suggest that this is not a new argument, that we know already that electronic mediation is no substitute for the face to face and that whatever value we ascribe to the latter, it is not transferable once distances are mediated. But although the basic argument that I attempt to outline in what follows is recognizable and familiar, I hope I will be able to throw some new light upon it as I try to define the elements of a position that at least offers the terms for a debate on the moral consequences of electronic mediation.

Infinity

I will begin with me. As a child I would, from time to time, write my name and address as follows:

> Roger Saul Silverstone
> 21 Brancote Road
> Oxton
> Birkenhead
> Cheshire, England, UK, Europe, the World, the Solar System, the Universe, Infinity

And in so doing I would move, progressively, from the known to the unknown, though with me always, and of course, at the center. But in this projection of myself from the apparent security of home to the increasing distance and incomprehensibility of what was beyond reach and actually beyond imagination, I was at the same time displacing myself from the center, and in that displacement acknowledging, albeit unconsciously, that I was just a speck, that movement through the ether was both an extension of my power and the force of my identity into global space and simultaneously an expression of the insignificance of that power and the weakness and vulnerability of that identity. There was, in my childhood fantasy, somewhere else, something else, something that I could not comprehend but that I knew existed and that, arguably, by virtue of my knowledge of its existence gave a certain reality to my own.

René Descartes (1940) had a similar—but a rather more radical—thought. Toward the end of his Third Meditation he had this to say: "And I must not imagine that I do not apprehend the infinite by a true idea, but only by the negation of the finite, in the same way that I comprehend repose and darkness by the negation of motion and light: since, on the contrary, I clearly perceive that there is more reality in the infinite substance than in the finite, and therefore that in some way I possess the perception ... of the infinite before that of the finite, that is, the perception of God before that of myself, for how could I know that I doubt, desire, or that something is wanting in me, and that I am not wholly perfect, if I possessed no idea of a being more perfect than myself, by comparison of which I knew the deficiencies of nature" (78). The key idea here lies in the second half of this. It is the argument that there is something that we know, or have a sense of, that precedes our capacity to be: there is something before being, something that limits our being and is irreducible to our being. There is something out there that in no way can be held or contained or even understood fully. It is this recognition that makes us human, because through it we see our limits and we gain a measure of our strengths and weaknesses. In such acknowledgment we can come to terms with the reality of our doubts and desires, and in recognizing this reality, we can claim our humanity: the painful acceptance of our vulnerability.

Emmanuel Levinas takes this idea as the foundation of his moral philosophy and uses it as the stick with which to beat much of modern Western thinking, particularly the phenomenology of Martin Heidegger, for its reductive insistence on the singularity of the self as the locus of experience and as the foundation of being. Levinas takes issue with modernism's dreams of omnipotence, drawing a fundamental ethical lesson, negatively, from this reduction. It is because there will always be something that we know we cannot know and because there will always be something, someone, some aspect of someone, beyond our reach and beyond our comprehension—something, perhaps only metaphorically, that precedes us—that we can discover who we are. But, most crucially (and I will come back to this shortly) we learn through this recognition of the irreducible otherness of the world to accept our responsibility for our place in the world and for the other who occupies that world alongside us, whom we will never, ever, know quite entirely.

It is this argument that I want briefly to trace, for it opens up, as it has also for Zygmunt Bauman, an agenda for understanding the limits of moral sensibility as it has emerged through modernity that in both Bauman's arguments and my own finds its way into a critique of technology and mediation. Bauman's ambition lies in the exploration of what he calls a postmodern ethics; mine, more modestly, is to explore the idea of what I am calling *proper distance*.

Proper Distance

What do I mean by proper distance? There are a number of different ways of answering the question.

Let me begin etymologically and say something about the word "proper." The word "proper" (Latin *proprius*, one's own, special, particular, peculiar) has, in English, a number of related but quite distinct meanings that make it both useful and suggestive in the context of what I want to say. "Proper" has both descriptive and evaluative senses. Its first meaning refers to the sense of belonging: it is a property or a quality of a thing—the stars, for example, have their proper motion. It also refers to that quality of ownership as being distinctive: a proper name as opposed to a common name.

The second meaning emerges when the term is applied to a situation of conformity with a rule: when something is accurate, exact, or correct or when something is strictly the case, genuine, true, or real, we use the word "proper." So when something or someone is excellent, admirable, commendable, fine, goodly, or of high quality, we can say of it or them, perhaps slightly archaically, that they are proper: a proper person.

Third, we use the word "proper" to refer to something that is adapted to some purpose or requirement, that it is fit, apt, suitable, fitting or befitting, or when it is especially appropriate to the circumstances or conditions at hand. In this sense "proper" is what something should be or what is required: what one ought to do or have or use. It is a synonym, almost, for right; for example, one might say, "This is a proper time" to do something. Such a sense, finally, leads to a use of the word "proper" to describe and adjudge something or someone that conforms with social ethics or with the demands or usages of society, polite or otherwise. We talk about behaving properly or improperly.

"Proper" is not a word we use much in media or new media research. It is a modern rather than a postmodern term. It speaks of value: of the normative, as well as of the descriptive. But in its principal manifestations—as distinctive, correct, and ethically or socially appropriate—it commends itself to me, properly, as a way of approaching the question of distance and of providing an opening into a critical inquiry into the ethics of the media, both old and new.

And so to distance. There is often quite a fundamental confusion in much of the writing on the new geography of the Internet. Time-space distanciation, or compression, or what Frances Cairncross (1997) has called the death of distance, suggests a profound and illegitimate elision between two kinds of distance: the spatial and the social. The presumption in these discussions is that the electronic mediation of physical or material connection provides at the same time social or psychic connection. The technologically enabled transformation of time and space that marked the entry into the modern world certainly provided new conditions and possibilities for communication, communication that provided connection despite physical separation. Yet the paradoxes at the heart of such communication, although noted, as Ithiel de Sola Pool (1977), for example, famously noted them, have been insufficiently investigated, above all for their consequences for our relationships to each other. My point is that distance is not just a material, a geographical, or even a social category, but it is, by virtue of both and as a product of their interrelation, a moral category. The overcoming of distance requires more than technology and indeed more than the creation of a public sphere. It requires proximity.

Zygmunt Bauman (1993) makes the following assertion:

> Modern society specialised in the refurbishment of the social space: it aimed at the creation of a public space in which there was to be *no moral proximity*. Proximity is the realm of intimacy and morality; distance is the realm of estrangement and the Law ... . (83) If post-modernity is a retreat from the blind alleys into which radically pursued ambitions of modernity have led, a postmodern ethics would be one that readmits the Other as a neighbour, as the close-to-hand-*and*-mind, into the hard core of the moral self, back from the wasteland of calculated interests to which it had been exiled; an ethics that restores the autonomous moral significance of proximity; an ethics that recasts the Other as the crucial character in the process through which the moral self comes into its own (83–84).

"Proximity" is close here to what I have called "proper distance." Proper distance involves contact: the close at hand but also close to mind (Levinas 1981/1998: 86). Bauman, in his analysis of the proximal and of the ethics of distance, traces modernity's progressive refusal of the intimate and the individually responsible, a refusal that the activities of law and the state paradoxically impose on social life. Technology is a crucial component of this process, and horrendously so in his analysis of the Holocaust. Proximity involves also, as we shall see, responsibility. And responsibility, individual responsibility, has also been progressively denied by modernity and its technological handmaidens.

Where Bauman sees proximity as a synonym for closeness, however, and sees in technology an ethical juggernaut, I want to pose proper distance as a firmer basis for enquiring into the possibilities of a moral life, and I want to push back somewhat from the technologically determinant. In the relation to the first, it should be pointed out (Silverstone 1999) that we can be blinded morally by the too close at hand just as easily as we can be by the too far removed.

Closeness, even intimacy, does not guarantee recognition or responsibility; it can invite, conceivably, either blank resistance or, alternatively, incorporation. As Levinas (1981/1998) notes: "Proximity is to be described as extending the subject in its very subjectivity … . [Proximity,] the one-for-the-other … is not a configuration produced in the soul. It is an immediacy older than the abstractness of nature. Nor is it fusion; it is contact with the other. To be in contact is neither to invest the other and annul his alterity, nor to suppress myself in the other. In contact itself the touching and the touched separate, as though the touched moved off, was always already other, did not have anything in common with me" (86).

Levinas's notion of proximity preserves the separation of myself and the other, a separation that ensures the possibilities of both respect and responsibility for the other. It is a separation in which the notion of touch (elsewhere he writes of the caress) is central. For touch requires the sensitivity of, and to, distance in which there is recognition of the irreducible difference of the other as well as a sharing of identity with her or him. It is in this paradox of connection and separateness and in the ambiguities that we as individuals have to resolve in our relationships with the other that the creation of an ethical or moral life becomes, or does not become, possible.

I am proposing that the notion, but above all the achievement, of proper distance both sensitizes us to these ambiguities and provides the opportunity to surmount them. It recognizes that in our relationships to each other, in their flux and fluidity, we are confronted by a whole range of technological and discursive mediations that destabilize, in both directions, the proper distance that we must create and sustain if we are to act ethically. We have to determine, perhaps case by case, what that proper distance is or might be when we are confronted with both familiar and novel appearances or representations of the other. And we have to understand, of course, that in such cases there is no prix fixe, no singular, and no permanent. Neither can proper distance, like everything else that is meaningful in social life, be taken for granted nor is it pregiven. It has to be worked for. It has to be produced.

Distance can be proper (correct, distinctive, and ethically appropriate) or it can be improper. If improper distance can be, and is, created both through the general waxing and waning of modernity, as well as more precisely in the mediations that electronic technologies provide for us, then it follows that we can use the notion of *proper* distance as a tool to measure and to repair our failures in our communication with the other and in our reporting of the world in such a way that our capacity to act is enabled and preserved (cf. Boltanski 1999). And it follows too that we can use it as a way of interrogating those arguments, most recently in the analysis of the Internet, that mistake connection for closeness and closeness for commitment and confuse reciprocity for responsibility. But before we do this in a more deliberative way, it is necessary to dig a little more deeply into the nature of that ethical relation and the conditions of its possibility.

Strangers and Neighbors

The media, that is the broadcast media, have always fulfilled the function of creating some sense of proper distance, or at least they have tried, or claimed to be able, to do so. The reporting of world events, the production of news, the fictional representation of the past, the critical interrogation of the private lives of public figures, the exploration of the ordinariness of everyday life—all involve, in one way or another, a negotiation between the familiar and the strange, as the media try, forlornly, to resolve the essential ambiguities and ambivalences of contemporary life. As I have argued on many occasions, their task is to create some kind of comfort and pleasure for those on the receiving end of such mediations, some comfort and pleasure in the appearance of the strange as not too strange and the familiar as not too familiar. Such mediations, however, also tend to produce, in practice, a kind of polarization in the determinations of such distance: that the unfamiliar is either pushed to a point beyond strangeness, beyond reach and beyond humanity, on the one hand (the Iraqi leadership both during the Gulf War and now), or drawn so close as to be indistinguishable from ourselves on the other (the many representations of the everyday lives of citizens in other countries, as if the latter were in every respect just like us, really) (Silverstone 1999).

The new media, especially the Internet, in palpably challenging the one-to-many mediation of television, radio, and the press, and notwithstanding their evolutionary development from other forms of one-to-one electronic mediation, shift the terms of both the debate and the problem. They do so precisely insofar as they do enable that one-to-one-ness, or that many-to-many-ness, that e-mails and chatrooms and groupware offer. And it is this arguably transcendent characteristic, which involves, or might be called, the personalization of the other—that the person at the other end of the communication is a person rather than a thing, or an image or an event, and that I may be required to interact with that other, or she with me—is what I want now to evaluate. The Internet's claim is for interactivity, not uniquely perhaps, but centrally and essentially (Downes and McMillan 2000). But the notion of interactivity begs a number of questions, above all about its very nature and its capacity to connect interlocutors in new and significant ways. It also raises the question, though this has not been much discussed in the literature, of the moral status of those who communicate with each other and of the ethical status of the kind of communications that are generated online.

I want to suggest that this question of status requires, initially at least, a consideration of the difference between strangers and neighbors and that it requires, in a rather more focused way than I have yet attempted, a consideration of the difference between physical and social distance.

In premodern societies the differences between neighbors and strangers or aliens were rigidly enforced and accepted. Bauman (1993) suggests that for a large part of human history "an alien could enter the radius of physical proximity only in one of three capacities: either as an enemy to be fought and expelled, or as an admittedly temporary guest to be confined to special quarters and rendered harmless by strict observance of the isolating ritual, or as a neighbour-to-be, in which case he had to be made like [a] neighbour, that is to behave like the neighbours do" (150).

Modernity undermined the clarity, certainty, and defensibility of the boundary between strangers and neighbors. As Georg Simmel (1908/1971) has famously noted, the stranger is "the wanderer who comes today *and stays tomorrow*" and is close to us "insofar as we feel between him and ourselves similarities of nationality or social position, of occupation or of general human nature. He is far from us insofar as these similarities extend beyond him and us, and connect us only because they connect a great many people" (147, emphasis added). What characterizes the stranger in modernity is precisely her ambiguity. We can neither avoid her, nor can we be sure of her status, and indeed of our own status as she might judge it (we are all strangers to each other now). In a world of both geographical and social mobility—what Bauman (2000) calls liquid modernity and John Urry (2000) calls the postsocietal—we are confronted, perhaps as never before, by a nomadic universe in which the cognitive, aesthetic, and moral boundaries between ourselves and others can neither be clearly identified nor consistently defended. We cannot be indifferent to, nor exclude, the stranger who can no longer be defined by her difference. Yet we cannot, because of that indefinable difference, completely include her either. The stranger *is* the neighbor, and we are all neighbors to one another now.

This is the problem of what I want to call *ambiguity 1*, the ambiguity that is inevitable when relationships with the other require the creation of manageable social *distance* under circumstances of otherwise determined physical *closeness*. And because both the cognitive and aesthetic spacing in our relationships to strangers is, in modern life, such a continuous problem, it produces ambivalence, a sense of moral and ethical indecisiveness in our relationships with the other. I want to go further to suggest, however, that in electronic space these positionings are reversed and that the problem of the stranger is, consequently, the obverse to what it is in physical space, though it is still a problem. In electronic space we are confronted with the situation of determined, and arguably uniform, physical *distance*, and the moral task is, somehow or another, to create manageable social *closeness*. This is the problem of what I want to call *ambiguity 2*. But I want to suggest that it is generated by, and generates, similar ambivalence, an ambivalence present therefore both in physical and cyberspace, an ambivalence that requires an equivalent, and an equivalently difficult, moral response. Are there any strangers in cyberspace? Are there any neighbors?

This ambivalence comes not just from not knowing how to make sense of the other, but also from not knowing how to act in relation to the other: how to be, how to care, how to take responsibility. In the multiply converging worlds of technology, mediation, and social and geographical mobilities, it may be, as many have argued, that we are doomed to ambiguity and ambivalence, but this does not mean that we should avoid confronting it.

References

Bauman, Z. (1993) *Postmodern Ethics*. Oxford: Blackwell.

Bauman, Z. (2000) *Liquid Modernity*. Cambridge: Polity Press.

Boltanski, L. (1999) *Distant Suffering: Morality, Media, Politics*. Cambridge: Cambridge University Press.

Cairncross, F. (1997) *The Death of Distance: How the Communications Revolution Will Change Our Lives*. London: Orion Business Books.

de Sola Pool, I. (ed.) (1977) *The Social Impact of the Telephone*. Cambridge: MIT Press.

Descartes, R. (1940) "Meditations on First Philosophy." In T. V. Smith and M. Grene (eds.), *From Descartes to Locke*. Chicago: Chicago University Press, 49–113.

Downes, E. J., and S. McMillan (2000) "Defining Interactivity: A Qualitative Identification of Key Dimensions." *New Media and Society*, 2(2), 157–180.

Levinas, E. (1981/1998) *Otherwise than Being. Or Beyond Essence*. Pittsburgh: Duquesne University Press.

Silverstone, R. (1999) *Why Study the Media?* London: Sage.

Simmel, G. (1908/1971) "The Stranger." In D. E. Levine (ed.), *Georg Simmel: On Individuality and Social Forms*. Chicago: Chicago University Press, 143–149.

Urry, J. (2000) *Sociology beyond Societies: Mobilities for the Twenty-First Century*. London: Routledge.

Reading 4.2

Privacy Is Freedom

Robert Scheer

WHAT IS THE ROLE OF PRIVACY in the twenty-first century? To the leaders of Internet commerce, whose basic business model involves exploiting the minutiae of their customers' lives, the very idea of privacy has been treated as, at best, an anachronism of the predigital age. Meanwhile, those desiring to keep their personal data from prying eyes claim it as an unconditional constitutional right.

After making a pro-privacy pretense, in his company's early years, Facebook founder Mark Zuckerberg began steadily advancing the argument that privacy is a luxury being willingly tossed aside by customers preferring convenience. "People have really gotten comfortable not only sharing more information and different kinds, but more openly and with more people," he said while accepting a Crunchie award in San Francisco in January 2010. "That social norm is just something that has evolved over time. We view it as our role in the system to constantly be innovating and be updating what our system is to reflect what the current social norms are."[1]

Instead of viewing the protection of privacy as a business's obligation to his customer base, Zuckerberg suggested that the very concept of personal privacy could be gradually disappearing. "[F]our years ago, when Facebook was getting started, most people didn't want to put up any information about themselves on the Internet," he told an interviewer at the Web 2.0 Summit in 2008.[2]

> Right? So, we got people through this really big hurdle of wanting to put up their full name, or real picture, mobile phone number. ... I would expect that, you know, next year, people will share twice as much information as they are this year. And

Robert Scheer, "Privacy is Freedom," *They Know Everything About You: How Data-Collecting Corporations and Snooping Government Agencies Are Destroying Democracy*, pp. 79-102, 221-224. Copyright © 2015 by Perseus Books Group. Reprinted with permission.

then, the year after that, they'll share twice as much information as they are next year ... as long as the stream of information is just constantly increasing, and we're doing our job, and ... our role, and kind of like pushing that forward, then I think that, you know ... that's just been the best strategy for us.[3]

In other words, let's keep pushing customers to give up a little more privacy every day until they have none left. This has, of course, been the norm in an industry based on customers clicking an "agree" button to approve privacy terms and conditions contracts designed to be unreadable—and to go unread. (As Sun Microsystems chief executive Scott McNealy famously said way back in 1999, "You have zero privacy anyway. Get over it.")[4]

Zuckerberg went further in his 2010 statement, chastising those given to an older business model based on caution over privacy and instead praising companies (like his) that could easily rise above such obviously out-of-date concerns: "A lot of companies would be trapped by the conventions and their legacies of what they've built, doing a privacy change. ... But we view that as a really important thing, to always keep a beginner's mind and what would we do if we were starting the company now, and we decided that these would be the social norms now and we just went for it."

An even darker defense of the end-of-privacy doctrine had been offered a month earlier by Google's Eric Schmidt, who impugned the innocence of consumers who worry about snooping by Google and other companies. "If you have something that you don't want anyone to know, maybe you shouldn't be doing it in the first place," Schmidt stated in an interview for a December 2009 *CNBC Special*, "Inside the Mind of Google."[5]

The ability of the fast-growing Internet data-mining companies to trivialize privacy concerns succeeded because the target audience of younger consumers was either indifferent to invasions of their privacy or ignorant of the extent and depth of that data collection. It was remarkable that an American social culture that had for so long been moored to a notion of individual sovereignty predicated on the ability to develop one's identity, ideas, and mores in private, had, in a wink, become willing to surrender any such notion.

Americans had fought and died for the right to have privately developed papers, conversations, friendships, and diaries, especially in our homes. Yet here we were as a society voluntarily moving so much of that into digital spaces owned and managed by corporations we have no control over. This relinquishing of the most private information about one's essence and aspirations became the norm in a shockingly short period, examined only lightly and in passing. As we shared more and more with ever-widening social networks, it seemed okay as long as the companies securely stored this precious data, to be used only to enhance the consumer experience. We counted on the self-interest of the corporation not to harm us, not to bite the hand that feeds.

But the Snowden revelations changed all that by exposing how easily the government could access—and indeed was accessing—our personal info. That troubling confluence between the corporate world and the state caught the public's attention in a way that Internet companies feared might be game changing, threatening the culture of trust needed to continue gathering that data.

Also straining global confidence in Internet commerce was the shock of those outside the country who had bought into the myth that US-based multinationals were international in their obligations, but who now found them to be subservient to the whims of Washington.[6] That was a message that US companies, up against a saturated domestic market for their products, found particularly alarming, since they depend on global growth to please shareholders.

A suddenly anxious Zuckerberg felt compelled to communicate his concerns to the president as well as to the larger public. Ten months after the first Snowden revelations, Zuckerberg posted on Facebook the following *cri de coeur* to air his concerns over the enduring costs of the ongoing firestorm. It is long but worth reading as a coming-of-age manifesto from one of the Internet's *wunderkinder*:

> As the world becomes more complex and governments everywhere struggle, trust in the Internet is more important today than ever.
>
> The Internet is our shared space. It helps us connect. It spreads opportunity. It enables us to learn. It gives us a voice. It makes us stronger and safer together.
>
> To keep the Internet strong, we need to keep it secure. That's why at Facebook we spend a lot of our energy making our services and the whole Internet safer and more secure. We encrypt communications, we use secure protocols for traffic, we encourage people to use multiple factors for authentication and we go out of our way to help fix issues we find in other people's services.
>
> The Internet works because most people and companies do the same. We work together to create this secure environment and make our shared space even better for the world.
>
> This is why I've been so confused and frustrated by the repeated reports of the behavior of the US government. When our engineers work tirelessly to improve security, we imagine we're protecting you against criminals, not our own government.[7]

He ended by stating that he had called Obama "to express my frustration over the damage the government is creating for all of our future," but there is no indication the president got the message.[8] Obama continued to let his national security adviser James Clapper lead him about by the nose while joining him in treating whistleblower Snowden, whose courage is the only reason we learned what was going on, as one of the nation's most dangerous fugitives. Obama's Justice Department had chosen to forget all about the Fourth Amendment that protects citizens against the unwarranted searches of both state and federal governments, as Zuckerberg's lawyers would soon point out in court filings.

Soon after Zuckerberg's post, his company was embroiled in a lawsuit with the district attorney of Manhattan, who had sought the private data of 381 of Facebook's customers. In this particular situation, Facebook took the high road in defending its customers' privacy, as the record of the company's court filings would indicate. But the disclosure of that exemplary role on the part of Facebook in June 2014 (discussed following) was drowned out by the clamor of stories about Facebook's own manipulation of its customers' data in ways that many thought shameful, if not criminal.

A thorough report by Robinson Meyer on June 28, 2014, in *The Atlantic* magazine revealed that Facebook permitted data scientists to manipulate the "news feed" of almost 700,000 of its users in a study to determine whether users' moods could be manipulated through "emotional contagion." As Meyer reported, "Some people were shown content with a preponderance of happy and positive words; some were shown content analyzed as sadder than average. And when the week was over, these manipulated users were more likely to post either especially positive or negative words themselves."[9]

The study in question, which took place the week of January 11, 2012, and was published in the June 17, 2014, issue of the prestigious *Proceedings of the National Academy of Sciences*, indeed showed that "emotions expressed by friends, via online social networks, influence our own moods, constituting, to our knowledge, the first experimental evidence for massive-scale contagion via social networks."[10]

The story in *The Atlantic* was shared by thousands of readers and elicited numerous angry comments. The *New York Times* story on the study captured the essence of the outrage in its opening sentence: "To Facebook, we are all lab rats."[11] More negative responses to Facebook poured in—proof, one could conclude, of the emotional contagion of anger and outrage.

In a post on Facebook on that same day in June, Adam D. I. Kramer, a Facebook data scientist, fell on his sword, conceding that he wrote and designed the experiment in addition to co-writing the study with Professor Jeffrey T. Hancock and then-doctoral student Jamie E. Guillory of Cornell University's departments of Communication and Information Science.

Kramer's claim for the study was that "we care about the emotional impact of Facebook and the people that use our product. We felt that it was important to investigate the common worry that seeing friends post positive content leads to people feeling negative or left out. At the same time, we were concerned that exposure to friends' negativity might lead people to avoid visiting Facebook. ... And at the end of the day, the actual impact on people in the experiment was the minimal amount to statistically detect it. ... [O]ur goal was never to upset anyone. ... In hindsight, the research benefits of the paper may not have justified all of this anxiety."[12]

For its part, Cornell was prompted to issue a statement making clear that Hancock and Guillory merely analyzed the results of the research previously conducted by Facebook and did not have access to user data. "Their work was limited to initial discussions, analyzing the research results and working with colleagues from Facebook to prepare the peer-reviewed paper," said Cornell.[13]

But more disconcerting than the results of that study was the fact that Facebook had turned 689,003 of its 1.2 billion users into unsuspecting subjects in a deliberate attempt to manipulate their emotions. As *New York Times* tech writer Vindu Goel noted in his article, "The uproar highlights the immense control Facebook exerts over what its users see. When someone logs in, there are typically about 1,500 items the company could display in that person's news feed, but the service shows only about 300 of them."[14] That is, despite the company's endless turnout of tools that purportedly allow users to curate the content shown in news feeds, Facebook—not the user population—is the real author of our social media stories.

The totalitarian overtones of this thought-control experiment were more chilling after a year of discoveries of cooperation between the NSA and Internet companies like Facebook.

***

The news feed controversy exposed a Facebook reality its users might already have known if they followed the company's critics, or read its jargon-ridden 9,000-word terms-of-service agreement. But judging from the shocked reaction, few had thought analytically about the implications of Facebook's ordering of the data its users and advertisers generate. As Cornell communications scholar Tarleton Gillespie put it in the wake of the controversy, it left many users with "a deeper discomfort about an information environment where the content is ours but the selection is theirs."[15]

Gillespie spelled out the sea change in communications technology represented by social networks as a sharp break from previous models of the mass delivery of information. "On the one hand, there had been the safe and sound 'trusted interpersonal information conduits'—namely, the post office system and the trunk lines managed by telephone companies that were designed to be neutral carriers of information but not curators prioritizing the content via an algorithm of importance.[16] We expected them not to curate or even monitor that content," Gillespie wrote. "[I]n fact we made it illegal to do otherwise; we expected that our communication would be delivered, for a fee, and we understood the service as the commodity, not the information it conveyed."[17]

He continued to explain that the opposite was true for broadcast programming and the content of newspapers and magazines, which were explicitly curated offerings; we were consciously choosing—and often actually paying—to consume filtered presentations produced by professionals.

Social networks such as Facebook represent a confusion of the two, however, with users generally expecting the former and instead getting an automated version of the latter.[18] They are neither fish nor fowl, and while Facebook seems to be a neutral carrier of data, like the old post office system, it also dips into the "mail" and responds to its content by prioritizing future deliveries, attaching relevant advertising, and hiding what it considers junk.

The end result is that your information becomes the raw material for a new commodity the company manages for its own purposes—binding users ever more tightly to Facebook as their social home base on the Internet. But to monetize clicks, the company's research will most definitely also include exploiting purchasing tastes to benefit Facebook's true customers, the advertisers who want to sell you something. They are paying, after all; you are not.

Sheryl Sandberg, second in command at Facebook, admitted the news feed manipulations were an effort to improve commercial marketing (rather than a high-minded academic project). "This was part of ongoing research companies do to test different products, and that was what it was; it was poorly communicated," she said. "And for that communication we apologize. We never meant to upset you."[19]

But the message was clear that the heads of Facebook were embarrassed not by doing something creepy and manipulative but, rather, by having been caught. Of course, they never meant to upset Facebook users by making them feel they were part of some experiment in social control. Yet this was just business as usual, albeit not something on which they want the public to focus.

As Jaron Lanier warned in a *New York Times* op-ed published days after the release of the emotional-contagion study, "This is only one early publication about a whole new frontier in the manipulation of people, and Facebook shouldn't be singled out as a villain. ... Now that we know that a social network proprietor can engineer emotions for the multitudes to a slight degree, we need to consider that further research on amplifying that capacity might take place. Stealth emotional manipulation could be channeled to sell things (you suddenly find that you feel better after buying from a particular store, for instance), but it might also be used to exert influence in a multitude of other ways. Research has also shown that voting behavior can be influenced by undetectable social networking maneuvering, for example."[20]

Undetectable, because the news feed feature of Facebook, notwithstanding the disclaimers of the wordy terms-of-service agreement, manages to convey a sense of automated neutrality, in much the same way Google and Yahoo do with their searches. There is a thumb on the scale that users are lulled into ignoring, "[a]nd Facebook is complicit in this confusion," said

Cornell professor Gillespie, "as they often present themselves as a trusted information conduit, and have been oblique about the way they curate our content into their commodity."[21]

This presents a persistent contradiction for Facebook because its basic attraction is that it is simply a reliable communication tool for friends and family (admittedly an unrealistic expectation for a service that is provided free of charge), but the company's profit model requires it to find ever more ingenious ways to commodify a customer's curiosity or personal data.

Furthermore, the power of social networks to define reality makes them targets for governments that have their own stake in manipulating public opinion. (China, for example, has attempted to block the use of such networks inside its borders.) The ability to alter the thinking or emotions of large numbers of people would have obvious appeal to political demagogues, and some observers were quick to connect the Facebook experiment with the US Department of Defense's controversial Minerva Research Initiative.

Launched in December 2008 with $50 million, Minerva is a tool for the Pentagon to fund academic research by theoretically independent scholars on subjects it is interested in, such as China, terrorism, and political activism, "to improve DoD's basic understanding of the social, cultural, behavioral, and political forces that shape regions of the world of strategic importance to the US."[22]

Disturbingly, some of the research they commissioned seemed to be aimed at understanding how to control or prevent public dissent inside the United States through surveillance and manipulation of information flows, like those curated by social networks. When it turned out that one of those on the Minerva gravy train was the same Cornell prof who headed the analysis of the Facebook news feed study, warning flags were raised for civil libertarians.

While Cornell officials said that Jeffrey Hancock did not use his Pentagon funding specifically for the Facebook study, the "emotional contagion" survey was consistent with both his overall focus on "psychological and interpersonal dynamics of social media, deception, and language"[23] and the study the university spearheaded, which was managed by the Air Force and designed to develop an empirical model "of the dynamics of social movement mobilization and contagions."[24]

The Pentagon's project, slated to be funded through 2017, "aims to determine 'the critical mass (tipping point)' of social contagions by studying their 'digital traces' in the cases of 'the 2011 Egyptian revolution, the 2011 Russian Duma elections, the 2012 Nigerian fuel subsidy crisis and the 2013 Gazi Park protests in Turkey,'" reported global security scholar Dr. Nafeez Ahmed, writing in the *Guardian*.[25]

Hancock's work is a clear and ominous link between market manipulation of consumer taste, Facebook's bread-and-butter goal, and the potential ability to use those same tactics to engineer public consent for government policies. (The Air Force study focused on Twitter posts "to identify individuals mobilized in a social contagion and when they become mobilized.") Other Minerva-funded projects cover similar terrain; examples include a study awarded to the University of Washington to research the origination, characteristics, and likely consequences of political movements as well as a study titled "Who Does Not Become a Terrorist, and Why?" that, according to Ahmed, frighteningly conflated peaceful activists with "supporters of political violence."

Ahmed argues that NSA mass surveillance "is partially motivated to prepare for the destabilizing impact of coming environmental, energy and economic shocks." He finds support from other concerned academics, including James Petras, Bartle Professor of Sociology at New York's Binghamton University, who says that Minerva-funded social scientists linked to US counterinsurgency operations are involved in the "study of emotions in stoking or quelling ideologically driven movements," including how "to counteract grassroots movements."[26]

In the end, the motives of Internet companies engaged in the creative exploration of their customers' data, or those of the academics who facilitate this, may not matter very much if government agencies, in the United States or elsewhere, can simply seize that data and perform their own extensive exploration of the "contagions" involved, the better to cause or eliminate them.

In other words, the news feeds or timelines of social media can be surveilled to locate agitators and predict legal "rebellions," and, if the next logical step is taken, can be manipulated through deletion, addition, or changes in algorithms to block the spread of dissenting or "dangerous" ideas.

In June 2014, as Facebook was attempting to deal with the controversy over its own manipulation of news feeds, the company went into court to prevent the district attorney of Manhattan from taking similar liberties with the privacy of nearly four hundred site users who were unaware of the government's access to their data. Suddenly, Facebook, which had previously cooperated with various federal and state agencies, was on the warpath, ostensibly to protect the privacy of its clients in the post-Snowden era.

To read memorandums of law filed in support of Facebook's case against the attorney general's demand for data is to encounter a born-again belief in the intrinsic wisdom of the Fourth Amendment. "These warrants fail to include date restrictions or any other criteria to limit the voluminous data sought, nor do they provide for procedures to minimize the collection or retention of information that is unrelated to the investigation. The warrants' extraordinary reach and lack of particularity render them constitutionally defective under state and federal law and should be quashed," wrote Facebook's attorneys. "In the alternative, Facebook should be permitted to provide notice to the people whose accounts are subject to these warrants to afford an opportunity to object to the expansive scope."[27]

There is an inherent irony in this language made obvious when one considers that Facebook's own customers are never afforded an opportunity to know, let alone object to, the scope of the personal data that it has gathered on them. So, too, the fact that this vast trove of data the government is unreasonably demanding is already in the hands of Facebook, to be freely exploited for advertising sales and other sources of profit. But this irony disappears if one accepts Facebook's argument that the Fourth Amendment provides a restraint only against *government* searches and therefore becomes an issue only when its agents can invade their massive collections of data.

Crucially, Facebook invoked the Fourth Amendment's ban on warrantless searches, noting that the amendment was designed to prevent government and not corporate overreach. Clearly, if Facebook had been transparent in collecting customer data, with individuals' explicit approval, then this would have been a matter of private consensual commerce that does not fall under the Constitution's protections.

But in fact it is a fit matter of government regulation of business behavior, as the Federal Trade Commission (FTC) pointed out in challenging Facebook's possible mining of the data acquired in the course of its purchase of WhatsApp.

WhatsApp customers had supplied their information on the basis of that company's privacy policy restricting such mining, meaning Facebook was possibly breaking fraud laws by violating that binding agreement. However, fraud is not a constitutional violation, and the WhatsApp customers could not claim to be suffering the loss of Fourth Amendment rights, since those apply only to intrusive or abusive government actions.

What the Fourth Amendment clearly does prohibit, as Facebook's lawyers pointed out quite strenuously in their briefs versus the New York district attorney, is warrantless general searches by the government, and that applies even if the route to that data is through the files maintained by a third party, which in this instance is Facebook.

In this particular case, the DA was on a fishing expedition to find evidence that people claiming medical disability were cheating, a search that should have required a specific warrant. Pointing out that they were appealing the warrant's demand that Facebook "collect and turn over virtually all communications, data, and information from 381 Facebook accounts," and that only the holders of 62 of those accounts were even charged with any crime, Facebook correctly argued that the prosecutor's overreach represented a clear violation of the Fourth Amendment protections to which Facebook's clients were entitled.

"The trial court's refusal to quash the bulk warrants was erroneous and should be reversed. The Fourth Amendment does not permit the Government to seize, examine, and keep indefinitely the private messages, photographs, videos, and other communications of nearly 400 people—the vast majority of whom will never know that the government has obtained and continues to possess their personal information," the brief stated. "Nor does the First Amendment permit the government to forbid Facebook from ever disclosing what it has been compelled to do—even after the government has concluded its investigation."[28]

That last objection, to a government agency being able to require that a private company not inform its customers of possible violations of their rights, is particularly crucial. By what perversion of the hallowed American concept of an informed citizenry ever vigilant to deprivations of their freedom could such a gag order not violate the meaning of the First Amendment?

Facebook was appealing to the New York State Supreme Court appellate division to overrule the decision of a lower trial court that held the gag order valid, but the same argument could be made against a similar order imposed on communications companies by the federal courts that prevented them from discussing NSA and other government-agency spying on citizens.

One key issue here is whether third parties like Facebook and Google have legal standing to protect their customers' constitutional rights. Facebook's lawyers argued that permitting the government to rummage through the data collected in Facebook accounts would be analogous to government agencies hiring a private contractor to conduct a broad warrantless search in someone's home, a clear violation of the Fourth Amendment: "The Government's bulk warrants, which demand 'all' communications and information in 24 broad categories from the 381 targeted accounts, are the digital equivalent of seizing everything in someone's home. Except here, it is not a single home but an entire neighborhood of nearly 400 homes. The vast scope of the government's search and seizure here would be unthinkable in the physical world."[29]

***

This extension of the constitutional protection against unreasonable searches in the physical world to the digital world is, of course, the heart of the modern challenge to government surveillance overreach. Obviously, the founders did not have in mind a "digital home." However, in June 2014, the Supreme Court delivered a groundbreaking decision extending Fourth Amendment protection to the data on a mobile device found on or near an arrested person. This victory for civil libertarians clearly set a precedent for protecting other digital collections, including those housed on Facebook.

As Chief Justice John Roberts argued in *Riley v. California,* the information digitally housed on a mobile device—or, by extension, a Facebook page—is so vast that searching through it represents a warrantless search without probable cause that is banned by the Fourth Amendment. An individual therefore has a reasonable expectation that this material will be treated as private and searched only pursuant to a specific warrant alleging probable cause of a crime.

The lack of such specificity, obviously not present in the district attorney's broad scan of the entire data collection housed on almost 400 Facebook users' pages, denies the essence of the constitutional protections. As Justice Roberts wrote: "Modern cell phones are not just another technological convenience. ... With all they contain and all they may reveal, they hold for many Americans 'the privacies of life.'"[30]

So, too, do Facebook pages represent revelations of the privacies of life. The Supreme Court marker on privacy established that the digital world, instead of reducing the constitutional protection of privacy to a quaint anachronism, has in fact rendered those protections far more compelling, due to the vast amounts of data in digital collections.

"Before cell phones," Roberts wrote, in an opinion with obvious ramifications for all other digital databases, "a search of a person was limited by physical realities and tended as a general matter to constitute only a narrow intrusion on privacy. ... Today it is no exaggeration to say that many of the more than ninety percent of Americans who own a cell phone keep on their person a digital record of nearly every aspect of their lives—from the mundane to the intimate."[31]

This extension of the protections that the founders afforded to even the most meager of traditional homes—treating a hut as a castle in establishing privacy as a fundamental human right—to homes in the digital world is perhaps the most dramatic evidence that the Constitution is a living document, fully capable of being adapted to a vastly changed world. Not doing so, Roberts argued, "is like saying a ride on horseback is materially indistinguishable from a flight to the moon."

Instead of concluding that modern technology renders privacy demands untenable, Roberts argued that those protections had to be expanded to provide meaningful privacy protection in a technologically far more invasive era. "The sources of potential pertinent information are virtually unlimited," he wrote, noting that failing to restrict warrantless searches of the digital home "would in effect give 'police officers unbridled discretion to rummage at will among a person's private effects.'"

In their appeal, Facebook's attorneys demonstrated just how invasive that unbridled rummage could be. Even many of the 1.2 billion users of Facebook forget how much of themselves they are revealing:

> People use Facebook to share information about themselves, much of it personal. This information often includes:
>
> - The person's age, religion, city of birth, educational affiliations, employment, family members, children, grandchildren, partner, friends, places visited, favorite music, favorite movies, favorite television shows, favorite books, favorite quotes, things "Liked," events to attend, affiliated groups, fitness, sexual orientation, relationship status, political views;
> - The person's thoughts about: religion, sexual orientation, relationship status, political views, future aspirations, values, ethics, ideology, current

events, fashion, friends, public figures, celebrity, lifestyle, celebrations, grief, frustrations, infidelity, social interactions, or intimate behavior;
- The person's photographs and videos of: him- or herself, children/family, friends, third parties, ultrasounds, medical experiences, food, lifestyle, pets/animals, travel/vacations, celebrations, music, art, humor, entertainment;
- The person's private hardships meant to be shared only with friends; and
- The person's intimate diary entries, including reflections, criticisms, and stories about daily life.[32]

This is just the sort of personal information the Fourth Amendment was designed to protect against warrantless searches. But given Facebook's acknowledgment that it is in fact collecting and storing such information, one has to ask why? Why collect such detailed and intimate information if you have already learned that the federal government, as represented by the NSA and other agencies, can routinely tap into that information? What is the likelihood of governments abroad doing the same? If Facebook and other Internet companies cannot guarantee the security of the data they collect, or even, as this case demonstrates, alert their customers to the risks involved, why collect or store the data at all?

The answer becomes apparent in what we have learned of the basic business model that ensures the profitability of most Internet companies. The data is collected not because government agencies require it but, rather, because the companies themselves want to exploit it, for profit. Consider the ethical implications of doing just that under an overtly totalitarian government enabling a degree of surveillance of the individual of unprecedented proportions. Perhaps Facebook trusts the US government more, but isn't that a choice its customers should make about the use of their data? In any case, Facebook has already shown that it is in a position to manipulate the choices its customers make, and what assurance can the company provide that it is impervious to any government's use of that same set of manipulative tools?

While Facebook, Twitter, and other social media companies have been applauded for indirectly helping dissidents in countries like Egypt and Ukraine by providing a decentralized, free, "real-time," and difficult-to-disrupt alternative communication system, what assurance can they give that those activities have not been appropriated by the very governments the protesters sought to challenge?

The reality is that most of us spend our days freely surrendering personal data out of convenience, whether to enhance a shopping experience or to build a friendship, while in denial—or simply unaware—of the fact that at the same moment all of it is being made available to government officials whose motives are inscrutable and potentially repressive.

***

In order to conform to the fourth amendment's restrictions on unreasonable searches, wiretapping phone conversations has long been carefully restricted by court rulings, whether conducted by private detectives or government agents. All of the world's democratic governments, even without the specific restraint of that amendment, manage to strictly regulate the physical taps placed on phone lines to listen in and record conversations.

In the predigital age, physical intrusion on phone lines was required to intercept calls, but, today, undetected copying of signals has made the process much easier. So much so that in 2007 Google, in the course of cruising neighborhoods with vehicles designed mainly to collect photographic images to complement Google Maps, also had the ability to pick up and record data from homes connected to Wi-Fi networks. Google's equipment was able to collect basic data from those network connections, "location-based" service IP addresses, and payload information including usernames, personal emails, passwords, and documents.

By May 2010, when confronted over this practice, Google admitted it had inadvertently collected six hundred gigabytes of such data in thirty different countries.[33] Several class action lawsuits were filed accusing Google of having violated the federal Wiretap Act. Google lost the case both in district and appellate courts, and in June 2014 the Supreme Court refused to overturn the lower-court decisions and allowed the case to proceed.

The Supreme Court decision, coming a week after its sweeping affirmation of privacy protection for mobile devices obtained by police during an arrest, was interpreted as a shift in direction by the high court toward a reaffirmation of the importance of privacy in the digital age. Its significance for Google was less about tapping into home networks with its Google mapping trucks, which the company had agreed to stop doing, and more about important projects the company was launching that had even clearer privacy issues. As the *New York Times* reported, the court's ruling "[undermined] the search company's efforts to put a troublesome episode to rest even as it plans to become more deeply embedded in consumers' lives."[34]

That last phrase is the rub. In an earlier time, the General Electric Company boasted that "progress is our most important product"; it can fairly be argued that a comparable slogan for Google today could replace *progress* with *intrusion*. Expansion plans at Google involve more effectively mining ever-larger collections of data. The *Times* report noted why the Supreme Court's increased attention to privacy came at an awkward moment for the company: "Google's annual developers conference last week showcased the company's wide-ranging agenda to expand its technology from desktop computers and mobile devices to the home, the body, and vehicles. Google's new devices will communicate and share data, requiring a great deal of trust by users that all this information will not be used in unauthorized or unexpected ways."[35]

This is a concern of consumers throughout the world, and it has been greatly enhanced in the aftermath of the Snowden revelations. Suddenly, the arrogant insistence of Google's Schmidt or Facebook's Zuckerberg about privacy being merely an anachronistic obsession of the technologically primitive, the perverted, or the outright criminal begins to ring hollow.

For much of human history, the line between the government and the private individual was quite clearly marked, whether under rule of the British Crown or in the new republic born in the rebellion of the colonies. Arguably, the clearest distinction between Anglo-Saxon legal experience and its alternatives resided in a profound respect for the innate rights of the individual against societal sources of power, be they derived from church or government.

The English common law that restrained the crown and informed the mindset of the American colonialists contained the seeds of a notion of individual space, an inviolate personal sovereignty that guided the writing of the Fourth Amendment into the Bill of Rights. One's house, as humble as that dwelling might be, was safeguarded from the warrantless searches by agents of the crown, and when that right came to be ignored by the English administrators over the American colonies, it sparked the revolution as much as any factor.

That was the judgment of no less an expert on the origins of the American Revolution than a young John Adams, who witnessed the patriot James Otis delivering a speech denouncing the British Crown's use of general warrants and writs of assistance to invade the homes of colonialists. Chief Justice John Roberts cited that incident as foundational in offering his majority opinion in the mobile devices decision:

> In 1761, the patriot James Otis delivered a speech in Boston denouncing the use of writs of assistance. A young John Adams was there, and he would later write that "every man of a crowded audience appeared to me to go away, as I did, ready to take up arms against writs of assistance." According to Adams, Otis's speech was "the first scene of the first act of opposition to the arbitrary claims of Great Britain. Then and there the child Independence was born."[36]

By positioning the right to privacy so clearly as a motivation for the break from English rule and the establishment of the republic, Roberts offered the clearest defense of a constitutional protection for privacy, a word actually absent from the Constitution itself. With that opinion a year after the first revelations by Edward Snowden regarding the enormous loss of privacy to government surveillance, a unanimous majority of the Supreme Court unexpectedly drew a firm line in defense of privacy as a constitutionally protected right.

The justices did this not by addressing the abuses of privacy by the NSA, which would have required significant self-criticism on the part of the court, since Chief Justice Roberts was responsible for appointing judges to the FISA court that approved the scope of NSA spying.

Instead, this same Roberts wrote a dazzling opinion in the cell phone case that enjoyed unanimous support across the ideological divide that has defined this court in recent decades. His defense of privacy in the age of the Internet set as clear a standard on the subject as the nation has ever enjoyed through its judicial system.

Prior to the Roberts opinion, the perception had been growing in the burgeoning Internet industry—which profited so mightily from the exploitation of privacy—that the very notion of privacy was an anachronism. Since the massive flow of previously private data was essential to the new tools and toys provided free of charge by firms like Google and Facebook, the right to mine that data was simply their payment in return.

The corollary justification for the end of privacy was in part a technical one: the data stream would be too costly and difficult to restrict in the name of privacy; the very vastness of the data collected had become the compelling reason to ignore demands for protection of individual privacy by granting consumers meaningful control over their own data. That was a judgment made by most of the lower courts, including the two that had ruled in the cases reviewed by the Supreme Court that formed the basis of the Roberts opinion.

But what Roberts did, much to the surprise of industry lawyers, was to stand the complexity argument on its head. He asserted that it was precisely the scope of the data collected in the case of devices acquired by police during an arrest that made it unwise to allow those same police to search the phones' various stored databases. This landmark decision provides an unequivocal answer on the critical role of privacy in the conception of the Fourth Amendment. Roberts did this in his conclusion by reminding us that because of the most rapid of technological changes, the threat to privacy has never been greater.

The question that Roberts's decision left unanswered is to what degree this broad extension of cell phone privacy protection applies to the even larger collections of similarly personal data held by federal agencies, beginning with the NSA. Until the Snowden revelations, there was no serious national debate or understanding about the scope of the federal government's assault on privacy in the digital age. But now that issue, of far greater consequence but organically quite similar to the one dealt with by Roberts in his decision, strongly and clearly demands the court's attention.

Notes

1. Marshall Kirkpatrick, "Facebook's Zuckerberg Says the Age of Privacy Is Over," *ReadWrite*, January 9, 2010, http://readwrite.com/2010/01/09/facebooks_zuckerberg_says_the_age_of_privacy_is_ov.
2. Michael Zimmer, "Mark Zuckerberg's Theory of Privacy," *Washington Post*, February 3, 2014, http://www.washingtonpost.com/lifestyle/style/mark-zuckerbergs-theory-of-privacy/2014/02/03/2c-1d780a-8cea-11e3-95dd-36ff657a4dae_story.html.

3. Ibid.
4. Polly Sprenger, "Sun on Privacy: 'Get Over It,'" *Wired*, January 26, 1999.
5. "Google CEO on Privacy: 'If You Have Something You Don't Want Anyone to Know, Maybe You Shouldn't Be Doing It'" (video), *Huffington Post*, March 18, 2010.
6. Claire Cain Miller, "Revelations of N.S.A. Spying Cost U.S. Tech Companies," *New York Times*, March 21, 2014, http://www.nytimes.com/2014/03/22/business/fallout-from-snowden-hurting-bottom-line-of-tech-companies.html.
7. Mark Zuckerberg, "Mark Zuckerberg (Official Page)—March 13, 2014 Post," Facebook, March 13, 2014, https://www.facebook.com/zuck/posts/10101301165605491.
8. Ibid.
9. Robinson Meyer, "Everything We Know About Facebook's Secret Mood Manipulation Experiment," *The Atlantic*, June 28, 2014.
10. Adam D. I. Kramer, Jamie E. Guillory, and Jeffrey T. Hancock, "Experimental Evidence of Massive-Scale Emotional Contagion Through Social Networks," *Proceedings of the National Academy of Sciences* 111 (June 17, 2014): 87–89, http://www.pnas.org/.
11. Vindu Goel, "Facebook Tinkers with Users' Emotions in News Feed Experiment, Stirring Outcry," *New York Times*, June 30, 2014, http://www.nytimes.com/2014/06/30/technology/facebook-tinkers-with-users-emotions-in-news-feed-experiment-stirring-outcry.html?_r=0.
12. Adam D. I. Kramer, https://www.facebook.com/akramer/posts/10152987150867796.
13. Quoted in John Carberry, "Media Statement on Cornell University's Role in Facebook 'Emotional Contagion' Research," Cornell University Media Relations Office, June 30, 2014, http://mediarelations.cornell.edu/2014/06/30/media-statement-on-cornell-universitys-role-in-facebook-emotional-contagion-research/.
14. Goel, "Facebook Tinkers with Users' Emotions in News Feed Experiment, Stirring Outcry."
15. Tarleton Gillespie, "Facebook's Algorithm—Why Our Assumptions Are Wrong, and Our Concerns Are Right," *Culture Digitally*, July 4, 2014, http://culturedigitally.org/2014/07/facebooks-algorithm-why-our-assumptions-are-wrong-and-our-concerns-are-right.
16. Ibid.
17. Ibid.
18. Ibid.
19. R. Jai Krishna, "Sandberg: Facebook Study Was 'Poorly Communicated,'" *Wall Street Journal*, July 2, 2014, http://blogs.wsj.com/digits/2014/07/02/facebooks-sandberg-apologizes-for-news-feed-experiment/.
20. Jaron Lanier, "Should Facebook Manipulate Users?," *New York Times*, June 30, 2014, http://www.nytimes.com/2014/07/01/opinion/jaron-lanier-on-lack-of-transparency-in-facebook-study.html.
21. Gillespie, "Facebook's Algorithm—Why Our Assumptions Are Wrong, and Our Concerns Are Right."
22. "Program History & Overview," The Minerva Initiative, August 12, 2014, http://minerva.dtic.mil/overview.html.

23. Cornell University, Department of Communication, "Department Faculty and Academic Staff," 2014, https://communication.cals.cornell.edu/people/faculty-and-academic-staff.
24. Nafeez Ahmed, "Pentagon Preparing for Mass Civil Breakdown," *Guardian*, July 4, 2014, http://www.theguardian.com/environment/earth-insight/2014/jun/12/pentagon-mass-civil-breakdown.
25. Ibid.
26. Ibid.
27. "Facebook Case over Search Warrants for User Information," *New York Times*, June 26, 2014, http://www.nytimes.com/interactive/2014/06/26/technology/facebook-search-warrants-case-documents.html.
28. "In Re 381 Search Warrants Directed to Facebook, Inc. and Dated July 23, 2013," New York State Supreme Court Appellate Division—First Department, July 23, 2013, https://www.eff.org/files/2014/06/26/fbopening_brief_in_re_381_search_warrants.pdf.
29. "Facebook's Brief Seeking Review of the Case on Searches," Document Cloud-NYT News, *New York Times*, July 23, 2013, https://www.documentcloud.org/documents/1209712-facebooks-brief-seeking-review-of-the-case-on.html.
30. "Supreme Court of the United States—Riley vs. California Opinions," Supreme Court, June 25, 2014, http://www.supremecourt.gov/opinions/13pdf/13-132_8l9c.pdf.
31. Ibid.
32. "In Re 381 Search Warrants Directed to Facebook, Inc. and Dated July 23, 2013."
33. "Google to Give Governments Street View Data," *New York Times*, June 3, 2010, http://www.nytimes.com/2010/06/04/business/global/04google.html.
34. David Streitfeld, "Supreme Court Rejects Google's Street View Appeal" (blog), *New York Times*, June 30, 2014, http://bits.blogs.nytimes.com/2014/06/30/supreme-court-rejects-googles-street-view-appeal/?assetType=nyt_now.
35. Ibid.
36. Mark Walsh, "A "View" from the Court: Some Morning Joe Before Digital Day" (blog), *SCOTUSblog*, June 25, 2014.

Post-Reading Questions

1. The author presents evidence that consumer privacy is rapidly declining. Leaders of major corporations argue that the concept of personal privacy is gradually disappearing and that privacy concerns are antiquated and "out-of-date" and that consumers freely surrender their privacy. One executive argued that "if you have something that you don't want anyone to know, maybe you shouldn't be doing it in the first place." Is privacy and are privacy concerns outdated? Choose a position and defend it.
2. The author argues that data-collecting corporations and government agencies are using social media platforms like Facebook, which collect extensive amounts of personal data, to conduct social experiments, and market goods and services on information shared by consumers on "secure" social media platforms. Do these activities in fact compromise freedom? Please explain your answer.

Videos Retrieved from the Internet

"Ethics, Computers and Security"

https://www.youtube.com/watch?v=ubwmFcXvxdc&feature=emb_logo

This is a university lecture on the topic.

"Cyber Security Training: Becoming an Ethical Hacker"

https://www.youtube.com/watch?v=KkgY0903m14&feature=emb_logo

This is a training video on offensive hacking.

"The Complete Ethical Hacking Course"

https://www.youtube.com/watch?v=fDeLtKUxTmM&feature=emb_logo

This is a private training film on the topic.

Internet Sites on Ethics and Cyber Security

This is a discussion of the need for IT security professionals to have ethical standards and training.

"Tough Challenges in Cyber Security"

https://securityintelligence.com/tough-challenges-cybersecurity-ethics/

This article discusses the need for students to receive ethical training before entering the profession.

"In Search of an Ethical Code for Cybersecurity"

https://www.infosecurity-magazine.com/magazine-features/search-ethical-code-cybersecurity/

This article discusses the issues and challenges for ethics in the profession.

"Cybersecurity: A Major Concern and a Great Business Opportunity"

https://www.forbes.com/sites/miltonezrati/2018/09/05/cyber-security-a-major-concern-and-a-great-business-opportunity/#20cc11c13e26

The article addresses the current and future needs of cyber security.

"The State of Cybersecurity in 2018: What Do the Experts Think?"

https://www.pandasecurity.com/mediacenter/news/cybersecurity-2018-what-experts-think/

This is a comprehensive discussion of the current issues in cyber security.

Section V

Redefining Internal Environmental Ethics

*"It's not about making the right choice. It's about
making a choice and making it right."*
J.R. Rim

IN SECTION 5, TWO COMPREHENSIVE SUSTAINABILITY articles by Paula Alexander are presented for the reader. In the first article, "Ethics of Business Decision Making" the author raises the question, "What should be the standards use to evaluate ethical business decisions in the workplace?" In daily decisions, leaders must select from a multitude of ethical standards such as rights, justice, virtue ethics, and ethics of care. Also, a leader's personal integrity is also involved in the leader's ability to create an ethical workplace culture.

The author examines what ethical standards address ethical decision making. "Property rights" are grounded in John Locke's social contract theory that property is a natural right and is derived from an individual's labor, and "right of contract" is fundamental to a capitalist society for all adults. The author notes that a recurring challenge for leaders is how to balance property rights and contractual rights. She acknowledges that new rights are evolving.

Two forms of justice are discussed: procedural due process and distributive justice. Procedural justice addresses whether a fairness standard is met according to the courts' interpretations based on the U.S. Constitution. Distributive justice is based on who gets what and how much. The concepts of justice are further discussed by reviewing Rawl's writing.

Other standards discussed are utilitarianism, which addresses the greatest good for the greatest number of individuals; minority rights as protected under the U.S. Constitution; the Disclosure Rule, which examines transparency; Kant's categorical imperatives to do one's duty; ethics of care; and virtue ethics.

The author closes with a review of Kohlberg's "Stages of Moral Reasoning" and deciding on what is a moral dilemma.

In the second reading by Paula Alexander, "Sustainable Environmental Management," the author notes that risks are inherent in the workplace. Thus, risk management is considered a leader's fundamental responsibility. In managing the triple bottom line for an economically, socially, and environmentally sustaining business, leaders must constantly be reviewing production and consumption practices. Poor practices resulted in the Exxon Valdez and BP Deep Water Horizon oil spills, Chernobyl, Three Mile Island, and Fukushima nuclear power plants, which are discussed in terms of both technological and social choices. The author designs a "Probability-Impact Matrix" that rates the probably and risks associated with an environmental or technological disaster. The model discusses high probability-high impact events, high probability-low impact events, low probability-high impact events, and low probability-low impact events.

Other topics discussed include unintended negative consequences, free goods, negative externalities, sustainable production, sustainability, sustainable development, and the Kyoto protocol, and issues in sustainable supply chain management.

The author concludes with a case study on Starbucks sustainability practices.

Pre-Reading Questions

- How important is the triple-bottom line for business?
- What is the concept of materiality and how much of an influence does it have on business decisions?
- Where have you observed global sustainability initiated?

Reading 5.1

Ethics of Business Decision Making
Paula Alexander

New Property Rights and Human Rights

New property rights and human rights are evolving. Most of us sustain our lives not by living from the returns generated by our ownership of capital or our ownership of land but by the fruit of our labor. We own our hands and our bodies and live from the fruit of our labor, which includes knowledge work.[1]

Jobs and education become the basis for people's income earning capacity. A person's job and education are fundamental to their economic well-being. However, the right to an education and the right to a job are not established rights, like property rights and rights of contract. Moreover, our right to Social Security, which provides income in the event of disability and in retirement, and to Medicare, which provides medical care during retirement are evolving as *new property rights*.

These newly recognized new property rights sometimes conflict with traditional individual property rights. For example, the Supreme Court of New Jersey has interpreted the New Jersey Constitution's equal protection clause to require equal access to education. The New Jersey Supreme Court stated that funding education on the basis of property taxes is unconstitutional; richer towns had better education systems when schools were funded by municipal property taxes, while poorer towns were disadvantaged. The New Jersey Supreme Court required a state-wide tax as the basis to fund the New Jersey public schools. The solution adopted was the New Jersey income tax to fund the New Jersey public schools.[2] However, there is no federally recognized right to an equal education.[3]

In addition, there is no "guarantee" of employment in the United States, and the Congress struggles with employment policy. For example, the predominant employment relationship

Paula Alexander, "Ethics of Business Decision Making," *Corporate Social Irresponsibility*, pp. 60-69, 72-74. Copyright © 2015 by Taylor & Francis Group. Reprinted with permission.

is "at will" in the US, and unemployment is predominantly a problem of the individual person who is unemployed. However, there are significant differences across countries about the right to work. For example, in spring 2006, France was gripped by strikes because legislation was passed that adversely affected younger workers' rights to their jobs: workers under age 26 years who had worked for their company less than two years could be laid off without cause, in contrast to the usual procedures for layoffs under French law.[4] The law was eventually revoked after the widespread social movements that occurred in France.

Some rights have been recognized as fundamental human rights. Thus, for example, the United Nations identified basic human rights and is pressing for a global recognition of these rights, irrespective of the form of government or its governing documents. The right to own property is considered a fundamental human right in the UN Declaration of Human Rights.

Employers are faced with the challenge of respecting and implementing fundamental human rights of their employees and perhaps other stakeholders. For example, Unocal was charged with responsibility for the human rights violations by the Myanmar (Burmese) government in the construction of the natural gas pipeline across Burma. Although the responsibility of Unocal for the human rights violations was never fully litigated, Unocal decided to settle the case after the Ninth Circuit Court of Appeals permitted the litigation to go forward. A fuller consideration of the dilemma faced by Unocal is given in the end of chapter case. Challenges of respecting worker rights is considered in Chapters 10 and 11 on labor markets.

Justice Standards

A *justice standard* is an alternative to a rights standard for deciding ethical dilemmas. Justice standards are based on two perspectives: procedural due process and distributive justice. *Procedural due process* addresses whether a fairness standard is met by the actions taken in a controversy or disputed situation. Procedural due process addresses the fairness of the dispute resolution process itself, such as the impartiality of the decision maker in the controversy. The United States Constitution in its Fifth, Fourteenth and Sixth Amendments, guarantees procedural due process.[5] The Fourteen Amendment guarantees US citizens that they may not be deprived of life, liberty or property without due process of law; however, with due process, one can be deprived of life, liberty and property. The Fourteenth Amendment also promises the equal protection of the laws to United States citizens, establishing a principle of non-discrimination in the application of law. The Fifth Amendment promises procedural due process in federal proceedings while the Sixth Amendment establishes the right to trial by a jury of one's peers in criminal proceedings.

The concept of equal protection is expansive and undergoing evolution in its application. For example, in June 2003, the United States Supreme Court struck down a Texas law prohibiting homosexual relations.[6] The Texas law was struck down as violating the Due Process Clause of the Fourteenth Amendment. In the aftermath of the *Lawrence v. Texas* decision, Wal-Mart, the largest private employer in the United States, announced that it would not discriminate against its workers based on their sexual orientation.[7] Although Title VII law constrains employers against gender discrimination, discrimination based on sexual orientation is not prohibited by federal law, so that companies must make choices about their policies affecting their gay and lesbian employees. Certain states, such as New Jersey, prohibit discrimination based on sexual orientation. Moreover, the Massachusetts Supreme Court interpreted the equal protection clause of the Massachusetts Constitution as requiring gay marriage; homosexual individuals must have the same protections of the laws as heterosexual individuals.[8] Massachusetts was the first state to do so.

Distributive justice is oriented to who gets what and how much. Conflicts among stakeholders arise about what is an appropriate distribution of the goods and rewards of society or, conversely, the bads of society. John Rawls developed a provocative theory on the just distribution of social goods and bads.

John Rawls, *A Theory of Justice*. John Rawls, in his book, *A Theory of Justice*,[9] proposes an innovative approach to distributive justice. Many philosophers as well as politicians have addressed the question of what constitutes a fair or just society. For example, Karl Marx protested the social dysfunctions and social inequalities associated with the rise of capitalism in the early stages of the industrial revolution. In the twentieth century, Russia and China developed communist systems to attempt to construct a fair or just society, attempting to minimize differentials in wealth, power, privilege and status.

Rawls addresses the question: must differentials in wealth, power, privilege and status be minimized in order to have a just society? Do we have to seek the lowest common denominator? Russia and Communist China have been unsuccessful in creating a classless society, in part because leadership requires differentials in power and access to resources; with these differentials, differences in status also become magnified.[10] Also, differences in natural abilities and talents are inherent in human populations. The demise of the USSR and the transition of the People's Republic of China to a market-driven economy reveal that the socialist or communist systems did not succeed in establishing classless societies, wherein differentials in wealth, power, privilege and status are abolished.

Rawls asks the question: under what conditions would the privileged or top dogs as well as underdogs buy into the social arrangements? Typically, top dogs have a vested interest in status quo, while underdogs foment change. Rawls proposes to construct a society in everyone would "buy into" the social arrangements, irrespective of whether they were born as top dogs or underdogs.[11]

Rawls' solution is that a just society is one in which the differentials accruing to the top dogs work to the advantage of the underdogs, so that the less privileged benefit by the greater wealth, power, privilege and status of the top dogs. However, this principle is a limiting factor on permissible differentials in the distribution of goods. Any differentials in wealth, power, privilege or status that do not work to the benefit of the underdogs would be taxed away under a distributive justice principle.[12] Rawls' solution does not require the minimization of differentials in social goods.

Utilitarianism. *Utilitarianism* evaluates a solution as just as that choice that creates the greatest good to the greatest number of individuals. A utilitarian standard might lead to conclusion, in the Johns Manville case for example, that it would be ethical to continue production of asbestos products. The executives of the Johns Manville Company might have invoked a utilitarian standard in addressing the issue whether asbestos should be used for industrial products requiring fire-retardant properties, even after they knew that asbestos can harm workers who mined and produced asbestos products. Moreover, the bankruptcy settlement of Johns Manville arguably created a just solution under a utilitarian analysis: were the fund established by the bankruptcy settlement not have been created, early claimants would have exhausted the resources of the firm; the bankruptcy permitted latter claimants to be compensated too.

However, application of a utilitarian standard can trammel the rights of minorities, since minorities are by definition not members of the majority served by the utilitarian solution.

Minority Rights

A majoritarian or utilitarian standard may trammel *rights of minorities*. The UN Declaration on Human Right speaks to the rights of minorities. The US Bill of Rights, the first ten amendments to the Constitution of 1789, guarantees rights of minorities. Moreover, under a constitutionally based system of checks and balances, the role of the judiciary is to protect minorities from having their rights trammeled by a majoritarian standard. In addition, an important role of a leader to is to protect voices of minorities. Small group studies show that groups in which the correct solution was held by a minority voice within the group adopt correct solutions more frequently if they have an effective leader compared to groups without an effective leader. A rights perspective on the asbestos problem at Johns Manville would require that the safety of workers who mined and manufactured asbestos products would be protected and the workers give informed consent to work under the hazardous condition, even if the public benefits from the use of asbestos in public buildings as a fire retardant.

Other Standards by Which to Judge Ethical Dilemmas

The Disclosure Rule

The Disclosure Rule is a test whether some action withstands the light of day. The *Disclosure Rule* goes to materiality of information; information is material if a prudent decision maker or investor would want to have this information to make the decision or investment. Beech-Nut apple juice fraudulently advertised its baby juice as 100% natural.[13] Beech-Nut executives, in the face of an order to submit juice samples to the New York Department of Agriculture, moved the subpoenaed product under cover of darkness to New Jersey, thus creating a barrier to the New York Department of Agriculture's jurisdiction to test the product. The act of transferring the apple juice under cover of night across state lines might have created feedback to the Beech-Nut executives that something was awry; that they cannot in good faith argue that the apple juice is not adulterated.

Likewise the disclosure rule would have been useful to Philip Morris Tobacco when it undertook a country-specific study of Eastern European markets, promoting the advantages to the Czech Republic of having low barriers to the importation of cigarettes because the polity saves $1,200 by each smoker's early death.[14] The American Legacy Foundation ran an ad carried by all major newspapers, except the *Wall Street Journal*, which disclosed the study and its marketing pitch. Philip Morris apologized in a press release to the *Wall Street Journal* and immediately to put an end to future studies.[15] The disclosure rule would have prevented Philip Morris' commissioning the study and saved it the great embarrassment caused by the disclosure of its marketing plan.

The Categorical Imperative

The *categorical imperative* or the principle of universalizability of Immanuel Kant addresses the ethics of behavior which, when generalized, might harm the social fabric and whether an individual would make exception for himself or herself given special circumstances. The test is whether the exception could be generalized to others similarly situated. The rule of *universalizability* extends a similar right of act to others similarly situated and serves as a test as to whether behavior is ethical. For example, stealing in general is wrong or immoral, but stealing to prevent yourself or others from starvation is ethically permissible. The principle of universalizability was illustrated in *Doctor Zhivago*, when Zhivago is stealing wood to burn to keep his family warm during the Moscow winter; his brother, an officer of the Red army, sees him, but lets him go, reflecting that one man stealing wood is pathetic, but all men stealing wood is dangerous.

Also, the ethics of polluting and dumping are subject to the test of universalizability. For example, many homeowners dump leftover gasoline for lawn mowers at the end of the mowing season, rather than take the gasoline to the recycling/disposal center, which also charges the homeowner for the costs of disposal. The problem with simply dumping the gasoline, even in one's own yard, is that the gasoline can seep down to the water table and pollute the groundwater. Although the damage caused by a single instance of dumping gasoline might be tolerated by the environment, if all homeowners disposed of their gasoline in this manner, a major problem of groundwater contamination would likely develop. Therefore, dumping does not pass the universalizability test.

Reciprocity or Test of Reversibility

Reciprocity or *test of reversibility* embodies the rule, "Do unto Others as You Would Have Them Do unto You"—or your family and loved ones. The test of reciprocity, or reflexivity, is another aspect of Kant's categorical imperative. The Ford Pinto case is an example of failure of *test of reciprocity*. The Ford executives who decided to market Ford Pinto knowing that it was subject to fire upon low speed rear-end collision would not make the decision to manufacture the car with this defect, then pay damages, were they themselves, their wives or children to be burned then be paid damages. The test of reciprocity or reversibility would clarify the ethics of the cost–benefit approach Ford used with the Pinto.[16]

Feelings about a Choice

The *gut test* tests the ethics of a decision based on the decision maker's emotional response to his or her choice. The *red face test* is a heuristic rule this author learned from her mentor at NYU Law School; I have found the red face test gives particularly useful guidance for making innovative arguments in my legal practice. Attorneys push the envelope; the red face test queries whether the attorney can make an innovative argument without blushing. The *gag test* is somewhat similar to the red face test. The gag test queries whether the attorney can make an innovative argument without choking on his or her words.

The "*smell test*" can be useful in addressing questions of conflicts of interest and the appearance of impropriety. For example, does the award of a contract by the board of a company to a board member pass the "smell test"?

Each of the feeling-based tests, the gut test, the red face test, the gag test, and the smell test, is based on an emotional response to an ethical decision and uses self-based feedback to the decision maker. The feeling-based tests tie to the managerial skill, emotional intelligence. The emergence of emotional intelligence as a key managerial skill lends authenticity and supports the use of feelings-based tests of the ethics of a decision.[17]

Personal Integrity

Lawrence Kohlberg's Stages of Moral Reasoning

Lawrence Kohlberg has articulated a developmental theory of moral decision making.[18] Kohlberg has identified stages of moral reasoning related to an individual's development: a pre-conventional stage, a conventional stage and a post-conventional or principled stage.[19] These stages parallel the stages of cognitive development identified by Jean Piaget.[20]

At the pre-conventional level, children identify as moral those rules established by their parents as right or wrong.[21] That is good that satisfies the child's needs. In the second stage of pre-conventional moral reasoning, the individual engages in social exchange and follows rules in his or her self-interest. The pre-conventional level is a stage which lasts up to age nine years, when the individual is focused on himself or herself. The conventional level of moral reasoning occurs between ages nine years and adolescence. At the conventional level, children start to understand the point of view of the other; they understand expectations of their reference group; morality is seen as conforming to the obligations and expectations of their reference group, including parents, teachers and their peers. The post-conventional level of moral reasoning can be achieved by adolescents and adults and corresponds to Piaget's cognitive stage of formal reasoning. In the post-conventional level of moral reasoning, individuals understand that different groups have different standards of rules and laws; morality is seen as upholding the social contract of one's group. Utilitarianism, achieving the greatest good for the greatest number, is characteristic of Kohlberg's first stage of post-conventional moral reasoning. In the second stage of post-conventional moral reasoning, the individual makes decisions based on universal ethical principles, involving individual rights and justice principles.

Ethics of Care

The *ethics of care*[22] approach, developed from the criticism that Kohlberg's stages of moral reasoning, with its emphasis on rights and obligations, is gender biased.[23] Carol Gilligan, a professor of education at Harvard University who had an interest in the psycho-social development of adolescent girls, conducted extensive interviews with young women. Gilligan developed her approach from these interviews, as *In a Different Voice*.[24] Later Gilligan interviewed women considering abortion after *Roe v. Wade*, the United States Supreme Court decision that decided that women have a legal right to abortion.[25] The *Roe v. Wade* decision grounded its approach in a privacy right inferred in the United States Constitution and a woman's right to autonomy over her own body.[26]

However, Gilligan found that the women considering whether to have an abortion after the legalization of abortion by the *Roe v. Wade* decision were not basing their decision on their rights but on their relationships. "I was listening at the time to women who were pregnant and thinking about abortion in the immediate aftermath of the *Roe v. Wade* decision.

Women's concerns were often driven by experiences of disconnection which rendered relationships difficult to maintain, but their voices carried a sense of connection, of living and acting in a web of relationships which went against the grain of the prevailing discourse of individual rights and freedom."[27]

Duty of Care. A duty of care is owed by a parent to a child, by spouses to each other, by a teacher to a student, by a manufacturer to its customers. A duty of care is recognized in the law of torts. A tort is an injury to another that is actionable at law. A tort is committed when: 1) a duty of care is owed to another; 2) that duty of care is breached; and 3) an injury is incurred that is proximately caused by the breach of the duty of care owed to the other person. There is no duty of rescue among strangers, if the person in peril was not put in peril by the act of the other stranger; however, if a stranger acts as a Good Samaritan, the rescuer owes a duty not to further injury the imperiled person by the rescuer's negligence. The concept of duty of care ties the ethics of care to concepts of rights and justice. Moreover, care is a virtue fundamental to good human development.[38] Care ethics would urge the view that caring and caring relationships are essential to human flourishing, a concept central to virtue ethics.

Virtue Ethics

Virtue ethics focuses on the character of the individual actor or decision maker. Virtue ethics is based on Plato and Aristotle's examination of the basis for well-being in the republic or state.[29] The goal is human flourishing. Human flourishing is achieved by citizens of virtue or good character who exercise practical wisdom.

There are different perspectives on virtues, defined as mind sets, habits or dispositions to act by a human agent. Thomas Aquinas, for example, identifies "cardinal virtues," including prudence, temperance, justice and courage or fortitude. Vices are also identified; the Christian tradition identifies seven "capital" or "deadly" sins, including greed, lust, anger, envy, sloth, gluttony and pride. Other traditions identify important or fundamental virtues differently. For example, Robert Thurman, a professor at Columbia University and a noted Buddhist scholar, in his recent book, *Infinite Life: Seven Virtues for Living Well*, identifies the Buddhist approach to virtues as: generosity, morality, tolerance, creativity, contemplation, wisdom and art (of living).[30]

Personal Vision

Personal vision, a habit of "highly effective people,"[31] is a component of managerial decision making. Personal vision and values underlie the individual manager's values and decision framework. A cognitive-based approach to decision making, Image Theory, considers values and personal principles the basis for choice and decision making.[32] Decisions are adopted, according to Image Theory, only if a particular choice is compatible with the individual's values, goals and strategies. Individual managers might very productively engage in a process of values clarification, surfacing their decision framework and the personal values they would use to decide ethical dilemmas.

Conflicts of Interest

A touchstone of personal integrity is the ability and willingness of an individual to recognize and to resolve conflicts of interest. The tests of ethical decision making that use an individual's emotional response to a decision, the red face test, the gag test and the gut test, require an informed or sensitive conscience.[33] The Freudian defense mechanisms, denial, rationalization and reaction formation, can interfere with an individual's recognition and coping with conflict of interest issues. […] many of the corporate scandals were related to fraudulent earnings management practices, which justified stock price increases and that were tied to executive compensation, a policy that creates a conflict of interest between the personal interests of the manager and the interests of the enterprise in transparency and fair dealing in the market. Conflicts of interest were an important factor in the Enron failure; for example, the Board of Directors suspended the Enron code of conduct about conflicts of interest.

Moreover, it is possible that the conflicts of interest between patients and shareholders in for-profit medical enterprise is so fundamental that the best interests of patients cannot be served by a for-profit organizational structure.[34] The drive to cut costs in order to maximize profits, serving the interests of providers of equity capital, may so directly conflict with the best interests of patients that the for-profit medical services organizations may not be an appropriate form or organization for the delivery of health care services. It may be that the conflicts of interest between patients, stockholders and managers are such that the interests of patients become sacrificed to the interests of stockholders and managers of the for-profit medical services organizations. This dilemma and conflict of interest has been recognized in the public health literature, where studies show a higher mortality rate and other adverse indicants of patient care for patients in for-profit hospitals.[35]

Deciding Ethical Dilemmas

In deciding specific ethical dilemmas, an individual must decide which standard of judgment is appropriate for specific cases or in specific situations. The decision maker can test the standards of judgment and undertake an ethical evaluation of each standard using stakeholder analysis. Using a decision matrix, managers can evaluate whether the proposed act is ethical under a given standard. The decision matrix should list the alternative standards of decision making as well as the stakeholders and determine whether or not the proposed action is ethical as to each stakeholder. See Table 5.1.1 for a method to test choices about ethical dilemmas.

TABLE 5.1.1 Which Standards of Judgment for Deciding Ethical Dilemmas?

	Stakeholder										
	Customer	Employees	Shareholders	Executive Management	Suppliers of Debt Capital	Suppliers of Raw Materials	Competitors	Community Where the Firm Operates	Environment	Regulators	Others Impacted by Management Actions (Specify)
Standard of Judgment	Ethical? What acts are required by this standard?	Ethical? What acts are required by this standard?	Ethical? What acts are required by this standard?	Ethical? What acts are required by this standard?	Ethical? What acts are required by this standard?	Ethical? What acts are required by this standard?	Ethical? What acts are required by this standard?	Ethical? What acts are required by this standard?	Ethical? What acts are required by this standard?	Ethical? What acts are required by this standard?	Ethical? What acts are required by this standard?
Property rights											
Rights of contract											
Human Rights											
Procedural Justice											
Distributive Justice											
Utilitarianism											
Disclosure Rule											
Universalizability											
Reversibility											
Red face test/ Gag test/Smell test											
Gut test											
Ethics of Care											
Virtue Ethics											

Notes

1. Karl Marx protested the status of workers who owned only their hands, i.e., the labor factor of production, at the time when capital was becoming a key resource in the production process. The exploitation of labor during the Industrial Revolution was the subject of Karl Marx's *Das Kapital*.
2. In addition, the New Jersey Supreme Court has required richer towns to have "affordable housing."
3. *San Antonio Independent School District v. Rodriguez*, 411 U.S. 1 (1973).
4. Elaine Sciolino, "French Protests Over Youth Labor Law Spread to 150 Cities and Towns," *New York Times*, March 19, 2006, http://www.nytimes.com/2006/03/19/international/europe/19paris.html?_r=0.
5. The Fourteenth Amendment is one of the reconstruction amendments. The Thirteenth, Fourteenth and Fifteenth Amendments to the United States Constitution, together known as the reconstruction amendments, abolish slavery and promise due process and the equal protection of the laws to the former slaves who became newly recognized U.S. citizens.
6. *Lawrence v. Texas*, 539 U.S. 558, '123 S. Ct. 2472 (2003). *Lawrence v. Texas* over-ruled a prior Supreme Court decision upholding the constitutionality of a Georgia sodomy statute, *Bowers v. Hardwick*, 478 U.S. 186 (1986).
7. Joshua Partlow, "Wal-Mart Forbids Bias Against Gays: New Policy, Hailed by Rights Groups, Follows Corporate Trend" *Washington Post*, Thursday, July 3, 2003.
8. Supreme Judicial Court of Massachusetts.

    Opinions of The Justices to the Senate.

    Feb. 3, 2004.

    Background: Senate requested opinion on constitutionality of bill which prohibits same-sex couples from entering into marriage, but allows them to form civil unions with all benefits, protections, rights, and responsibilities of marriage. Holding: The Supreme Judicial Court held as a matter of first impression that the bill violates the equal protection and due process requirements of the state constitution. Question answered.
9. John Rawls, *A Theory of Justice* (Cambridge, MA: Belknap, Harvard University Press, 1971).
10. Reinhard Bendix and Seymour Martin Lipset, ed., *Class, Status and Power: A Reader in Social Stratification* (New York: Free Press, 1963).
11. Rawls invokes a "veil of ignorance," whereby people do not know their position in the social hierarchy.
12. For example, the tax proposals of Jeremy Rifkin in his book, *The End of Work: The Decline of the Global Labor Force and the Dawn of the Post-Market Era* (New York: Putnam, 1995) and of Robert Reich in his book, *The Work of Nations: Preparing Ourselves for 21st Century Capitalism* (New York: Vintage, 1992), although not central to their major theses, address distributive justice issues and recommend tax-based solutions.
13. Leonard Buder, "Beech-Nut Is Fined $2 Million for Sale of Fake Apple Juice," *New York Times*, Nov. 14, 1987.
14. Lee Dembart, "Tobacco Giant's Analysis Says Premature Deaths Cut Costs in Pensions and Health Care: Critics Assail Philip Morris Report on Smoking," *New York Times*, July 18, 2001.

15. Gordon Fairclough, "Philip Morris Apologizes for Report Touting Benefits of Smokers' Deaths," *Wall Street Journal,* July 26, 2001.
16. Mark Dowie, "Pinto Madness," *Mother Jones,* Sept./Oct. 1977.
17. James Goleman, *Emotional Intelligence: Why It Can Matter More Than IQ* (New York: Bantam, 1995).
18. Lawrence Kohlberg, "Moral Stages and Moralization: The Cognitive-Developmental Approach," in *Moral Development and Behavior: Theory, Research, and Social Issues,* ed. Thomas Lickona, consulting eds. Gilbert Geis and Lawrence Kohlberg (New York: Holt, Rinehart and Winston, 1976). Lawrence Kohlberg, *The Philosophy of Moral Development* (New York: Harper & Row, 1981). Carol Gilligan, *In a Different Voice: Psychological Theory and Women's Development* (Cambridge: Harvard University Press, 1982). Jeanne M. Logsdon and Kristi Yuthas, "Corporate Social Performance, Stakeholder Orientation and Organizational Moral Development," *Journal of Business Ethics* 16 (1997): 11–36.
19. Kohlberg, "Moral Stages and Moralization." See also Kohlberg, *The Philosophy of Moral Development.*
20. Piaget, in his *Theory of Cognitive Development,* has identified specific stages in the cognitive development of children. Kohlberg has identified specific stages in the moral development of children. Individuals' cognitive development and their ability to engage in moral reasoning and decision making are interdependent.
21. The super-ego or conscience develops in the child in interaction with the parent. The voice of the parent becomes internalized as the super-ego or conscience. In transactional analysis, the super-ego is called the parent. See Thomas Anthony Harris, *I'm OK, You're OK* (New York: Harper & Row, 1969).
22. Carol Gilligan, *In a Different Voice.*
23. "When I began the work that led to In a Different Voice (1982), the framework was invisible. To study psychology at that time was like seeing a picture without seeing the frame, and the picture of the human world had become so large and all-encompassing that it looked like reality or a mirror of reality, rather than a representation. It was startling then to discover that women for the most part were not included in research on psychological development, or when included were marginalized or interpreted within a theoretical bias where the child and the adult were assumed to be male and the male was taken as the norm … . Bringing women's voices into psychology posed an interpretive challenge: how to listen to women in women's terms, rather than assimilating women's voices to the existing theoretical framework. And this led to a paradigm shift."
    Gilligan, "Hearing the Difference: Theorizing the Connection," *Hypatia* 10, no. 2 (Spring 1995): 120.
24. Gilligan, *In a Different Voice.*
25. Gilligan, "Hearing the Difference," 120.
26. 410 U.S. 113 (1973).
27. Gilligan, "Hearing the Difference," 120.
28. Raja Halwani, "Care Ethics and Virtue Ethics," *Hypatia* 18, no. 3 (Summer 2003): 161.
29. Plato, *The Republic.*
30. Robert Thurman, *Infinite Life: Seven Virtues for Living Well* (New York: Riverhead Books, 2004). Generosity, morality, tolerance, creativity, contemplation, wisdom and art (of living).

31. Stephen Covey, *Seven Habits of Highly Effective People* (New York: Free Press, 1989). See also Peter Senge, *The Fifth Discipline: The Art and Practice of the Learning Organization* (New York: Doubleday/Currency, 1990).
32. Kevin Morrell, "Decision Making and Business Ethics: The Implication of Using Image Theory in Preference to Rational Choice," *Journal of Business Ethics* 50, no. 3 (March 2004): 239–52.
33. The conscience is the super-ego, in terms of Freudian theory of personality.
34. Vince Galloro, "Regulators Scrutinize Oklahoma Nursing Home Company," *Modern Healthcare* 31, no. 16 (April 16, 2001): 17.
35. Charlene Harrington, Steffie Woolhandler, Joseph Multan, Helen Carrillo, and David Himmelstein, "Does Investor Ownership of Nursing Homes Compromise the Quality of Care?," *American Journal of Public Health* 91, no. 9 (September 2001): 1452–55. See also Steffie Woolhandler and David Himmelstein "Payments for Care at Private For-Profit and Private Not-for-Profit Hospitals: A Systematic Review and Metaanalysis," *Canadian Medical Association Journal*, 170 no. 12 (June 2004): 1817–24.

Reading 5.2

Sustainable Environmental Management

Paula Alexander

Chapter Introduction

Risks are inherent in the process of production. Corporate responsibility and ethical management practice mandate that executives proactively manage such risks and act to minimize negative externalities. The principle "first do no harm" takes on particular meaning for environmental management. Leading corporation citizens are managing for the triple bottom line—for economically, socially and environmentally sustainable enterprise. Sustainable production and consumption are global concerns, addressed by partnerships between corporations, governments, non-governmental organizations, and coordinated in important ways by the United Nations.

Chapter Goal and Learning Objectives

Chapter Goal: To identify ways in which enterprise can engage in sustainable environmental management.

Learning Objectives:

1. Identify the risks inherent in production and alternative risk management strategies.
2. Discuss managing for the triple bottom line and corporate initiatives to "go green."
3. Relate sustainable production to sustainable consumption and global initiatives for sustainability.
4. Discuss the conflict of interest among roles of individuals: as consumers seeking low price, as workers desiring job security and as citizens desiring quality of life.

Paula Alexander, "Sustainable Environmental Management," *Corporate Social Irresponsibility*, pp. 236-246, 251-256. Copyright © 2015 by Taylor & Francis Group. Reprinted with permission.

Risks Inherent in the Technology of Production

Risks are inherent in the production process. *Risk management* thus becomes a key responsibility of ethical and socially responsible management. Different risks are associated with different production technologies. For example, the risk of explosion is inherent in process production technologies, such as nuclear power generation and oil refining. Oil spills and well blowouts are a risk of drilling for oil and of oil transport.[1] The Exxon Valdez accident in 1989 was not the largest oil spill, but it caused the most environmental damage because it occurred in an enclosed area, Prince William Sound, Alaska, rather than in the open seas.[2] Although oil spills are a risk inherent in oil drilling and transport, human factors, including alcohol abuse by the captain of the tanker, caused and aggravated the Exxon Valdez spill. Human factors were also a factor in the BP oil spill of 2010 in the Gulf of Mexico, which was the largest oil well blowout and the largest unintended oil spill.[3]

A comparison of the Chernobyl accident with the nuclear power plant accident at Three Mile Island, Pennsylvania, and the Fukushima nuclear power plant meltdown in Japan illustrates not only the risks inherent in technology but also demonstrates social choices about the allocation of risks. The technology used to generate nuclear energy, and the structure of the Chernobyl nuclear power plant, externalized more risk on the general public than did the Three Mile Island nuclear power plant.[4] The Chernobyl plant used graphite rods and did not use a cement containment structure. The construction of the Chernobyl nuclear power plant thereby externalized risk on the surrounding community by its construction, whereas the nuclear power plant at Three Mile Island was constructed so as to reduce the risks on the surrounding community.[5] Social choices were at work in the choices about the construction and management of both the Chernobyl and the Three Mile Island nuclear power plants.

In addition, TEPCO, the manager of the Fukoshima nuclear power plant that melted down after an earthquake and tsunami in March 2011, externalized risks and costs on the surrounding community in the construction and management of the meltdown in 2011. TEPCO recognized the option of flooding the Daiichi reactor with seawater but did not do so because the seawater would corrode the equipment.[6] The report of the Carnegie Foundation for Peace also concluded that social and cultural factors figured in TEPCO's failure to manage the risks of external events, such as the tsunami that flooded the Fukushima plant.[7]

Safety measures are often considered overhead costs that can be deferred in tight budget situations, rather than costs integral to the production process. This was illustrated in the operation by Union Carbide and its subsidiaries of the Bhopal plant in India (see Figure 5.2.1).

> **Figure 5.2.1** The Good, the Bad or the Ugly: The Bhopal Accident
>
> The Bhopal accident occurred as a result of an explosion in a process production technology of producing the pesticide Sevin. An intermediate product of the production process methyl isocyanate (MIC) is unstable when mixed with water. Water was added to the MIC storage tank at the Union Carbide plant in Bhopal, India. The environmental and human injuries from the explosion of the Union Carbide plant in Bhopal resulted in large measure from the failure to manage the risks involved in the production process.[8] These included: the failure to have the storage tanks cooled with a refrigeration system; the failure to have spare storage tanks available; the failure to have functional vent gas scrubbers; and the failure to have functional flare towers to burn off released gases.
> Questions for discussion:
>
> 1. Is there an ethical obligation to shut-down operations, rather than to continue low-cost/shoe string operations, if continuing production is unsafe?
> 2. Is compliance with local law enough with respect to safety of operations and pollution? What about the international double standard? Manufacturers in the United States are subject to OSHA and EPA regulation and requirements. Note that there is a similar manufacturing facility in West Virginia.
> 3. In view of the risks of manufacturing MIC, could/should Union Carbide have negotiated with the government of India regarding the latter's requirement that even intermediate products be manufactured in India, if they are to be sold there? Should Union Carbide have stopped producing Sevin, and withdrawn from the Indian market, if the government of India continued to require the manufacture of MIC there?

Social choices, including choices about who bears the downside risk, are reflected in the regulatory requirements for the construction and operation of nuclear power plants and other production operations.

Assessment of Risk: Probability-Impact Matrix

A *probability-impact matrix* manifests the probability and the risk of an environmental or other disaster. A probability-impact matrix rates the probability of event as high or low and the impact of an event as high or low, yielding four possible outcomes: a high-probability/high-impact event, a low-probability/high-impact event, a high-probability/low-impact event and a low-probability/low-impact event.

The management of high-probability, high-impact risks must be given priority, as well as insured. For example, the risk assessment done by the Federal Emergency Management Agency in 2001 projected the environmental and other risks to New Orleans of a force five hurricane, such as Hurricane Katrina that actually devastated New Orleans in August 2005.[9] The New Orleans *Times-Picayune*, as well as PBS, attempted to arouse public concern over the risks to the Gulf Coast of a large-scale hurricane. In that respect, the devastation wrought in New Orleans in 2005 was predicted as a high-probability, high-impact event. The failure to manage the high-probability/high-impact event was a strategic management and governmental failure.

High-probability, low-impact events must also be managed via control processes and standard operating procedures and methods. Although any single event may be "low impact," because the risk of the occurrence is high, resources will be frittered away unless high-probability/low-impact events are managed, thereby reducing risks and lowering the impacts. Management of *low-probability/high-impact* events was previously neglected or relegated to a contingency plan. The Exxon Valdez spill was a low-probability/high-impact event. The probability of an oil spill such as occurred with the Exxon Valdez was assessed at one in 240 years. However, the risks were mis-conceptualized because the oil spill would not necessarily occur in the 240th year; although the risk of a spill of the magnitude that occurred in the Exxon Valdez spill was only one time in 240 years, the event could occur randomly over the entire period. Moreover, the agencies responsible for managing the contingency plan for a spill in Alaska, including Alyeska, had been lulled into complacency and were unprepared for the emergency oil spill from the Exxon Valdez. The unpreparedness for the Exxon Valdez spill was similar to the unpreparedness of Union Carbide India for the Bhopal accident. In both cases, the mechanisms required for managing an actual accident were out of commission. Moreover, the probability of the oil well blowout that occurred in the Gulf of Mexico in April 2010 was considered so remote that the United States Mineral Mining Service did not require a risk analysis.[10]

TABLE 5.2.1 Probability-Impact Matrix

Impact	Probability	
	High	Low
High	High-Probability/High-Impact Event	Low-Probability/High-Impact Event
Low	High-Probability/Low-Impact Event	Low-Probability/Low-Impact Event

Risk management strategies for managing *low-probability, high-impact* events have gained legitimacy from an understanding of the most currently accepted theory accounting for the extinction of the dinosaurs.[11] The currently accepted explanation for the sudden extinction of the dinosaurs is that a comet hit the earth, falling into a fault in the ocean. The hit spewed up so much volcanic ash that the sunlight was blocked; plants, which are dependent for photosynthesis on sunlight, died; as a result, the plant-eating dinosaurs died, followed by the carnivorous dinosaurs. Since the consequences of a low-probability, high-impact event can be devastating, risk management strategies should incorporate contingency planning as well as insure for such events. *Low-probability, low-impact* events are appropriately self-insured. Since risks are inherent in the production process, risk management is an essential aspect of effective and ethical, socially responsible management.

Unintended Negative Consequences

Unintended negative consequences may result from production processes or even consumption patterns.[12] Rachel Carson, with the publication in 1962 of her book *Silent Spring*,[13] explained the unintended negative consequences of the pesticide DDT. The publication of *Silent Spring* launched the environmental movement in the United States and perhaps globally. Ecologists are concerned about long-term system consequences to ecological systems, particularly unintended negative consequences of production processes, the probability of which increase with interdependence within a system. The devastating effects of Hurricane Katrina experienced by the United States Gulf Coast, and particularly the city of New Orleans in Louisiana, were an unintended negative consequence of the flood management program for the Mississippi River. The ecological systems effects of barricading the Mississippi River by constructing levies for flood prevention caused the erosion of the wetlands that serve as a barrier to storm systems from Gulf of Mexico flooding.[14] The Army Corps of Engineers is now trying to reverse the damage to the ecological systems created by the leveeing of the Mississippi River. New levies are being built that can open to permit flooding and re-silting of the Mississippi Delta. However, the allocations of monies needed to remedy the environmental degradation of the Mississippi Delta and to correct identified risks was considered a political issue by Congress, rather than a matter of national security.[15]

Part of the problem of managing unintended negative consequences of production processes or consumption patterns is that the unintended negative consequences occur over the long term and the causal links may be complex and even uncertain. Moreover, some natural resources used in production have been conceptualized as "free goods."

Free Goods

The air and water used in enterprise production processes have been considered *free goods*.[16] Economists have reconceptualized land, traditionally considered a factor of production (see Table 5.2.1), as *natural capital*.[17] Natural capital is defined as "natural resources and the ecological systems that provide vital life-support services."[18] Ecological concerns about sustainability of enterprise production systems often involve natural capital, including air and water. Ethical concerns are also raised about who pays the costs when companies pollute natural resources that have been used as free goods and when land itself becomes contaminated.

Negative Externalities

Negative externalities occur when the full costs of production are not internalized by the producing company. For example, if clean air, obtained as a free good, is inputted as a component of the production process, but that air is reintroduced back to the atmosphere in a polluted form, then a negative externality has been created. The same may happen with water, which is often obtained as a free good. For example, production plants are often located along a river; the river water is used for cooling purposes or to rotate a turbine engine. If the water used in the production process is reintroduced to the environment in a degraded or polluted form, then a negative externality has been created. This happened for example, when California Public Gas and Electric added hexavalent chromium to the water used in its cooling towers and then stored the wastewater on their property in unlined collection ponds.[19] An additional example is given by the pollution of the waterbed in Woburn, Massachusetts. The disposal of waste products deriving from the production processes by a number of businesses in Woburn, Massachusetts, caused the land to be degraded and the waterbed to become polluted in the town of Woburn.[20] Even raised water temperatures can cause changes to the ecological system when re-introduced to a river. Although companies may "own" the land that becomes contaminated, issues of *intergenerational fairness* are raised if the land or the underlying waterbeds become polluted.

The costs of negative externalities such as polluted air, polluted water, and contaminated soil are often paid by third parties, such as the community where a firm operates. For example, the communities in Woburn, Massachusetts, suffered higher rates of leukemia as a result of the dumping of the toxic wastes on the land and the resultant contamination of the wells in Woburn. The residents of Hinkley and Kettleman, California, also experienced higher rates of cancer as a result of California Public Gas and Electric's utilization of chromium six in its compressors. Union Carbide also externalized its costs of production onto the community where it operated in Bhopal, India. By failing to manage the risks inherent in the production process, and by failing to properly maintain required safety systems, Union Carbide suffered an industrial accident that caused damage to the environment and especially to the people living near the plant. More recently, China's Songhua River became polluted by an explosion at the China National Petroleum plant, a benzene manufacturing plant in Jilin. Benzene flowed into the river; since benzene is carcinogenic, water supplies to Harbin, a city along the river, were cut off in November 2005 so to prevent harm to the households from the polluted water.[21] The impact of the toxic pollution of the Songhua River crossed national boundaries, affecting Russia by the downstream pollution.[22]

Strip mining is another example of production process that externalizes damage to the environment on the surrounding community. Where the mining companies do not remediate the land that they have mined for natural resources, externalized costs are borne by the community in the form of ugliness and degradation of the land, as well as ill health effects from the air and water pollution caused by the mountaintop removal strip mining.[23] Congress has enacted legislation, the effect of which is to prevent or remediate the negative externalities of strip mining. The Surface Mining Control and Reclamation Act, passed by Congress in 1977, requires coal mining companies to meet certain environmental standards and to restore the land to its original condition, unless the mining company shows that the flattened land will be used for commercial development. The Clean Water Act, also passed by Congress in 1977,[24] prohibits coal companies from dumping mining waste into streams. Companies were prohibited in 1999 by a federal court in West Virginia from burying streams with the mountaintop soil and rocks.[25] However in 2002, the Bush administration changed the rule to permit the burial of streams by mountaintop removal strip mining.[26] This change in regulation met with opposition from environmental groups, including the Sierra Club.[27] The Army Corps of Engineers subsequently suspended the licenses of four mining companies for mountaintop removal coal mining.[28] Mountaintop removal represents a conflict among stakeholders about the utilization of a particular production technology and the impact of that technology on the environment and surrounding community.

Sustainable Production

The creation of negative externalities results in the underpricing of the goods produced, since the essence of a negative externality is that enterprise fails to incorporate the full costs of production into the product price. Products would be priced higher if the product price incorporates the costs of cleaning the air or the water used in the production process. Consumers must be willing to pay the increased priced of products if corporations are to effectively eliminate the externalization of production costs and the creation of negative externalities.

The costs of production in less economically developed countries (LEDCs) may be lower due to a less stringent regulatory environment. As a consequence, enterprises in some LEDCs may be permitted to externalize costs to the environment or to workers in the form of unsafe working conditions. When the North American Free Trade Agreement (NAFTA) was being negotiated between the United States, Canada, and Mexico, there was a concern that products manufactured in Mexico would have a competitive advantage because Mexico has a less stringent regulatory environment than Canada or the United States. Therefore, the North American Commission for Environment Cooperation was established in addition to the creation of NAFTA's environmental standards.[29] The North American Commission for Environmental Cooperation addresses transnational, continental environmental concerns and was intended to create synergistic effects by cooperation among the nations participating in NAFTA.

In managing enterprise relationships with the environment, ending negative externalities is a first step. Remediating environmental degradation is a second step, by such means as the Land Reclamation Act discussed previously. But in the long run, companies and countries must engage in sustainable production. For example, the soccer ball industry, whose production is concentrated in LEDCs, has been criticized for exposing workers to toxic fumes and for using child labor. The World Federation of the Sporting Goods Industry participated in a global form for sports and environment in conjunction with the United Nations Environmental Programme. The third global forum for the World Federation of the Sporting Goods Industry developed the Global Sports Alliance Principles for socially responsible production of sporting goods, committing the sporting goods industry to principles of sustainable production and to the reduction of environmental harms, including toxic and chemical wastes generated in the production process. These principles were embodied as The Lahore/Sialkot Declaration on Corporate Responsibility.[30]

Sustainability

Sustainability addresses the long-term consequences of an enterprise's production system and questions whether the long-term consequences can be sustained or whether those consequences lead to the long-term degradation of the system. *Ecological systems theory* is used to evaluate enterprise sustainability. Ecological systems theory views *ecological systems* as *closed systems*. Viewing the ecological system as a closed system forces producers and consumers to assess the consequences of their production and consumption patterns. Under a closed system approach, negative consequences cannot be ignored; they must be taken into account. Ecological systems theory focuses particularly on unintended negative consequences of production systems. *The Lorax* by Dr. Seuss, nominally a children's book, uses an allegory to explain the interdependencies within an ecological system and illustrates the unintended negative consequences of that production system.[31]

Americans, with the history and experience of frontier, can easily fall prey to an "open system" approach, whereby the negative by-products of a production system can be externalized to the frontier. For example, testing of nuclear weapons was done in the deserts of Nevada[32] and high-level nuclear waste products originally were stored in Hanford, Washington. The assumptions underlying these actions were that no living beings would experience the negative consequences of nuclear testing or disposal of nuclear by-products. However, the storage containers deteriorated at Hanford, requiring re-containment.[33] In 1982, Congress provided that high-level nuclear waste requiring long-term storage be stored at the Nevada nuclear test site in Yucca Mountain, which was formed from a volcano.[34] Now some ecologists are concerned that the fissures in the mountain will allow the escape of radiation from the stored nuclear waste products.[35]

Sustainable Development

Sustainable economic development emphasizes sustainable consumption patterns and the role of women and households who are primarily responsible for consumption patterns and the generation of waste products. Developed, high-income countries presently are engaged in non-sustainable patterns of consumption, including energy consumption, and generate waste products that are injurious to the environment. The non-sustainability of the industrialized world's consumption patterns is evident by the principle of universalizability: if the less developed countries and their populations engaged in the consumption patterns and production patterns of the developed world, those patterns of consumption and production would be injurious to the environment and would exhaust natural resources. Sustainability efforts, therefore, focus on the use of renewable resources and methods of production and consumption that are less wasteful and that generate fewer waste products.

The United Nations has exerted significant leadership in raising awareness about sustainable development and in developing principles for sustainable development.[36] The United Nations Environmental Programme (UNEP) was established in 1972 after the Stockholm conference on the human environment. UNEP then established the Intergovernmental Panel on Climate Change in 1988. The Intergovernmental Panel on Climate Change convenes an international group of scientists that support the United Nations Framework Convention on Climate Change. The United National Framework Convention on Climate Change was negotiated as the outcome of the first Earth Summit held in Rio de Janeiro, Brazil in 1992. The Earth Summit also issued the Rio Declaration on Environment and Development. The

Rio Declaration provides principles for sustainable development.[37] The principles for sustainable development articulated in the Rio Declaration, while recognizing national sovereignty, include a concern for environmental needs across generations, i.e., future generations as well as present generations, and the goal of eradicating poverty on a global basis, as well as a concern that nations do not externalize their environmental problems onto the surrounding nations.[38, 39]

The United Nations Commission on Sustainable Development was also created in 1992. It oversees the implementation of the Rio Declaration, as well as Agenda 21, an environmental program deriving from the Earth Summit held in 1992.[40] These principles were reaffirmed by the World Summit on Sustainable Development held in Johannesburg, South Africa, September 2002. Sustainable consumption and production and energy for sustainable development are the recent foci of the Commission on Sustainable Development.[41] Energy utilization and the impact of energy utilization on the environment, including air pollution and global warming are of great concern to the UNEP and other agencies concerned with long-term effects of our production and consumption patterns on the environment.

The Kyoto Protocol and Global Warming

The Kyoto Protocol was developed as a means of addressing climate change resulting from human activities.[42] The Kyoto Protocol was negotiated in 1997 and amends the United Nations Framework Convention on Climate Change, which was concluded at the Earth Summit in Rio de Janeiro in 1992. The Kyoto Protocol has the goal of reducing greenhouse gas emissions and mitigating global warming and consequent global climate change. *Global warming* is the phenomenon that the earth's atmosphere and oceans are increasing their average temperature.[43] These temperature changes are thought to result from human activities and their impact on the natural environment, particularly *greenhouse gas emissions.* Greenhouse gas emissions include the release of carbon dioxide, methane gas, nitrous oxide, ozone, hydrofluorocarbons, perfluorocarbons and sulfur hexafluoride. Greenhouse gas emissions result from, among other processes, the mining and combustion of fossil fuels. Reforestation reduces greenhouse gas emissions, because plants use carbon dioxide as a component of photosynthesis, and environmental strategies for climate control include reforestation programs. The impact of global warming is to reduce ice masses at the Artic and Antarctic, thus raising the sea level and increasing storm systems and flooding. Also as ocean temperatures rise, life forms in the sea can be affected.

The signatories to the Kyoto Protocol agreed that the industrialized nations will reduce greenhouse gas emissions to below 1990 levels by the year 2012.[44] The United States did not ratify the Kyoto Protocol, which came into force in February 2005. The Bush administration withdrew support for the Kyoto protocol in early 2001. President Bush criticized the

Kyoto Protocol for failing to require LEDCs to curb greenhouse gas emissions. There may be some merit to this concern: for example, Russia ratified the Kyoto Protocol in November 2004, thereby creating the conditions for the Kyoto Protocol to come into force, as it did in February 2005. However, because of the collapse of the economies of many states of the former Soviet Union, Russia does not have to reduce its emissions and in fact may sell credits to other nations that are obligated under the Kyoto Protocol to reduce their emissions.[45] Efforts for sustainable production methods become more urgent as the LEDCs undergo economic development and industrialization.

The Intergovernment Panel on Climate Change won the Noble Peace Prize in 2007, shared with Vice President Al Gore.[46] The Intergovernment Panel on Climate Change issues reports on climate change that "created an ever-broader informed consensus about the connection between human activities and global warming. Thousands of scientists and officials from over one hundred countries have collaborated to achieve greater certainty as to the scale of the warming." Al Gore wrote and promoted a book, *An Inconvenient Truth*, as well as an earlier bestseller, *Earth in the Balance*; he was honored as a politician who raised awareness and created social action to correct global warming.

Cap and Trade

Cap and trade is a system for managing enterprise and even a nation's carbon footprint. Proposals for cap and trade were brought before the US Congress but never passed. Instead, the EPA implemented regulations limiting greenhouse gas emissions through its New Source Performance Standards; these standards included rules for cross-state air pollution.[47] And in 2013, President Barack Obama issued an executive order to create a task force of governors and mayors to consider ways to deal with the impacts of climate change, such as extreme weather, including 2012's Superstorm Sandy.[48] And in 2014, the United States Supreme Court upheld the authority of the EPA to issues CO2 standards but limited regulation to "stationary sources" that are already subject to EPA standards, and upheld its rules on cross-state air pollution.[49]

Notes

1. See Jonathan L. Ramseur, *Oil Spills in U.S. Coastal Waters: Background and Governance*, Congressional Research Office, January 11, 2012, http://www.fas.org/sgp/crs/misc/RL33705.pdf.
2. National Response Team, *The Exxon Valdez Oil Spill: A Report to the President: Executive Summary*, Environmental Protection Agency, May 1989, http://www2.epa.gov/aboutepa/exxon-valdez-oil-spill-report-president-executive-summary. Also, view *Dead Ahead: The Exxon Valdez Disaster*, directed by Paul Seed (HBO Films, 1992), http://www.youtube.com/watch?v=bXtsB4G0ohg.

3. The story of the BP Oil Well blowout was the subject of the end of chapter case for Chapter 2 on stakeholder management. See also, "Oil Spill Fast Facts," *CNN Library*, last modified April 8, 2014, http://www.cnn.com/2013/07/13/world/oil-spills-fastfacts/index.html. The greatest oil spill was the deliberate dumping of oil into the Persian Gulf by Iraqi armed forces during the 1991 Gulf War.

4. "The Chernobyl reactors are of the RBMK type. These are high-power, pressure-tube reactors, moderated with graphite and cooled with water."

    "To stop the fire and prevent a criticality accident as well as further substantial release of fission products, boron and sand were dumped on the reactor from the air. In addition, the damaged unit was entombed in a concrete 'sarcophagus,' to limit further release of radioactive material."

    "U.S. reactors have different plant designs, broader shutdown margins, robust containment structures, and operational controls to protect them against the combination of lapses that led to the accident at Chernobyl."

    "Backgrounder on Chernobyl Nuclear Power Plant Accident," *United States Nuclear Regulatory Commission*, last modified Apr. 25, 2014, http://www.nrc.gov/reading-rm/doc-collections/fact-sheets/chernobyl-bg.html.

5. The accident at the Three Mile Island Unit 2 (TMI-2) nuclear power plant near Middletown, Pennsylvania, on March 28, 1979, was the most serious in U.S. commercial nuclear power plant operating history, even though it led to no deaths or injuries to plant workers or members of the nearby community. But it brought about sweeping changes involving emergency response planning, reactor operator training, human factors engineering, radiation protection, and many other areas of nuclear power plant operations. It also caused the U.S. Nuclear Regulatory Commission to tighten and heighten its regulatory oversight. "Three Mile Island Accident," *United States Nuclear Regulatory Commission*, last modified 2014, http://www.nrc.gov/reading-rm/doc-collections/fact-sheets/3mile-isle.pdf.

6. Fumiya Tanabe, "Analysis of Core Melt Accident in Fukushima Daiichi-Unit 1 Nuclear Reactor," *Journal of Nuclear Science and Technology* 18, no. 8 (2011): 1135–39.

7. James M. Acton and Mark Hibbs, Why Fukushima Was Preventable, (Washington, DC: Carnegie Foundation for Peace, March 6, 2012), http://carnegieendowment.org/files/fukushima.pdf. This report serves as the end of chapter case for this chapter.

8. See Dan Kurzman, *A Killing Wind: Inside Union Carbide and the Bhopal Catastrophe* (New York: McGraw-Hill, 1987).

9. "In 2001, the Federal Emergency Management Agency ranked a major hurricane strike on New Orleans as 'among the three likeliest, most catastrophic disasters facing this country,' directly behind a terrorist strike on New York City." See "How Not to Prepare for a Hurricane," *The Progress Report*, Aug. 30, 2005, http://www.alternet.org/story/24799.

10. The National Environment Policy Act (NEPA) and a Review of MMS NEPA Documents Prepared for the National Commission on BP Deepwater Horizon Oil Spill and Offshore Drilling, October 19, 2010, report developed by Meg Caldwell, Executive Director of the Center for Ocean Solutions, Debbie Sivas, Luke W. Cole

Professor of Environmental Law and Director of the Stanford Environmental Law Clinic, and Kimiko Narita (Stanford J.D./M.S. '11), research assistant at the Center for Ocean Solutions, http://energyseminar.stanford.edu/sites/all/files/eventpdf/The%20National%20Environmental%20Policy%20Act%20(NEPA)%20and%20a%20Review%20of%20MMS%20NEPA%20Documents.pdf.

11. "Dinosaur Extinction," *National Geographic*, last modified 2014, http://science.nationalgeographic.com/science/prehistoric-world/dinosaur-extinction/.

12. The unintended ecological effects of consumption patterns is a reason why the United Nations Environmental Programme and other related agencies emphasize sustainable consumption, as well as sustainable production.

13. Rachel Carson, *Silent Spring* (Boston: Houghton Mifflin Company, The Riverside Press: 1962).

14. *Disappearing Delta Overview*:

    "Three years ago this month, NOW presented a two-part story on the disappearance of the Mississippi River delta. 'Losing Ground,' uncovered how one of the biggest civil engineering projects in U.S. history—the leveeing of the Mississippi River—had brought Louisiana and the nation to the brink of what could be the most costly environmental disaster in history. In 'The City in a Bowl,' NOW examined another ominous effect of this crisis—the risk that a massive hurricane could drown New Orleans. Hurricane Katrina has now made these predictions a reality."

    See Transcript, "City in a Bowl," *NOW with Bill Moyers*, PBS.org, Sept. 20, 2002, http://www.pbs.org/now/transcript/transcript_neworleans.html. See also Transcript, "Losing Ground," *NOW with Bill Moyers*, PBS.org, Sept. 26, 2002, http://www.pbs.org/now/transcript/transcript_delta.html and "New Orleans and the Delta," *NOW with Bill Moyers*, PBS.org, Sept. 2, 2005, http://www.pbs.org/now/science/neworleans.html.

15. Eric Berger, "Keeping Its Head above Water: New Orleans Faces Doomsday Scenario," *Houston Chronicle*, Dec. 1, 2001. See also Eric Lincoln, "Old Plans Revived for Category 5 Hurricane Protection," *United States Army Corps of Engineers*, Sept.–Oct. 2004. A category five hurricane was considered a 1 in 500-year-event.

16. Free goods are defined by Samuelson and Nordhaus as: "Those goods that are not economic goods. Like air or seawater, they exist in such large quantities that they need not be rationed out among those wishing to use them. Thus, their market price is zero." Economic goods are defined as: "A good that is scarce relative to the total amount of it that is desired. It must therefore be rationed, usually by charging a positive price." Paul A. Samuelson and William D. Nordhaus, *Economics*, 18th ed. (Boston: Irwin/McGraw-Hill, 1998).

17. Paul Hawken, *Growing a Business* (New York: Simon and Schuster, 1987); Paul Hawken, *The Ecology of Commerce* (New York: HarperCollins, 1993); and Paul Hawken, Amory Lovins, and L. Hunter Lovins, *The Ecology of Commerce, Natural Capitalism: Creating the Next Industrial Revolution* (New York: Little, Brown and Company, 1999). See also *Paul Hawken*, last modified 2010, http://www.paulhawken.com.

18. This definition of natural capitalism is given by Paul Hawken, Amory Lovins and L. Hunter Lovins at their website, *Natural Capitalism*, last modified 2014, http://www.natcap.org/. See also Hawken, Lovins, and Lovins, *Natural Capitalism*.

19. See Annual Report filed by PG&E Corporation for fiscal year 2005, filed with SEC on Feb. 17, 2006, at http://pcg.client.shareholder.com/investors/financial_reports/EdgarDetail.cfm?CompanyID=PCG&CIK=75488&FID=1004980-06-67&SID=06-00&filings=UTILITY&formchoose=insider#FORM10K_HTM_COMPRESSORSTATIONCHROMIUMLITIGATION. See also Marc Lifsher, "PG&E's Toxic Plume Creeps Toward L.A. Water Supply," *LA Times*, Mar. 6, 2004. The toxic contamination in Hinkley, California, is dramatized in the movie *Erin Brockovich*, directed by Steven Soderbergh (Universal Pictures, 2000).

20. See the EPA description of the Woburn, Massachusetts, Superfund site cleanup, at "Waste Site Cleanup and Reuse in New England," *United States Environmental Protection Agency*, last modified Sept. 23, 2013, http://yosemite.epa.gov/r1/npl_pad.nsf/f52fa5c31fa8f5c885256adc0050b631/1E8F7D6FFCD9B-61B85256A0F00067136?OpenDocument. The toxic contamination in Woburn, Massachusetts was dramatized in the movie *A Civil Action*, directed by Steven Zaillian (Touchstone Pictures, 1998).

21. "A Chinese city of 3.8 million people closed schools and was trucking in drinking water Wednesday after shutting down its water system following a chemical plant explosion that officials said polluted a nearby river with toxic benzene.

    An explosion on Nov. 13 at a chemical plant in the nearby city of Jilin left the Songhua River, Harbin's main water source, polluted with benzene, a toxic, flammable liquid, the government said.

    Russian television reports said Wednesday that concern was growing over the pollution threat in the border city of Khabarovsk, about 700 kilometers down river from Harbin on the Songhua."

    "Chinese City Shuts off Water after Toxic Spill," *The Moscow Times*, Nov. 24, 2005, http://www.moscowtimes.ru/stories/2005/11/24/251.html.

22. "Russia plans to cut off drinking water supplies from River Amur to its far eastern city of Khabarovsk, which is threatened by a toxic benzene spill in China.

    Oleg Mitvol with the Russian environmental agency told the BBC heating would not be affected but tap water would be cut for a few days. He said fish from the Amur also would be contaminated.

    Chinese officials say they expect the spill to take two weeks to reach the Amur River. China's Songhua River flows into the Amur River separating China and Russia."

    "Russia braces for Chinese water pollution," United Press International, Nov. 24, 2005, http://www.sciencedaily.com/upi/?feed=TopNews&article=UPI-1-20051124-10464000-bc-russia-chinapollution-1stld.xml.

23. "Mountaintop mining is a form of surface coal mining in which explosives are used to access coal seams, generating large volumes of waste that bury adjacent streams. The resulting waste that then fills valleys and streams can significantly compromise water quality, often causing permanent damage to ecosystems and rendering streams unfit for drinking, fishing, and swimming. It is estimated that almost 2,000 miles of Appalachian headwater streams have been buried by mountaintop coal mining." "2011 News Releases: EPA Issues Final Guidance to Protect Water Quality in Appalachian Communities from Impacts of Mountaintop Mining/Agency to provide flexibility while

protecting environment and public health," *United States Environmental Protection Agency*, July 21, 2011, available at http://yosemite.epa.gov/opa/admpress.nsf/1e5ab1124055f3b28525781f0042ed40/1dabfc17944974d4852578d400561a13!OpenDocument. See also John McQuaid, "Mining the Mountains," *Smithsonian Magazine*, Jan. 2009, http://www.smithsonianmag.com/ecocenter-energy/mining-the-mountains-130454620/?no-ist. and "Beyond Coal: Destroying Mountains," *Sierra Club*, http://content.sierraclub.org/coal/mining-destroying-mountains.

24. The Clean Water Act amended the Federal Water Pollution Control Act of 1972.

25. However, in 2001, the Fourth Circuit Court of Appeals overturned the federal court ruling prohibiting coverage of streams; the fourth circuit ruled that the trial court did not have jurisdiction. The ruling left open the possibility that the practice could be appealed in state court. See James Dao, "Rule Change May Alter Strip-Mine Fight," *New York Times*, Jan. 26, 2004, http://www.nytimes.com/2004/01/26/national/26COAL.html. See also "Bush Administration Told by Congress and Court: Changing Environmental Rules to Allow Waste Dumps in Waters Violates the Clean Water Act," *EarthJustice*, May 8, 2002, http://www.earthjustice.org/news/display.html?ID=367.

26. Joby Warrick, "Appalachia Is Paying Price for White House Rule Change," *Washington Post*, Aug. 17, 2004, http://www.washingtonpost.com/wp-dyn/articles/A6462-2004Aug16.html. See also Dao, "Rule Change May Alter."

27. See for example, "Burying Valleys, Poisoning Streams," *New York Times*, Editorial of May 4, 2002, http://www.nytimes.com/2002/05/04/opinion/burying-valleys-poisoning-streams.html.

28. "Army Corps of Engineers Suspends Mountaintop Removal Mining Permits," *EarthJustice*, last modified June 8, 2006, http://www.earthjustice.org/news/press/2006/army-corps-of-engineers-suspends-mountaintop-removal-mining-permits.html. See also "Judge Rules Against Mountaintop Mining," *Associated Press/NBC News*, last modified June 14, 2007, http://www.nbcnews.com/id/19231612/#.U7CZqeLD_X4 and "Supreme Court Rejects Coal Industry Lawsuit, Defends EPA Veto of Mountaintop Removal Mine," *EarthJustice*, Mar. 24, 2014, http://www.democraticunderground.com/1014763706.

29. "Looking to the Future: Strategic Plan of the Commission for Environmental Cooperation 2005–2010," *Commission for Environmental Cooperation of North America*, last modified June 17, 2005, http://www.cec.org/pubs_docs/documents/index.cfm?varlan=english&ID=1761.

30. "The Lahore/Sialkot Declaration on Corporate Responsibility," *United Nations Environment Programme*, last modified Nov. 26, 2004, http://www.unep.org/Documents.Multilingual/Default.asp?DocumentID=412&ArticleID=4673&l=en.

31. Dr. Seuss, *The Lorax* (New York: Random House, 1971).

32. For information on Frenchman Flat, Nevada, the site of the first nuclear atmospheric test that took place in 1951, see Phil Garlington, "Nevada—Blasts From The Past: Touring A-Bomb Test Site," *The Seattle Times*, Jan. 25, 1998 and "Photo Library: Nevada National Security Site," *United States Department of Energy*, last modified Feb. 20, 2014, http://www.nv.doe.gov/library/photos/nts.aspx.

33. "Backgrounder on Radioactive Waste," *United States Nuclear Regulatory Commission*, last modified June 27, 2014, http://www.nrc.gov/reading-rm/doc-collections/fact-sheets/radwaste.html. See also "Hanford Nuclear Waste Cleanup Plant May Be Too Dangerous; Safety Issues Make Plans to Clean up a Mess Left Over from the Construction of the U.S. Nuclear Arsenal Uncertain," *Scientific American*, May 9, 2013.
34. "Topic: Yucca Mountain," *Las Vegas Sun*, last modified June 29, 2014, http://www.lasvegassun.com/news/topics/yucca-mountain/.
35. Ken Silverstein, "Nuclear Waste Will Never Be Laid to Rest at Yucca Mountain," *Forbes*, Aug. 24, 2013.
36. A global social movement on the environment occurred at this time, as discussed above earlier in this chapter, as well as in Chapters 5 and 7.
37. "Agenda 21," *United Nations Environment Programme*, last modified 2014, http://www.unep.org/Documents.Multilingual/Default.asp?DocumentID=52.
38. This happened, as discussed above by the environmental spill in China, which affected Russia down river.
39. The Chernobyl explosion spread a nuclear cloud over Europe, and in fact, the Russians failed to disclose the Chernobyl nuclear accident. Its occurrence was discovered by an air monitoring station in Scandinavia. "Soviet Minds Sheltered From Catastrophes," *New York Times*, Editorial of May 15, 1986.
40. "AGENDA 21 United Nations Conference on Environment & Development," Rio de Janeiro, Brazil, June 3–14, 1992, United Nations Sustainable Development Knowledge Platform, http://sustainabledevelopment.un.org/content/documents/Agenda21.pdf.
41. "Trends in Sustainable Development," 2006, United Nations Sustainable Development Knowledge Platform, http://sustainabledevelopment.un.org/content/documents/trends_rpt2006.pdf.
42. Its full title is the Kyoto Protocol to the United Nations Framework Convention on Climate Change.
43. "Global Warming," Wikipedia, last modified June 27, 2014, http://en.wikipedia.org/wiki/Global_warming.
44. "Kyoto Protocol to the United Nations Framework Convention on Climate Change," United Nations Framework Convention on Climate Change, last modified 2014, http://unfccc.int/resource/docs/convkp/kpeng.html.
45. "Kyoto Protocol," United Nations Framework Convention on Climate Change, last modified 2014, http://unfccc.int/kyoto_protocol/items/2830.php.
46. O. Edenhofer et al., eds., "IPCC, 2014: Summary for Policymakers," Climate Change 2014, Mitigation of Climate Change. Contribution of Working Group III to the Fifth Assessment Report of the Intergovernmental Panel on Climate Change (New York: Cambridge University Press, 2014).
47. Brad Plumer, "Is U.S. Climate Policy Better Off Without Cap-and-Trade?," *Washington Post*, Oct. 25, 2012.
48. Federal Leadership in Environmental, Energy and Economic Performance—Exec. Order No. 13,514 (Oct. 25, 2009), http://www.whitehouse.gov/administration/eop/ceq/sustainability.
49. *Utility Air Regulatory Group v. Environmental Protection Agency*, _ U.S. _ (2014). See Adam Liptak, "Justices Uphold Emission Limits on Big Industry," *New York Times*, June 23, 2014.
50.

Applied Ethics Case

As one of the world's largest automobile manufacturers, Toyota adopted a code of conduct, known as the "Toyota Way," designed as a corporate social guideline for all employees. The Toyota Way statement incorporated 14 principles:

1. Base your management decisions on a long-term philosophy, even at the expense of short-term financial goals
2. Create continuous process flows to bring problems to the surface
3. Use "pull" marketing distribution and promotion systems to avoid over-production
4. Level out the manufacturing workload
5. Build a culture of stopping to fix problems to get quality right the first time
6. Recognize standards as the foundation for continuous improvement and employee empowerment
7. Use visual control so problems are not hidden
8. Use only reliable, thoroughly tested technology that serves people and processes
9. Develop leaders who thoroughly understand the work, live the philosophy, and teach it to others
10. Have exceptional people and teams who follow the company's philosophy
11. Respect the extended network of partners and suppliers by challenging them and helping them improve
12. Personally overview issues to thoroughly understand the situations
13. Make decisions slowly by consensus, thoroughly consider all the options, and then implement decisions rapidly
14. Become a learning organization through relentless reflection and continuous improvement

In the fall of 2007, Toyota recalled 55,000 automobiles for floor mats that ran the risk of sliding forward and trapping the gas pedal. This floor mat and gas pedal issue became a public concern when a 2009 Lexus suddenly accelerated out of control, hit another car, fell down an embankment, and caught fire. The American National Highway Traffic Safety Administration (NHTSA) had initiated nine separate investigations into claims of acceleration by Toyota automobiles over the previous decade. Toyota recalled floor mats on 4.2 million vehicles, and company officials instructed dealers to remove the gas pedal and shorten it so it would not interfere with the floor mats.

In January 2010, Toyota officials announced a second recall of 2.3 million vehicles because of continued problems with the gas pedal. Toyota claimed the second recall was unrelated to the floor mat recall but also announced that 1.7 million Toyota vehicles were affected by both recalls. This second recall impacted over 50% of Toyota's U.S. annual sales for that year. That same month, Toyota officials announced that two million vehicles in Europe were recalled for the same problem. Thirty-four deaths were alleged due to the pedal entrapment/floor mat problem problems during this time period.

1. Although Toyota had a 14-point code of conduct, what went wrong? Compare Toyota's code to the readings' content.
2. What recommendations would you make to Toyota's leaders?

Post-Reading Questions

1. What are the standards of judgment to evaluate ethical business decisions in your place of employment? Are these standards appropriate for your industry? Why or why not?
2. Discuss the strengths and weaknesses of the probability/event matrix as applied to your place of employment? Which design best fits? Why?
3. Unintended negative consequences, free goods, negative externalities, sustainable production, sustainability, sustainable development, and sustainable supply chain management are all important in today's global workplace. Which are the three most important to your company?

Videos Retrieved from the Internet

"Microsoft video—A Sustainable Future"

https://www.youtube.com/watch?v=3KnIJoHibiQ

This is a futuristic video with touch glass displays everywhere, e-paper devices, random screens, you name it.

"What is Sustainability?"

https://www.youtube.com/watch?v=rmQby7adocM

A Penn State professor defines the topic of sustainability.

"Explaining Sustainability & Climate Change"

https://www.cultivatingcapital.com/sustainability-videos/

This clip is from a documentary film called *The Corporation* and features Ray Anderson, founder and CEO of Carpet Company Interface, talking about what caused him to change his paradigm.

"Averting the Climate Crisis"

https://www.cultivatingcapital.com/sustainability-videos/

This TED talk explains how energy efficiency and conservation are investments that pay for themselves and then dives into 15 ways that individuals can address climate change.

"Climate Change is Happening"

https://www.cultivatingcapital.com/sustainability-videos/

This video explains some of the science behind climate change and how economic systems will need to adapt.

Internet Sites on Sustainability

"Sustainable Manufacturing"

https://www.epa.gov/sustainability/sustainable-manufacturing

This is a government website on sustainability manufacturing practices.

"What is Sustainable Manufacturing?"

https://www.marlinwire.com/blog/what-is-sustainable-manufacturing-2

This is a blog on multiple aspects on the topic of sustainable manufacturing.

"Top 75 Sustainability Blogs, Websites & Influencers in 2020"

https://blog.feedspot.com/sustainability_blogs/

This is a reference for discussions on the topic of sustainability.

"The Internet and Sustainability: A Discussion Paper"

https://www.iisd.org/sites/default/files/publications/icts_internet_sustainability.pdf

Two experts in their respective fields discuss the topic.

"The Sustainability Sites Initiative"

http://www.sustainablesites.org/directory

This is a listing of corporate and government sites on the sustainability topic.

Section VI

Redefining the Role of Corporate Social Responsibility

"A culture that truly values ethical (and safe) behavior must be led by men and women committed to principle for its own sake, not solely for the purpose of compliance."
Thomas Krause

ETHICS OFTEN PLAYS A ROLE in an employee's decision to comply with safety rules and to participate in safety programs. An organization's ethical environment can also influence an individual's ethical perspective and behavior. Understanding the organization's ethical climate environment (culture) enables employees to develop a shared understanding of what leaders consider to be right and wrong within the organization's decision-making process. By assessing this ethical culture, a company can devise programs to enhance safety efforts, induce employee compliance and participation, and achieve a better safety record.

In section 6, the authors, E. Andrew Kapp and K. Praveen Parboteeah, introduce us to the concepts of ethics and safety in the article "Ethical Climate and Safety Performance." The authors studied 237 employees from five U.S. automobile component manufacturers. Ethical climate, safety compliance, and safety motivation were measured. The study's results showed that strong support was found for the influence of the organization's principled climate on safety-related behavior of the employees, with both greater safety compliance and more safety participation behavior reported among the plants displaying a principled ethical climate. The authors concluded with a discussion of ethical climate types and complementing safety initiatives.

The second article by Wayne Buck and Jeffrey Schaller, "Using Safety to Introduce Ethics into Operations Management Courses," discusses the importance of ethics, safety, and sustainability based on the United Nations declaration of 1987, "Sustainable development is development that meets the needs of the present without compromising the ability of future generations to meet their own needs."

The authors' research found that three aspects of sustainability, taught in universities, focused primarily on green products, green production, and corporate social responsibility. They shift their attention to safety within organizations and its distinct advantage for introducing ethical issues in operations management courses. They conclude their discussion with a suggested exercise for students.

Pre-Reading Questions

As you read the chapter articles, reflect on the following:
- How do the readings integrate with my understanding of ethics, safety, and sustainability?
- What concepts resonate with me?
- How do the articles strengthen my comprehensive understanding of the topic?

Reading 6.1

Ethical Climate and Safety Performance
Design Better Programs, Improve Compliance and Foster Participation

E. Andrew Kapp and K. Praveen Parboteeah

Abstract: Ethics can play a significant role in employees' decisions to comply with safety rules and participate in safety-enhancing initiatives. An organization's ethical environment can also influence employees' ethical perspective and behavior. One useful means for understanding this environment is ethical climate, which embodies the employees' shared understanding of what is considered right or wrong within that organization. By assessing its ethical climate, a company can devise better ways to reduce employee resistance to safety efforts, induce greater levels of compliance and participation, and achieve better safety.

ETHICS IS THE AREA OF PHILOSOPHY that deals with values and customs of a person or society—essentially how one determines what is right or wrong. As far back as Aristotle, ethics has been considered a fundamental driving force of human behavior.

The role that ethics plays in an organization's safety performance has been of interest to scholars and practitioners, although for fewer years. Writing from a Christian moral philosophical standpoint (specifically Roman Catholic theology), Angelini (1987) spells out the moral principles that should preside over the prevention of occupational injuries and illnesses. These principles include: 1) a precise concept of the worker as a human with dignity, not merely a means of production; 2) a clear acknowledgment of fundamental human rights including the right of workers to employment in a production system that does not endanger their physical welfare or jeopardize their moral integrity; and 3) a complete vision of prevention including the capacity to find a balance between absolute principles and concrete reality through the determination of acceptable risk.

Tidwell (2000) presents a review of the literature relating ethics to workplace safety, and concludes by establishing a safety and ethics framework. This framework is characterized by an organizational climate where safety is valued and openly discussed, and an employment relationship where employees have the freedom and responsibility to make individual choices about safety. Underlying this employment relationship is a set of obligations and duties shared by employer and employee. These duties include the duty of mutual loyalty, the duty of care owed to the employee, the right of the employee to be informed of the risks, and the right of the employee to refuse work where the risk is unacceptable.

Eckhardt (2001) also addresses the question of an employer's moral responsibility to provide "enough" safety. Accepting the definition of safety provided by Lowrance (1976), a condition with an acceptable level of risk, Eckhardt contemplates the question: When has a company fulfilled its moral duty to provide employees with a safe workplace? He presents an overview of major religious teachings and relevant moral philosophy, but leaves it to the reader to answer the question.

Birkner and Birkner (2000) present a conceptual model they call the ethical pyramid, by which management's ethical orientation influences employee's actions. According to Birkner and Birkner, the process of influencing employee behavior begins with management establishing a formal code of ethical conduct (the base of the pyramid) and reaches its apex with employees being held accountable for their behavior against those standards. To explore this important link between an organization's ethical framework and the safety behaviors of the employees, let's first discuss the concept of organizational ethical climate.

Ethical Climate

Organizational climate symbolizes what an organization truly values and is revealed through the shared perception of employees as to the kinds of behaviors that are encouraged, supported and rewarded within the organization. This shared perception of the accumulated expectations and corresponding rewards serves as a ready frame of reference for guiding the behaviors of the employees (Schneider, 1975). When applied to ethics, the organizational ethical climate refers to the specific shared perceptions of organizational practices and procedures that define what is considered right or wrong within the organization (Parboteeah & Kapp, 2008; Martin & Cullen, 2006; Victor & Cullen, 1987; 1988).

The Victor and Cullen typology of ethical climates consists of three basic ethical climates, each based on one of three prominent schools of normative ethics. These ethical climate types are: egoistic, benevolent and principled (sidebar at right).

TABLE 6.1.1 Representative Descriptions of Ethical Climate Types

Ethical Climate Type	Representative Descriptions
Egoistic	• In this company, people are mostly out for themselves. • People in this company are very concerned about what is best for themselves. • People are expected to do anything to further the company's interests.
Benevolent	• In this company, people look out for each other's good. • The major consideration is what is best for everyone in the company. • People in this company view team spirit as important.
Principled	• It is very important to strictly follow the company's rules and procedures here. • Successful people in this company obey the company policies. • In this company, the law or ethical code of their profession is the major consideration.

In an egoistic climate, company ethical norms support the pursuit of self-interest. An egoistic climate may exist, for example, in a car dealership or brokerage firm. In both organizations, employees are expected to make decisions that maximize their self-interest.

In a benevolent climate, company ethical norms support maximizing the interests of all members of the social group. A benevolent climate may develop in, for instance, a pharmaceuticals lab, where employees are expected to cooperate and help each other to achieve successful outcomes.

Finally, in the principled climate, company ethical norms support following universal principles regardless of situational variables. A principled climate may be present in public accounting firms where the organizational climate supports ethical decision making based mostly on the codes that govern the profession. Table 6.1.1 presents representative descriptions for identifying these ethical climates.

Ethical Climate and Employee Behavior

While no previous work has examined the relationship between ethical climate and safety-related behavior, investigations into the causes of other employee behaviors have employed the ethical climate model. Treviño, Butterfield and McCabe (1998) empirically examined the influence of ethical climate on unethical employee behavior. Included in their examination are the behaviors of employee theft and lying. They found that in organizations where ethical climates of self-interest (egoistic) dominated, there was greater incidence of unethical conduct. In contrast, in organizations with ethical climates emphasizing laws and professional standards (principled), they observed a decreased incidence of unethical behavior.

TABLE 6.1.2   Ethical Climate Types and Their Characteristics

Ethical Climate Type	Characteristic
Egoistic	Maximization of self-interest
Benevolent	The most good for the most people
Principled	Adherence to universal principles

Peterson (2002) investigated the relationship between ethical climate and deviant workplace behavior, with deviant behaviors defined as voluntary behavior that violates established organizational norms and threatens the well-being of the organization, its members or both. Peterson found that an employee-focused climate (benevolent) was associated with a decreased likelihood of production deviance, such as employees working on personal issues during company time or taking overly long breaks. Benevolent climates also experienced decreased likelihood of political deviance, such as blaming someone else for errors or spreading malicious gossip about a coworker. A rules-and-procedures climate (principled) was associated with a decreased likelihood of property deviance whereas the self-interest climate (egoistic) was associated with a greater likelihood of production deviance.

There has clearly been an interest in the role of ethics and the moral duty of management and employees in maintaining safe workplace (Angelini, 1987; Birkner & Birkner, 2000, Eckhardt, 2001; Tidwell, 2000), and previous research has shown an association between an organization's ethical climate and the occurrence of workplace deviance and unethical behavior (Peterson, 2002; Treviño, et al., 1998). However, no investigation has examined the role of ethics as a precursor of the individual worker's safety-related behavior. Let's now discuss this important, yet neglected, link between an organization's ethical climate and workplace safety behavior.

Ethical Climate and Safety Performance

A recent study of a medium-sized automotive component manufacturer in the midwestern U.S. examined the influence of ethical climate on safety-related behavior (Parboteeah & Kapp, 2008). An anonymous questionnaire was voluntarily completed by 237 hourly employees from five U.S. plants of a European multinational automotive component manufacturer

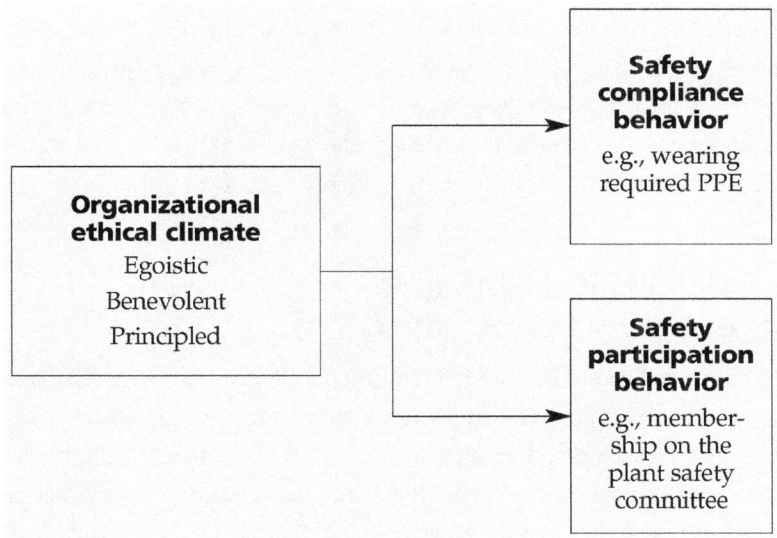

FIGURE 6.1.1 Ethical climate and safety-related behavior

measuring ethical climate (Victor & Cullen, 1987; 1988) and the safety compliance and safety participation behaviors of employees (Griffin & Neal, 2000).

Safety compliance behavior refers to the individual safe work practices of employees, and safety participation behavior represents those behaviors that support the organization's safety program. One example of safety compliance behavior is correctly wearing all the necessary PPE on the job. An instance of safety participation behavior would be volunteering for activities that help to improve workplace safety, such as joining the safety committee (Figure 6.1.1). The researchers developed measures based on the literature. As such, all measures (ethical climates, safety compliance and safety motivation) are valid and accurately represent what they are intended to measure. The researchers also found all measures to be reliable with Cronbach's alpha scores exceeding .70, thereby indicating strong agreement among respondents on the items.

Strong support was found for the influence of the organization's principled climate on the safety-related behavior of the employees, with both greater safety compliance ($\beta = .206$, $p < .01$) and more safety participation behavior ($\beta = .166$, $p < .05$) reported among the plants displaying a principled ethical climate. This company is known for maintaining a comprehensive formal safety program that includes an occupational safety and health management system (OHSAS 18001), a well-established 5S program (sort, straighten, shine, systemize and sustain), and a mandatory risk assessment and corrective measure development process with required participation from every manufacturing employee annually.

The results suggest that this company, with its principled climate and well-established safety program, is motivating employees to both comply with safety procedures and engage in safety-enhancing efforts. This organization's comprehensive safety program harmonized well with this strong principled ethical climate, yielding low injury rates among the five plants surveyed—days without lost-time injuries ranged from 250 to 2,379, with an average of 1,742.

Understanding Ethical Climate for Improved Safety Performance

While ethical climates tend to be somewhat controllable by managers (Cullen, et al., 1993), changing an organization's ethical climate is a major undertaking that requires substantial effort and resources—with no guarantee of success. A more practical approach may be to identify a company's ethical climate type (Table 6.1.3) and tailor the safety program to harmonize with that climate (sidebar at right).

Egoistic climates, those based on the ethical criterion of maximizing an entity's self-interest, may benefit from the inclusion of well-designed individual incentive systems that target safety-enhancing behaviors in safety programs. The critical success factor is to target specific safe behaviors, not the nonoccurrence or nonreporting of incidents. Specific behaviors can include both compliance with safe work practices such as wearing appropriate PPE for a given task, and participation in safety-enhancing activities such as contributing to an employee suggestion program or attending a facility safety committee meeting. The emphasis should be on specifying those desired behaviors and constantly rewarding them when they occur.

Benevolent climates, where being concerned with benefiting the greatest number of people is the norm, should frequently use safety messages that clearly communicate the

TABLE 6.1.3 Potential Indicators of Ethical Climate Type

Ethical climate type	Potential Indicators
Egoistic	• Individually oriented competitions in the company such as sales contests and injury-free workday records. • Profit sharing based on individual performance.
Benevolent	• Cooperative work systems such as autonomous work teams and job sharing. • Profit sharing based on work unit performance.
Principled	• Established company mission or values that employees can describe in their own words. • Frequent discussion among employees of local, national or global issues that relate to company performance.

possibility and consequences of injury, and the importance of using established safety procedures to avoid injury.

Ironically, keeping employees conscious of the potential for injury can be particularly challenging for a company with a low incidence of injuries. Under such conditions, where long spans of time pass without serious injury, safety can lose its predominant association with employees' well-being, and other issues become more highly associated with colleagues' welfare, such as the equitable distribution of workload among the team, or unbiased access to training and promotion opportunities. Without the consistent messages maintaining an awareness of the risk of injury, caring employees may take up other causes to benefit their colleagues. In a benevolent climate, the frequent use of safety messages becomes a means of encouraging safety compliance behavior as a way to benefit everyone in the company. Likewise, within a benevolent climate where the risks of injury are understood, participation in safety-enhancing activities maintains its importance as a meaningful and appropriate way to benefit colleagues.

Principled climates, where adherence to rules, laws and standards is the ethical criterion underlying all decisions, benefit from formalized safety programs. Safety in this climate would be well served by dedicating the time and resources to a comprehensive safety program focusing on established processes and procedures. An occupational safety and health management system such as ANSI Z10 or OHSAS 18001 would be a good investment for such an organization and would likely yield favorable results.

TABLE 6.1.4 Ethical Climate Type: Safety Program Element Summary

Ethical climate type	Complementing safety initiative
Egoistic	Individualized safety incentive system
Benevolent	Risk communications program
Principled	Safety management system

Conclusion

Evidence suggests that an organization's ethical environment influences employees' decisions to comply with safety rules and participate in safety-enhancing initiatives. An ethical climate assessment is a useful tool for understanding this environment. An organization's ethical climate offers unique insight into the ethical basis of employees' safety-related behavior. By understanding its ethical climate, a company can discover better ways to design safety and health programs to reduce employee resistance, achieve better safety compliance and encourage greater levels of participation in safety-enhancing initiatives.

References

Angelini, M. (1987). Ethical behavior for the prevention of injuries in the workplace. *Ergonomics, 30,* 231–237.

Aristotle. (2002). *Nicomachean ethics* (J. Sachs, Trans.). Newbury, MA: Focus Publishing/R. Pullins. (Original work published in 350 B.C.)

Birkner, L. & Birkner, R. (2000, Oct.). Assessing your firm's ethical climate. *Occupational Hazards, 62*(10), 141–142.

Cullen, J.B., Victor, B. & Bronson, J.W. (1993). The ethical climate questionnaire: An assessment of its development and validity. *Psychological Reports, 73,* 667–674.

Eckhardt, R. (2001, Aug.). The moral duty to provide workplace safety. *Professional Safety, 46*(8), 36–39.

Griffin, M.A. & Neal, A. (2000). Perceptions of safety at work: A framework for linking safety climate to safety performance, knowledge and motivation. *Journal of Occupational Health Psychology, 5*(3), 347–358.

Lowrance, W. (1976). *Of acceptable risk: Science and the determination of safety.* Los Altos, CA: William Kaufman.

Martin, K.D. & Cullen, J.B. (2006). Continuities and extensions of ethical climate theory: A meta-analytic review. *Journal of Business Ethics, 69*(2), 175–194.

Parboteeah, K. & Kapp, E. (2008). Ethical climates and safety-enhancing behaviors: An empirical test. *Journal of Business Ethics, 80*(3).

Peterson, D.K. (2002). Deviant workplace behavior and the organization's ethical climate. *Journal of Business and Psychology, 17*(1), 47–61.

Schneider, B. (1975). Organizational climates: An essay. *Personnel Psychology, 28*(4), 447–479.

Tidwell, A. (2000). Ethics, safety and managers. *Business & Professional Ethics Journal, 19,* 161–180.

Treviño, L.K., Butterfield, K. & McCabe, B. (1998). The ethical context in organizations: Influences on employee attitudes and behaviors. *Business Ethics Quarterly, 8*(3), 447–476.

Victor, B. & Cullen, J.B. (1987). A theory and measure of ethical climate in organizations. In W.C. Frederick (Ed.), *Research in corporate social performance* (pp. 57–71). Greenwich, CT: JAI Press.

Victor, B. & Cullen, J.B. (1988). The organizational bases of ethical work climates. *Administrative Science Quarterly, 33,* 101–125.

Reading 6.2

Using Safety to Introduce Ethics into Operations Management Courses

Wayne Buck and Jeffrey Schaller

Introduction

One of the most significant developments in operations management (OM) over the past decade or so has been growing attention to sustainability. This has become a focus of practical concern on the part of numerous companies, regulatory authorities, and nongovernmental organizations, as well as an important area of research for academics.[1]

The touchstone of nearly all definitions of sustainability was articulated by the United Nations in 1987: "Sustainable development is development that meets the needs of the present without compromising the ability of future generations to meet their own needs."[2] Despite the generality of this definition, the literature does seem to have reached a rough consensus on what sustainability means in OM. Kleindorfer, Singhal, and Wassenhove have traced the origins and evolution of the concept in OM. Their construct is founded on "a broad perspective on triple-bottom-line thinking, integrating profit, people and planet into culture, strategy, and operations of companies."[3] Many, if not most, definitions of sustainability in the OM literature reference this triple-bottom-line concept.[4]

Three aspects of sustainability have received the most attention: green products, green production, and socially responsible suppliers.[5] Health and safety (aside from working conditions at supplier factories) have received less attention in the OM literature.[6] This relative neglect of health and safety is reflected in OM teaching practice as well, which largely bypasses these issues.[7]

Within this context, it is not surprising that instructors interested in incorporating ethics in their OM courses do so through the topic of sustainability focusing almost exclusively on the "green" and supplier components, leaving health and safety aside.[8] Nonetheless, operating safely and delivering safe products to market are widely recognized ethical imperatives, and form an important component of corporate social responsibility.[9]

Wayne Buck and Jeffrey Schaller, "Using Safety to Introduce Ethics into Operations Management Courses," *Teaching Ethics Across the Management Curriculum*, Volume II: Principles and Applications, ed. Kemi Ogunyemi, pp. 137-161. Copyright © 2016 by Business Expert Press. Reprinted with permission.

In this chapter we argue that safety has distinctive advantages as an avenue for introducing ethical issues into OM courses. Further, this chapter suggests strategies for introducing safety as an ethical issue that neither crowd out existing OM topics nor take a hasty and superficial approach that implicitly devalues ethics and social responsibility.

Description of the Discipline of OM

OM is widely understood to be "the function responsible for planning, coordinating, and controlling the resources needed to produce a company's goods and services."[10] The scope of OM is an organization's productive activities. The success of an organization's OM function is traditionally measured along three dimensions: efficiency, timeliness, and quality. The aim of OM as an academic field is to develop theory, concepts, techniques, tools, and processes to help organizations achieve their productive performance targets. High levels of performance enable organizational success, whether that success is measured as increased competitiveness versus rivals and greater profitability or as more completely accomplishing the organization's mission.

Sustainability, in effect, adds yet another standard for evaluating how well an organization's productive activities are performing.[11] This significantly complicates the OM challenge.[12] First, it does so simply because sustainability adds more objectives to an already long list of objectives and thereby increases the number and complexity of the trade-offs that must be evaluated—now there are even more cakes that organizations cannot both eat and have.

Second, and more importantly for our purposes, sustainability introduces ethical considerations. Operations managers now face the possibility of having to make trade-offs between what is good for the organization and what is morally right. As we will see in the next section, making decisions that balance, for example cost and timeliness, are usually very different from decisions that require managers to balance, for example cost and safety.

Typical Ethical Issues in OM

Sustainability is widely considered to be an ethical imperative, a key aspect of social responsibility.[13] However, given the disparate nature of the objectives that have been linked to sustainability, and the fact that the task of this chapter is to help instructors introduce ethics and not sustainability into their OM courses, we need a criterion for which specific aspects of sustainability—and ultimately OM—are properly thought of as having ethical ramifications.

Before we discuss this criterion, however, we should make clear that our focus is what have been called "pro-organizational behaviors"—actions and decisions by managers intended to benefit the organization.[14] This contrasts to managerial behavior that benefits the manager at the expense of the organization. For example, a manager might embezzle funds, sexually harass a colleague, misappropriate company equipment, or select a supplier based on a personal interest instead of one that would be best for the organization. This focus is justified because we are interested in understanding how an organization should manage its operations, and when we talk about an organization doing something—manufacturing a product, setting work schedules, contracting with a supplier—we are implicitly referencing what individual managers do on behalf of their organizations.

A Criterion for Ethical Issues

The approach taken in this chapter is to identify which business decisions have an ethical aspect by referencing stakeholders' views on the proper basis for making those decisions. In the case of some decisions, reasonable stakeholders will not object to the organization making the decision solely on self-interested economic grounds. For these decisions, methods that compare and evaluate alternative courses of action on the basis of the economic costs and benefits to the organization itself are appropriate and acceptable to reasonable stakeholders. Decisions that pass this "test" are purely instrumental, and do not raise issues of moral right and wrong.

By contrast, a decision does have an ethical aspect if reasonable stakeholders would object to the organization making the decision solely on the basis of economic costs and benefits to itself. In other words, ethical issues arise when reasonable stakeholders would consider it inappropriate and unacceptable for an organization to make a decision strictly on the basis of self-interested economic and financial considerations.[15]

To illustrate how this criterion works, consider the following two examples. First, setting a target maximum defect rate in manufacturing computer microchips. Assuming that the microchips are intended as components in equipment whose failure would not threaten life or limb, a decision that factors in only production costs and the costs of defective chips (inspection, rework, return, customer complaints, reputation, etc.) in relation to revenue, is perfectly appropriate. A manager may quite reasonably decide to accept a higher than practically possible minimum defect rate because the costs of doing so are outweighed by the additional revenue—and because the costs of reducing the defect rate would not be outweighed by additional revenue. Customers, suppliers, employees, investors all understand and accept management making a decision about an acceptable defect rate based on a cost–benefit analysis. A business decision purely based on maximizing profitability, even if it meant a higher than necessary rate of defective computer chips, would be acceptable to stakeholders. Hence, in this case, decisions about what defect rate is acceptable do not have an ethical aspect—the business case is decisive and nonbusiness factors need not be considered.

The second example concerns contamination of a processed food product such as potato chips. In this case, a manager who accepts a given contamination risk because doing so maximizes profitability, when it is possible and practical to reduce that risk by giving up some profits, would be criticized by customers as "putting profits ahead of people." Contaminated potato chips are in a different category, in the eyes of stakeholders, than defective computer chips. People get sick, suffer long-term debilitating injuries, and die from eating contaminated food. Yet consumers have every right to expect the food they eat to be safe.[16] Just as poisoning a relative in order to acquire an inheritance is unethical, so it is widely acknowledged that it is unethical to poison people in order to make greater profits. These ethical judgments arise from the fact that we value human life and human well-being much more highly than mere things or money.

Of course, reasonable customers do not expect food-manufacturing businesses to completely forego cost–benefit analysis, nor do they believe that contamination risk should be reduced to zero, or that human health should be assigned an infinite dollar value. Reasonable customers will accept some limits to how much a company should spend to reduce contamination risk, but they will do so only if they perceive that the company and the people at the company care about their health beyond purely financial considerations. This is why OM decisions about how to manage food contamination risk have an ethical aspect, while decisions about managing rates of computer chip defects do not.

Safety as an Ethical Issue

Every business—every organization—has to make trade-offs between cost and safety. The snack foods company making potato chips could always spend more on pest control, mold detection, equipment cleaning, product testing, and employee training. Even though the marginal benefit of every additional dollar spent on safety is likely to diminish, nonetheless, there would likely be some improvement. But if the company insisted on continuing to increase safety spending as long as the marginal benefit was greater than zero, it would go out of business.

Managers cannot spend infinite amounts of money on safety, but how much? How safe does a car company, a drug company, or a processed food manufacturer need to make their products? How safe does a chemical process, airline flight, or medical procedure need to be? How accurate does a Certified Public Accountant (CPA) need to be in filling out a client's tax return? How complete does a pharmaceutical product disclosure need to be? At what point should a company stop testing, evaluating, and verifying its products, services, suppliers, and operations and bring them to market?

These ethical challenges arise from the fact that the question "how safe is safe enough?" cannot be answered using cost–benefit analysis. Profit and safety are, at bottom, incommensurable and cannot be weighed on the same scale. They are incommensurable because safety is an ethical and not simply an economic issue.

Of course, sometimes—perhaps more often than some managers believe—safety pays.[17] But sometimes it does not. In any case, when faced with specific operating decisions that must be made quickly, with limited and to some degree inaccurate information, it is often very unclear or uncertain whether safety will in fact pay, or if it will, when. And it is exactly this hard reality—that every business is faced with having to make hard, ethically laden choices between benefits to itself and risks to employees, customers, and the public—that serves as the entry point for ethics into OM. The fundamental OM ethical challenge is: how much risk can I (we) expose others to in order to gain some benefit for myself (ourselves)? This kind of challenge is ubiquitous in business, especially in OM. These are decisions not about balancing risk and reward for oneself, but risk to someone else versus benefits to oneself.[18]

As one of us has argued elsewhere, these types of challenges are not ethical dilemmas in the sense of a conflict of values.[19] They are better thought of as "ethical conundrums." They have no obvious right or wrong answers; they are "confusing or difficult problems."[20] These are tough problems to solve in large part because risk to others and benefit to oneself are incommensurable. The two cannot be measured on the same scale of economic analysis. This means that what is needed is not better, more accurate, more sophisticated calculation, but good ethical judgment.

We suggest that safety is an especially effective vehicle for raising ethical issues in OM courses. Safety is an easily appreciated value and of great interest to employees, customers, and the general public. Safety is directly tied to operating decisions, and many familiar business processes raise safety issues. And because of safety's connection to risk, safety is often (but not always) quantifiable in ways that enable incorporation into OM decision-making methods and models.

Types of Safety

The term "safety" covers a variety of distinct risks. Personal safety hazards (often termed occupational or worker safety) are the most widely recognized and studied in both the OM and safety literature. This type of safety concerns hazards to the health and well-being of individual workers, hazards that do not threaten the continued functioning of a facility as a whole.

Process safety hazards, by contrast, threaten the operations of the facility itself, have the potential to seriously disrupt, either temporarily or permanently, the facility's output, and the potential to kill or injure large numbers of people, either workers or the public.[21] Process safety hazards include fires and explosions, toxic releases, flooding, and large-scale physical destruction.

Product safety—the risk products pose to consumers—represents a third type of safety, and also has an ethical dimension. Consider the design of the General Motors (GM) ignition switch, which made the switch vulnerable to rotating into the "off" position, shutting down the engine, and disabling the airbags. This defectively designed switch is reported to have cost the lives of dozens of drivers and passengers.[22]

Ethics Teaching Strategy: Experiential Learning

Safety, whether personal, process, or product, is clearly a large field, with its own methods, concepts, principles, and practices.[23] Despite this, we believe that it is not necessary to add new material into existing courses in order to use safety to introduce ethics to OM students. The keys to success in this endeavor are (a) modest expectations combined with (b) an experiential approach.

First, we suggest that OM instructors seek to raise students' awareness of the reality that operating decisions have an ethical aspect, and to present them with that reality in the context of problems they are already solving. Success will be achieved when students come away from solving an OM problem realizing that the best solution cannot always be determined on the basis of purely technical, pragmatic, or economic reasoning. They do not need to have the tools to actually find the very best, most ethically informed, solution. Rather, the goal is to get students to recognize that at some point, for some OM decisions, the "best" solution is one that relies on ethical judgments and results in a decision that is less than optimum from a purely cost–benefit perspective.

Second, in addition to these modest expectations, we propose that experiential learning methods, not concept acquisition, are the best way to raise students' ethical awareness. What is needed is an approach that shows students why safety issues arise in production environments and shows them how safety is entwined with meeting production objectives. This showing may or may not be accompanied by formal discussion of safety issues, but in any case students will come away with a foundational experience that explicitly includes ethics in OM.

Simulations

Experiential teaching methods are especially appropriate in OM. This is because experiential learning opportunities in the form of production simulations are already in common use and have been shown to be effective.[24] Moreover, simulations are widely applied in OM practice to support decision making.[25]

Simulation games immerse students in the complexities, uncertainties, and ambiguities of decision making. They provide an opportunity for students to experience what it is like to feel the pressures of cost, production, time, and quality. Moreover, simulation games provide students with an opportunity to watch and reflect on their own revealed behavior as they react to the pressure to out-compete their classmates and struggle with the temptation to sacrifice other values for the sake of personal gain.[26]

One of us has developed and used, for a number of years, an operations-oriented simulation game in his business ethics class.[27] The simulation game, commercialized under the name "Deepwater," provides a concrete example of how OM simulations can be used to raise ethical issues and provides valuable general lessons for utilizing simulations.

In Deepwater, students manage the operations of a deep water oil production platform in the Gulf of Mexico. The objective is for students to operate at a profit, outperforming rival oil companies. The game is played over several rounds, typically 8 to 12. Students make operational decisions in each round about oil production, spending on maintenance and safety, crew size and training, and equipment overhauls. After a round closes, the simulation model processes the decisions and determines outcomes. Students receive reports on the outcomes of their decisions. These reports include not only operating and financial information, but information about worker injuries and fatalities, accidents including well blowouts, and social impacts such as pollution and the company's carbon footprint.

In Deepwater, students face several operational risks including personal accidents that can injure or kill individual workers and process accidents that can cause their oil well to blowout, potentially killing or injuring workers, causing an environmental disaster and putting the company on the sidelines for a portion of the simulation. Virtually all of the operating decisions that students face in Deepwater have an impact on both personal and process safety. The more oil they produce, for example, the greater the chances of an accident or blowout. The more spent on maintenance, the lower the chances of an accident or blowout.

It is important to note that outcomes in Deepwater are probabilistic. That is, the decisions students make affect the probability of certain events happening, but do not mechanistically determine those events. This is intended to capture the day-to-day reality of many OM decisions—and, for that matter, of most management decisions. Many traditional OM simulation games share this characteristic.[28]

In addition to being probabilistic, OM simulations utilized to raise ethical issues can usefully incorporate nonlinear functions. Nonlinear relationships—relationships between an independent and a dependent variable that display either diminishing or increasing returns to scale—are common in business and economics.

For example, after a certain point spending an additional dollar on training has less of an impact on reducing accidents than the first dollar had. Likewise, after a certain point each increment of additional production will raise defect rates more than the first increment. Understanding changing returns to scale is fundamental to making decisions about how to trade-off increased risk for increased benefits, or increased costs for decreased risk. Here too, many standard OM simulations display nonlinear behavior. In these simulations, small changes in production or inventory inputs can result in surprisingly large changes in throughput or inventory levels.

Consider the relationship between maintenance spending and blowout probability in Deepwater, which displays decreasing returns to scale (see Figure 6.2.1). As more money is spent on maintenance, the better the equipment condition, and the lower the chances of a blowout. Simulation players can improve their equipment's condition by producing less crude oil and by spending more on maintenance. What is the "right" level of maintenance spending? This is very difficult to say in the abstract, but one thing is clear: while increasing spending from $2.00/bbl to $3.00/bbl noticeably reduces the chances of a blowout, an increase from $10 to $12—or even $20!—provides only a very slight benefit.

So far we have simply recommended a set of design characteristics that make OM simulation games especially useful in raising ethical issues. We recommend that such simulation games be operationally and risk-oriented and model risk using probabilistic and nonlinear input–output functions. These design characteristics also have the benefit of being completely neutral on the question of how to resolve the resulting ethical issues. The ethical issues raised in simulation games with these design characteristics can be tackled using consequentialist, deontological, virtue ethics, care ethics, or any other ethical framework one might prefer.

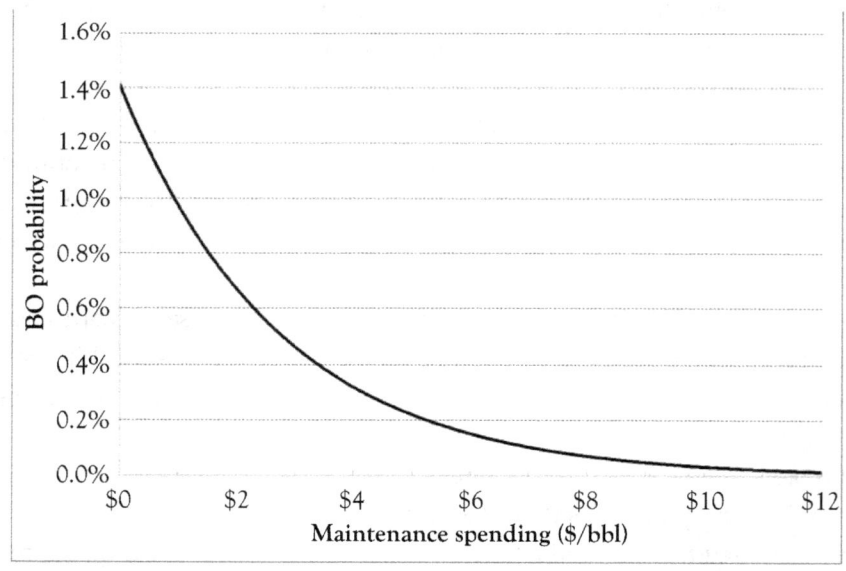

FIGURE 6.2.1 Maintenance spending versus blowout probability

The maintenance issue raised previously provides a good example of an ethical issue that arises in the context of the Deepwater simulation game: what is the ethically responsible level of spending on maintenance in a business that risks significant harm if things go badly? If a student playing the game wanted to make the ethically right decision, how much would he or she spend on maintenance?

Clearly, it would be unethical to spend no money on maintenance. The risks of a blowout or other problems that could harm employees or the environment would go much higher than they need be. Sooner or later—probably sooner—there would be an accident. But how much maintenance spending is enough? We cannot require managers to spend so much money on maintenance (or safety, or product quality, or service) that it is impossible to make a profit. And because the relationship between maintenance spending and blowing out is nonlinear, spending huge amounts of money on maintenance would in any case produce very little benefit compared to smaller amounts.

In the simulation, the baseline maintenance spending is $8.00 per barrel of oil produced. This is the amount recommended by the "manufacturer" of the oil rig and its equipment. Yet, even at this level, it is still possible for something to go wrong and a piece of equipment fail—even possible that the rig suffer a blowout. The chances are small at $8.00 per barrel, but still not zero.

Let's consider the option of spending less than $8.00 per barrel on maintenance in the simulation, say $7.75. Would this be irresponsible? A look at the graph shows that the increased risk is going to be quite small, so why not? If two players in the simulation are virtually tied in terms of profitability, would it really be irresponsible for one of them to shave a few pennies off of maintenance in order to out-compete the rival? And then the question arises, would it be irresponsible of the first competitor to "up the stakes" by shaving yet another $0.25 off their own spending?

There is no easy way to decide on the ethically responsible level of maintenance spending for a business such as deepwater offshore oil drilling. The purpose of drawing a student's attention to maintenance spending, equipment condition, blowout risk, and the (nonlinear) relationships between them is *not* to get them to learn how to make the "right decision." Rather, the objective is to encourage students to reflect on their own decision-making behavior as the simulation unfolds and note how that behavior changes under the pressure of pursuing profits in competition with each other. The benefit of participating in the simulation is not that students will discover the right "formula" for how much care to take in making management decisions. The value of the simulation is that it presents students with an opportunity to experience how their own judgments and decisions about the right degree of care are affected by the desire for profit and the pursuit of competitive advantage. Only after managers become aware of such effects on their own behavior will they be in a position to weigh economic considerations appropriately by bringing ethical judgment to bear.

Advice for Teachers Using Simulations

The success of an ethically oriented simulation requires that students reflect on their own simulation decision making and behavior.[29] This is, perhaps, the greatest challenge facing an instructor. Four years of experience with Deepwater has provided some insights into how to encourage productive self-reflection.

It is often assumed that reflection should take place after an experiential exercise ends and that the purpose of reflection is to get students to attend to their own individual subjective experience and then guide them to a deeper understanding of the significance of that experience.[30] Our own experience with Deepwater suggests that instructors should broaden the scope of reflection in two ways.

First, instructors should consider not only focusing on a student's subjective experience, but also on her actual behavior—that is, on the decisions she has made as a simulation player. A dual focus on subjective experience and actual behavior provides an opportunity for students to recognize any gaps that open up between what they think they did and what they actually did. When actual behavior becomes a subject for reflection, students have an opportunity to step back from a very natural absorption in their own individual decision-making and see those decisions in the context of the entire simulation. Moreover, by examining their own behavior in the context of the behavior of their classmates, students may see commonalities and differences that prompt them to reevaluate their own interpretations of why they made certain decisions.

Second, experience with Deepwater has shown that, especially for multi-round OM simulation games, there can be very real benefits to students from multiple reflection opportunities. We suggest that instructors initiate reflection even before the simulation begins, support an ongoing reflection process that parallels the simulation as it advances, and then, after the simulation has concluded, engage in the more traditional post-simulation reflection.

Consider first the need for a pre-experience reflection, which Kriz terms a "briefing" or "introduction."[31] A student's a priori understanding of why she is participating in an experiential exercise, her understanding of what the experience is supposed to accomplish and of how the experience is supposed to accomplish that end profoundly inform, shape, and color the experiences to come. Students asked to participate in simulation games are fully aware that these simulations are artifices, and thus in many important senses "fake."

Given that a simulation offers only a fake and not a real opportunity to manage a business, the success of a simulation depends on students approaching the simulation with the right attitudes, with appropriate expectations and with an understanding of the nature and limitations of the simulation. To benefit from a simulation, students need to "suspend their disbelief." They must learn to approach the simulation "as if" it were the reality itself while at the same time acknowledging, accepting, and even embracing its falsity. Unless the instructor prepares the student with the appropriate mindset, the simulation experience will be weak and impoverished, providing little of substance to reflect on during the post-experience debriefing activity. An initial briefing by the instructor on the experience ahead can be helpful in establishing the understanding and attitudes necessary for students to get the maximum benefit from a simulation.[32]

Moreover, as the experience unfolds the character and quality of a student's simulation experience is significantly determined by the student's own evolving mindset. A student can have a rich and useful learning experience only if the development of that mindset—of her attitudes, expectations, and understanding—is supported from the moment the simulation starts until it concludes.

For example, students who experience the simulation, as it proceeds, as in some way rigged to produce a specific outcome are unlikely to benefit from the simulation, and nothing said subsequently, in debriefing, could undo that experience. For students to have the "right" experiences—that is, the ones that the instructor intends for them to have—a certain trust in the instructor, a faith in the simulation itself, and a confidence in their own ability to play the simulation game well must be implanted and constantly nurtured. Students absorb a stream of new information during the course of the simulation, including round results and the moves of their competitors. This new information is subject to interpretation and reinterpretation by students in an attempt to make sense of their experiences. Instructors need to be aware of these interpretations and be available to influence those interpretations in ways that support the simulation's learning objectives. In particular, instructors need to intervene to instill and maintain student's trust, faith, and confidence in the simulation, and their own experiences.

Instructors should engage in a culminating, end-of-experience debriefing process immediately after the conclusion of a simulation. This will give students an opportunity to integrate multiple perspectives and share experiences and insights with each other. This final debriefing represents the culmination of the entire reflective process that has accompanied the simulation throughout.

This three-step process—initial briefing, responsive reflection during the course of the simulation, and a final debriefing—can dramatically enhance the effectiveness of a simulation game and improve student learning.

Ongoing assessment of students' experiences can be a valuable tool for supporting productive reflection. Assessment is often utilized in an attempt to measure learning outcomes, yet these outcomes are for many reasons the least tractable results of an experiential exercise.[33] Experience with Deepwater suggests that assessment can play a role not only in determining whether learning objectives have been met, but in better understanding of how they are being met and, if they are not being met, why. Assessments during the course of the simulation can help reveal the nature of students' unfolding simulation experience. They might, for example, uncover perceptions that the simulation is somehow "rigged" or unfairly manipulated by the instructor. Addressing these perceptions as early in the simulation as possible will clear obstacles to a successful simulation experience. And finally, assessments after the simulation concludes can provide the raw material to spark an extended in-class debriefing discussion about the entire simulation experience.

Developing Versus Developed Country Perspectives

Manufacturing facilities in developing countries tend to have three characteristics that are especially relevant for instructors who wish to use safety to introduce ethical considerations into OM. First, there tends to be less government regulation of workplace practices and weaker enforcement of process standards and best practices.[34] As a result, workers are injured at a significantly greater rate than in developed countries.[35] Moreover, individual managers are, paradoxically, in both a stronger and weaker position to improve safety at their facilities. They are in a stronger position simply in the sense that government inspectors and auditors play a smaller role, especially on a day-to-day basis, and hence are not in a position to "usurp" management decisions to the same degree as in developed countries.[36] Operational managers are, at the same time, more limited simply because their companies are often suppliers to large, more economically powerful buyers. As a result, the pressures to meet short-term production goals are often greater than they would be in developed countries, and production shortfalls have greater potential to significantly impact the supplier's relationship with buyers.

Second, operations managers in facilities operating in developing countries tend to have fewer resources available to them for capital improvements, routine maintenance, and quality control. As a result, implementation of new technologies to support increased safety tends to happen over a longer time frame; there is more of a practice of "making do" with existing parts and spares, refurbishing worn-out components rather than replacing them with brand new parts, and greater pressures to take shortcuts to resume production as quickly as possible.[37]

Third, manufacturing facilities in the developing world tend to be sited closer to significant population concentrations.[38] This not only increases risks to the public, but also means that students are more likely to have had experiences with these facilities and their operating practices.

While all three of these realities increase the safety challenges of operating in developing countries, they also provide instructors and students with many real-world experiences that can be fruitfully imported into the classroom.

Summary and Conclusion

This chapter suggests that OM instructors can use occupational, process, and product safety issues to introduce ethics into their courses. Safety is especially appropriate for raising ethical issues in OM courses because it is an easily appreciated value and of great interest to employees, customers, and the general public. Moreover, safety is directly tied to many operating decisions, and many familiar business processes raise safety issues. And because of safety's connection to risk, safety issues often arise naturally when presenting OM decision-making methods and models.

OM instructors should adopt modest expectations and employ an experiential approach for introducing ethics into their courses. Their aim should be to raise students' awareness of the ethical aspects of operating decisions, not to give students the concepts and tools to actually weigh ethical considerations and make good ethical judgments. Moreover, instructors can do this by taking advantage of the experiential exercises that are already a part of many OM courses.

Simulations, in particular, are a very common component of OM syllabi. We describe a concrete example of an operationally oriented simulation and explain how instructors can utilize their own existing OM teaching simulations to raise ethical issues.

OM instructors have readily available to them opportunities and methods for introducing ethical issues into their courses. This can be done (a) without crowding out any existing OM material, (b) without compromising a focus on production outcomes, while (c) nonetheless avoiding a hasty and superficial approach that implicitly devalues ethics.

Suggested Exercises/Projects

> Instructors should review existing syllabi and identify ways to add experiential learning opportunities, especially operationally oriented simulations, to strengthen student understanding of traditional OM concepts, methods, and practices. For this purpose, it would be useful to become familiar with some of the latest literature on experiential learning.[39]
>
> Consider the personal, process, and product safety implications of simulations currently in the syllabus. Develop strategies for using those implications to raise students' awareness of ethical issues. The following guidelines for identifying ethics-related aspects of OM simulations can be helpful:
>
> Identify the aspects of the simulation that require students to make decisions that impact risks to the well-being or interests of workers, the public, or other stakeholders. These risks might be greater exposure to occupational hazards, stresses on product or process quality control, or impacts on the quality of information or resources available to make future decisions.
>
> These risks do not need to be limited to those built into the simulation. Prompt students to think through the real-world implications of the OM problems being simulated.

It is not necessary to require students to factor those risks into their simulation decision making. Rather, focus on raising awareness and prompting discussion. This can often be done in the context of explicitly discussing the limitations of the simulation, especially as a necessary simplification of the totality of a real-world situation.

Avoid attempting to supplement the simulation with artificial ethical dilemmas such as presenting students with explicit opportunities to deceive competitors or falsify information.

As an example of applying these guidelines, consider the very simple cups manufacturing game.[40] Students work in a production line to assemble a tray of four paper cups, complete with lids, straws, and apply an adhesive colored dot. The first student supplies raw materials, the second places the cups in the tray, the third applies the dot, the fourth covers the cup with a lid, the fifth unwraps and inserts a straw, and the last student does quality control (QC) and ships the completed trays. The purpose of this game is to teach students about just-in-time manufacturing and the differences between push and pull production.

Even an OM game as simple as this provides opportunities to raise ethical issues. Consider, for example, quality control. The QC student must inspect each tray assembly. Those that are defective are tossed away; those that meet the quality standard are shipped. The risk here is shipping defective products to customers.

An instructor can take two different approaches to defining a quality standard: either allow the QC students in the game to set their own standards, or specify a standard for them. If students are allowed to set the standard and make their own judgments about quality, it is likely that they will reject very few assemblies. Assemblies are likely to be shipped with crooked lids and bent straws. Careful inspection for quality takes time, and tossing away assemblies reduces throughput. If the game is played competitively, team members will pressure the QC student to set a low quality bar and be very lenient in applying the standard.

If instead the instructor sets the quality standard, it should be specified in a way that is open to considerable interpretation and judgment. For example, if the standard is "dots must all face in the same direction," students will feel pressure to interpret the standard as "dots must all face in approximately the same direction."

In either case, the game does not have to be altered in any substantive way. Indeed, the instructor does not even need to mention the QC issue or enforce a quality standard. After the game is over, instructors can simply ask students to reflect on their own QC behavior and the extent to which substandard assemblies were shipped.

Notes

1. Gualandris et al. (2015); Linton, Klassen, and Jayaraman (2007); Seuring and Müller (2008).
2. WCED (1987).
3. Kleindorfer, Singhal, and Wassenhove (2005, 482).
4. For example, Carter and Easton (2011); Winter and Knemeyer (2013); Huchzermeier, Kohl, and Spinler (2014); Laasch and Conaway (2014).
5. Huchzermeier, Kohl, and Spinler (2014); Fan et al. (2014, 335).
6. Cantor (2008, 66); Das et al. (2008); De Koster, Stam, and Balk (2011); Pagell et al. (2014, 1161).
7. References to safety and safe operations, for example, are rare in the indices of the most widely used introductory operations management texts.
8. Huchzermeier, Kohl, and Spinler (2014).
9. Stewart, Ledgerwood, and May (1996); Zwetsloot (2004); Cantor (2008); Montero, Araque, and Rey (2009); Hart (2010); Lorenzo, Esqueda, and Larson (2010); Hart (2013); Hajmohammad and Vachon (2014).
10. Reid and Sanders (2012, 3).
11. Jiménez and Lorente (2001); Sustainability is not the only recent addition to strategic operational objectives—service, flexibility, and innovation have also been tossed in as "must achieve" priorities.
12. Devinney (2009); Wu and Pagell (2011); Longoni and Cagliano (2015).
13. Hajmohammad and Vachon (2014).
14. Umphress and Bingham (2011).
15. Notice that this criterion for ethical relevance applies not only to OM decisions, but to any decision an organization makes, whether that decision be in finance, human resources, marketing, or any other function.
16. "Blue Bell C.E.O. apologizes for recall" (2015).
17. Pagell et al. (2014).
18. Macpherson (2008).
19. Buck (2014).
20. Merriam-Webster (n.d.).
21. Hopkins (2009).
22. Mathews and Spector (2015).
23. Key journals include: *Safety Science, Journal of Safety Research, Journal of the Institution of Occupational Safety and Health, Journal of Safety Research, Accident Analysis and Prevention, Journal of Loss Prevention in the Process Industries, Reliability Engineering and System Safety, Process Safety and Environmental Protection Professional Safety*.
24. Lewis and Maylor (2007); Tan, Tse, and Chung (2010); Pasin and Giroux (2011).
25. Jahangirian et al. (2010).
26. Ezz, Loureiro-Koechlin, and Stergioulas (2012).
27. Buck (2014).

28. For example, production and inventory management simulations such as the Beer and Cups game are effective because students' intuitions about how the system will behave in response to certain strategies are usually completely wrong.
29. For example, Thatcher (1990); Crookall (2010); Hill and Lance (2002); Lederman (1992); Sims (2002).
30. For example, Sims (2002, 186).
31. Kriz (2010, 667–668).
32. See, for example, Snow, Gehlen, and Green (2002).
33. Mayer et al. (2011, 70).
34. Chen, Zhang, and Delaurentis (2014).
35. Hämäläinen, Saarel, and Takala (2009); Takala et al. (2014); Molla, Salgedo, and Lemu (2015).
36. Lorenzo, Esqueda, and Larson (2010).
37. Eti, Ogaji, and Probert (2005, 2006).
38. Porto and Freitas (1996); Renjith and Madhu (2010); Porto and Freitas (2003).
39. For example, Carnes (2014).
40. Ammar and Wright (1999); Lewis and Maylor (2007).

References

Ammar, S., and R. Wright. 1999. "Experiential Learning Activities in Operations Management." *International Transactions in Operational Research* 6, no. 2, pp. 183–97.

"Blue Bell C.E.O. Apologizes for Recall." 2015. *The New York Times*, April 21.

Buck, W.F. 2014. "A Theory of Business Ethics Simulation Games." *Journal of Business Ethics Education* 11, pp. 217–38.

Cantor, D.E. 2008. "Workplace Safety in the Supply Chain: A Review of the Literature and Call for Research." *The International Journal of Logistics Management* 19, no. 1, pp. 65–83.

Carnes, M.C. 2014. *Minds on Fire: How Role-Immersion Games Transform College.* Cambridge, MA: Harvard University Press.

Carter, C.R., and P.L. Easton. 2011. "Sustainable Supply Chain Management: Evolution and Future Directions." *International Journal of Physical Distribution and Logistics Management* 41, no. 1, pp. 46–62.

Chen, C., J. Zhang, and T. Delaurentis. 2014. "Quality Control in Food Supply Chain Management: An Analytical Model and Case Study of the Adulterated Milk Incident in China." *International Journal of Production Economics* 152, pp. 188–99.

Crookall, D. 2010. "Serious Games, Debriefing, and Simulation/Gaming as a Discipline." *Simulation and Gaming* 41, no. 6, pp. 898–920.

Das, A., M. Pagell, M. Behm, and A. Veltri. 2008. "Toward a Theory of the Linkages Between Safety and Quality." *Journal of Operations Management* 26, no. 4, pp. 521–35.

de Koster, R.B.M., D. Stam, and B.M. Balk. 2011. "Accidents Happen: The Influence of Safety-Specific Transformational Leadership, Safety Consciousness, and Hazard Reducing Systems on Warehouse Accidents." *Journal of Operations Management* 29, no. 7, pp. 753–65.

Devinney, T.M. 2009. "Is the Socially Responsible Corporation a Myth? The Good, the Bad, and the Ugly of Corporate Social Responsibility." *The Academy of Management Perspectives* 23, no. 2, pp. 44–56.

Eti, M.C., S.O.T. Ogaji, and S.D. Probert. 2005. "Maintenance Schemes and Their Implementation for the Afam Thermal-Power Station." *Applied Energy* 82, no. 3, pp. 255–65.

Eti, M.C., S.O.T. Ogaji, and S.D. Probert. 2006. "Strategic Maintenance-Management in Nigerian Industries." *Applied Energy* 83, no. 3, pp. 211–27.

Ezz, I., C. Loureiro-Koechlin, and L. Stergioulas. 2012. "An Investigation of the Use of Simulation Tools in Management Education." *Paper read at Proceedings of the 2012 Winter Simulation Conference*, December.

Fan, D., C. Lo, V. Ching, and C.W. Kan. 2014. "Occupational Health and Safety Issues in Operations Management: A Systematic and Citation Network Analysis Review." *International Journal of Production Economics* 158, pp. 334–44.

Gualandris, J., R.D. Klassen, S. Vachon, and M. Kalchschmidt. 2015. "Sustainable Evaluation and Verification in Supply Chains: Aligning and Leveraging Accountability to Stakeholders." *Journal of Operations Management* 38, pp. 1–13.

Hajmohammad, S., and S. Vachon. 2014. "Safety Culture: A Catalyst for Sustainable Development." *Journal of Business Ethics* 123, no. 2, pp. 263–81.

Hämäläinen, P., K.L. Saarela, and J. Takala. 2009. "Global Trend According to Estimated Number of Occupational Accidents and Fatal Work-Related Diseases at Region and Country Level." *Journal of Safety Research* 40, no. 2, pp. 125–39.

Hart, S.M. 2010. "Self-Regulation, Corporate Social Responsibility, and the Business Case: Do They Work in Achieving Workplace Equality and Safety?" *Journal of Business Ethics* 92, no. 4, pp. 585–600.

Hart, S.M. 2013. "The Crash of Cougar Flight 491: A Case Study of Offshore Safety and Corporate Social Responsibility." *Journal of Business Ethics* 113, pp. 1–23.

Hill, J.L., and C.G. Lance. 2002. "Debriefing Stress." *Simulation and Gaming* 33, no. 4, pp. 490–503.

Hopkins, A. 2009. "Thinking About Process Safety Indicators." *Safety Science* 47, no. 4, pp. 460–65.

Huchzermeier, A., E. Kohl, and S. Spinler. 2014. "Teaching Ethics in Operations Management." In *Teaching Ethics Across the Management Curriculum: A Handbook for International Faculty*, ed. K. Ogunyemi. New York: Business Expert Press.

Jahangirian, M., T. Eldabi, A. Naseer, L.K. Stergioulas, and T. Young. 2010. "Simulation in Manufacturing and Business: A Review." *European Journal of Operational Research* 203, no. 1, pp. 1–13.

Jiménez, J.D.B., and J.J.C. Lorente. 2001. "Environmental Performance as an Operations Objective." *International Journal of Operations and Production Management* 21, no. 12, pp. 1553–72.

Kleindorfer, P.R., K. Singhal, and L.N. Wassenhove. 2005. "Sustainable Operations Management." *Production and Operations Management* 14, no. 4, pp. 482–92.

Kriz, W.C. 2010. "A Systemic-Constructivist Approach to the Facilitation and Debriefing of Simulations and Games." *Simulation and Gaming* 41, no. 5, pp. 663–80.

Laasch, O., and R. Conaway. 2014. *Principles of Responsible Management: Glocal Sustainability, Responsibility, and Ethics*. New York, NY: Cengage Learning.

Lederman, L.C. 1992. "Debriefing: Toward a Systematic Assessment of Theory and Practice." *Simulation and Gaming* 23, no. 2, pp. 145–60.

Lewis, M.A., and H.R. Maylor. 2007. "Game Playing and Operations Management Education." *International Journal of Production Economics* 105, no. 1, pp. 134–49.

Linton, J.D., R. Klassen, and V. Jayaraman. 2007. "Sustainable Supply Chains: An Introduction." *Journal of Operations Management* 25, no. 6, pp. 1075–82.

Longoni, A., and R. Cagliano. 2015. "Environmental and Social Sustainability Priorities: Their Integration in Operations Strategies." *International Journal of Operations and Production Management* 35, no. 2, pp. 216–45.

Lorenzo, O., P. Esqueda, and J. Larson. 2010. "Safety and Ethics in the Global Workplace: Asymmetries in Culture and Infrastructure." *Journal of Business Ethics* 92, no. 1, pp. 87–106.

Macpherson, J.A.E. 2008. "Safety, Risk Acceptability, and Morality." *Science and Engineering Ethics* 14, no. 3, pp. 377–90.

Mathews, C.M., and M. Spector. 2015. "U.S. Weighs Wire-Fraud Charge Against GM Over Ignition Switch Recall." *The Wall Street Journal*, June 9.

Mayer, B.W., K.M. Dale, K.A. Fraccastoro, and G. Moss. 2011. "Improving Transfer of Learning: Relationship to Methods of Using Business Simulation." *Simulation and Gaming* 42, no. 1, pp. 64–84.

Merriam-Webster. n.d. "Conundrum." www.merriam-webster.com/dictionary/conundrum (accessed December 8, 2015).

Molla, G.A., W.B. Salgedo, and Y.K. Lemu. 2015. "Prevalence and Determinants of Work Related Injuries Among Small and Medium Scale Industry Workers in Bahir Dar Town, North West Ethiopia." *Annals of Occupational and Environmental Medicine* 27, no. 1, p. 12.

Montero, M.J., R.A. Araque, and J.M. Rey. 2009. "Occupational Health and Safety in the Framework of Corporate Social Responsibility." *Safety Science* 47, no. 10, pp. 1440–45.

Pagell, M., D. Johnston, A. Veltri, R. Klassen, and M. Biehl. 2014. "Is Safe Production an Oxymoron?" *Production and Operations Management* 23, no. 7, pp. 1161–75.

Pasin, F., and H. Giroux. 2011. "The Impact of a Simulation Game on Operations Management Education." *Computers and Education* 57, no. 1, pp. 1240–54.

Porto, M.F.S., and C.M. Freitas. 1996. "Major Chemical Accidents in Industrializing Countries: The Socio-Political Amplification of Risk." *Risk Analysis* 16, no. 1, pp. 19–29.

Porto, M.F.S., and C.M. Freitas. 2003. "Vulnerability and Industrial Hazards in Industrializing Countries: An Integrative Approach." *Futures* 35, no. 7, pp. 717–36.

Reid, R.D., and N.R. Sanders. 2012. *Operations Management*. 5th ed. New York: John Wiley and Sons.

Renjith, V., and G. Madhu. 2010. "Individual and Societal Risk Analysis and Mapping of Human Vulnerability to Chemical Accidents in the Vicinity of an Industrial Area." *International Journal of Applied Engineering Research* 1, no. 2, pp. 135–48.

Seuring, S., and M. Müller. 2008. "From a Literature Review to a Conceptual Framework for Sustainable Supply Chain Management." *Journal of Cleaner Production* 16, no. 15, pp. 1699–710.

Sims, R.R. 2002. "Debriefing Experiential Learning Exercises in Ethics Education." *Teaching Business Ethics* 6, no. 2, pp. 179–97.

Snow, S.C., F.L. Gehlen, and J.C. Green. 2002. "Different Ways to Introduce a Business Simulation: The Effect on Student Performance." *Simulation and Gaming* 33, no. 4, pp. 526–32.

Stewart, W.H., D.E. Ledgerwood, and R.C. May. 1996. "Educating Business Schools About Safety and Health is No Accident." *Journal of Business Ethics* 15, no. 8, pp. 919–26.

Takala, J., P. Hämäläinen, K.L. Saarela, L.Y. Yun, K. Manickam, T.W. Jin, P. Heng, C. Tjong, L.G. Kheng, and S. Lim. 2014. "Global Estimates of the Burden of Injury and Illness at Work in 2012." *Journal of Occupational and Environmental Hygiene* 11, no. 5, pp. 326–37.

Tan, K.H., Y.K. Tse, and P.L. Chung. 2010. "A Plug and Play Pathway Approach for Operations Management Games Development." *Computers and Education* 55, no. 1, pp. 109–17.

Thatcher, D.C. 1990. "Promoting Learning Through Games and Simulations." *Simulation and Gaming* 21, no. 3, pp. 262–73.

Umphress, E.E., and J.B. Bingham. 2011. "When Employees Do Bad Things for Good Reasons: Examining Unethical Pro-Organizational Behaviors." *Organization Science* 22, no. 3, pp. 621–40.

WCED (World Commission on Environment Development). 1987. *Our Common Future: Report of the World Commission on Environment and Development*. Oxford: Oxford University Press.

Winter, M., and A.M. Knemeyer. 2013. "Exploring the Integration of Sustainability and Supply Chain Management: Current State and Opportunities for Future Inquiry." *International Journal of Physical Distribution and Logistics Management* 43, no. 1, pp. 18–38.

Wu, Z., and M. Pagell. 2011. "Balancing Priorities: Decision-Making in Sustainable Supply Chain Management." *Journal of Operations Management* 29, no. 6, pp. 577–90.

Zwetsloot, G.I.J.M. 2004. *Corporate Social Responsibility and Safety and Health at Work*. Luxembourg: European Agency for Safety and Health at Work.

Post-Reading Questions

1. The author argued that safety concerns in operations management is an important sustainability concept and practice. Do you agree? Why or why not?
2. Corporate sustainability and sustainability in operations is considered to be an ethical imperative, but it is difficult to determine "how safe is safe enough?" across different industries. With this dilemma, how do companies know if they are acting ethically?
3. The author argues that the issues presented are ethical conundrums with no right or wrong answer and that good ethical judgment is needed to solve them. How do you measure and regulate good ethical judgment?

Applied Ethics Case: British Petroleum Deepwater Horizon

American oil companies' offshore oil drilling started in the 1930s, 1 mile off of the coast of Louisiana. Early efforts to pursue oil deposits in the Gulf of Mexico's were first focused in the shallow waters that hugged the coastline. Although offshore oil drilling in the Gulf was largely restricted to shallow waters (−656 feet), increasingly new and large oil field discoveries were deeper (+3,281 feet) below the surface of the ocean.

Deep water offshore oil drilling, with its increased technology, expense, and risk, required that the exploration investment would give a significant return on investment. In order to meet the world's increased demand for energy, British Petroleum (BP), like other companies, calculated with sophisticated business modeling where it could, and should, drill for oil while simultaneously mitigating risk to its capital, political, and social assets.

On the night of April 20, 2010, a natural gas surge erupted from within the drilling line of the BP Deepwater Horizon oil rig. This resulted in a massive fiery explosion that consumed the drilling platform and killed 11 workers. The semi-submersible drilling rig, leased to BP and operated by Transocean, a subsidiary of Halliburton, burned and sank, tearing from the sea floor the drilling pipe attached to the well drilled into a large oil deposit known as the Thunder Horse field. The tragic deaths and the property damage triggered immediate investigations by the Department of the Interior and the Department of Homeland Security the next day. However, there was no immediate concern about oil being spilled from the ruptured oil well. Federal safety regulations require that rigs such as BP's Deepwater Horizon have blowout containment equipment for just such a crisis. Two days after the explosion and after sending a remote-controlled robot to the underwater oil well site, BP reported that no oil was leaking, and it seemed that a worst crisis had been averted.

That assessment changed for the worse when, on April 24, BP reported that up to one thousand barrels per day were, in fact, leaking from the oil well. Three days later the U.S.

Coast Guard increased that estimate to five thousand barrels per day. By the end of April, the nation's attention was riveted on the BP Deepwater Horizon oil spill crisis and the ongoing, but failed, efforts by BP to cap the gushing oil leak.

By the middle of May, it was estimated twelve thousand to nineteen thousand barrels were escaping per day. On July 15, after several failed attempt at stopping the leak, BP lowered and tested a temporary cap for the well that would capture and divert oil to oil tanker ships above and/or close the well entirely until relief wells could be drilled. On July 16, the federal government and BP officials proclaimed that the cap test was successful and, after 89 days of free-flowing oil into the Gulf of Mexico, the BP Deepwater Horizon oil well was temporarily closed. On September 19, 2010 BP confirmed that the well was permanently sealed.

The criticism and scope of the crisis, safety standards, and social responsibility were overwhelming for BP's board of directors, and Tony Hayward's seven-year tenure as CEO ended on October 1, 2010. In the nearly four years that Hayward led the company, the count of reported recordable injury frequency (RIF) measuring the number of reported work-related incidents that result in a fatality or injury per 200,000 hours worked fell among employees and contractors—an admirable safety accomplishment for that industry. Yet there continued to be ethical, safety, and legal concerns for BP during Hayward's tenure.

1. Were Hayward's efforts to reform BP safety practices insufficient?
2. Had there not been enough time for Hayward to change the ethical culture of BP?
3. Is it impossible to change the ethical safety culture of a multi-national corporation? Why or why not?

Videos Retrieved from the Internet

"How Do You Define Accountability in a Safety Culture?"

https://www.youtube.com/watch?v=YrJFZF_lcdI

This is about developing accountability in an undefined organization culture.

Internet Sites on Ethical Climate and Safety

"Ethical Climate and Workplace Safety Behavior: An Empirical Investigation"

https://link.springer.com/article/10.1007/s10551-007-9452-y

This is an academic article examining the important but neglected link between workplace safety-enhancing behavior and ethics.

"Safety Culture or Safety Climate"

https://dealwithittraining.co.uk/the-difference-between-safety-culture-and-safety-climate/

This is an analysis of the use of the terms *safety culture* and *safety climate*.

"The Effects of Safety Culture and Ethical Leadership on Safety Performance"

https://commons.erau.edu/cgi/viewcontent.cgi?article=1200&context=edt

This is a dissertation exploring the topic.

"Ethical Climate, Ethics Stress, and the Job Satisfaction of Nurses and Social Workers in the United States"

https://www.sciencedirect.com/science/article/abs/pii/S0277953607003255

This is a review of the ethical culture and safety impacting nursing care.

"Ethical Culture"

https://www.ethicalsystems.org/content/corporate-culture

This is a discussion of how ethical culture represents "how we do things around here *in relation to ethics and ethical behavior in the organization.*"

"Ethical Issues in Patient Safety"

https://www.who.int/patientsafety/research/ethical_issues/en/

This is a World Health Organization document reflecting on the specific ethical questions that can arise in the conduct of patient safety research.

Section VII

Public Affairs and Ethical Business

"We do not say that a man who takes no interest in public affairs is a man who minds his own business. We say he has no business being here at all."
Pericles

Section 7 is a reading from Robert N. Lussier and Herbert Sherman's book *Business, Society, and Government Essentials: Strategy and Applied Ethics*. The section is a discussion of four major concepts. The first concept is a discussion of stakeholder management and ethics. In this section, the authors discuss the changing nature of business thinking from a shareholder to a stakeholder management approach and the need to ethically balance internal and external interests.

This section broadens the discussion of stakeholder management and applies it to public affairs and issues management. We first discuss public affairs activities and functions, then managing public affairs, followed by issues management, which is part of public affairs management. We end by explaining how issues management helps the business prevent and prepare to manage crises.

In the third section the authors provide an in-depth discussion of crises management including developing a crises team, monitoring and risk assessment, crises communication, and post-crises analysis.

Finally, the authors present their five-stage analysis for dealing with stakeholders. This five-stage strategic analysis presents a framework for critically thinking about issues and stakeholders in the professional and personal arenas.

Concepts discussed include issue identification, interested strategic stakeholders, incentives of stakeholders, information objectives, and interaction strategies. Throughout the reading cases are used to illustrate the various concepts presented by the authors.

Pre-Reading Questions

- What is stakeholder management?
- What is public affairs management?
- What is crises management?

Reading 7.1

Strategic Stakeholder and Ethical Public Affairs, Issues, and Crisis Management

Robert N. Lussier and Herbert Sherman

Learning Outcomes

In this chapter, you will find out the answers to these key questions:

- How do you use a stakeholder approach to management?
- What are public affairs and how do you manage them?
- How do you conduct a strategic analysis to develop strategies for dealing with public affairs?

After studying this chapter, you should be able to:

1. Describe stakeholder management and the need to balance stockholder and other stakeholder interests
2. Differentiate public affairs management from issues management
3. Identify the three-phase process of issues management
4. Define *crisis* and discuss the four stages of crisis management, including the 3 As of crisis communication
5. List and briefly describe the 5 Is of strategic analysis
6. Categorize the issue life cycle stages with the strategic focus for each stage
7. Define the following key terms (in order of appearance in the chapter):

stakeholder management	crisis management stages	objectives
strategic stakeholders	3As of crisis	writing objectives
public affairs (PA)	communication	model

Robert N. Lussier and Herbert Sherman, "Strategic Stakeholder and Ethical Public Affairs, Issues, and Crisis Management," *Business, Society, and Government Essentials: Strategy and Applied Ethics*, pp. 38-69, 72-74. Copyright © 2014 by Taylor & Francis Group. Reprinted with permission.

public affairs management	5 Is of strategic analysis	supportive information
issues management	issues to business	information strategies
issues management process	issues life cycle	interaction strategies
crisis	strategic stakeholders with incentives	

Chapter Outline

The Strategic Stakeholder Approach to Management and Ethics
    From the Stockholder to the Stakeholder Approach
    Stakeholder Management and Ethics
    Balancing Owner and Other Stakeholder Interests

Public Affairs and Issues Management
    Public Affairs Activities and Functions
    Public Affairs Management
    Issues Management
    Issues Management Can Preclude Crisis Management

Crisis Management
1. Developing the Crisis Team
2. Planning—Risk Assessment, Monitoring, and Crisis Prevention
3. Managing the Crisis—Communication
4. Analyzing Post Crisis

Strategic Analysis: The 5 Is
1. Issue Identification
2. Interested Strategic Stakeholders
3. Incentive of Stakeholders
4. Information—Objectives
5. Interaction Strategies

What's This Chapter About?

[...] The four major concept sections are closely interrelated.

    We begin with a discussion of the stakeholder approach to management and ethics. Next we discuss public affairs (how business interacts with stakeholders) and issues management (a public affairs management approach to interacting with stakeholders). Our third section extends issues management by describing how to identify and prevent potential crises and how to deal with crises that weren't prevented.

Our last section pulls the chapter together by presenting a five-stage strategic analysis for dealing with stakeholders. The 5 Is analysis presents a framework for critically thinking about issues and stakeholders in your personal and professional lives. It is a helpful guide in case analysis.

Case
Can Philip Morris Now Take a Breath of Fresh Air?

Victory is sweet, but is it really? The Philip Morris USA (PM) division of the Altria Group had been bombarded for many years by class action suits alleging that they knew their tobacco-based products were a major contributor to cancer-related illness for their consumers. In November 1998, the industry settled with 46 states for a total of $40 billion. Beginning in 1999, Philip Morris spent about $100 million per year on a TV campaign attempting to mitigate the highly negative publicity.[1]

Despite the settlement and the advertising campaigns, the problem was far from over. In April 2003, PM lost a $10.1 billion class action suit dealing with the claim of false advertising of light cigarettes.[2] CEO Louis Camilleri threatened to take the firm into bankruptcy. Altria's future was in doubt, and investors who normally focused on high dividends dumped the stock, despite its generous 9.1 percent yield. Some continued to shun Altria, despite a dividend yield that remained above 4 percent in 2005 and a low of 14 times next year's expected earnings trading range. Some major mutual fund managers said they weren't willing to risk owning the stock and watching the company possibly lose its litigation battles.[3]

However, the air seemed to clear after a 2005 decision in which the Illinois Supreme Court threw out the $10.1 billion class action lawsuit. Analysts claimed the court ruling was a major victory for PM and the Altria Group.[4] At the investor conference, Camilleri said the company was optimistic about its legal prospects and looked toward a highly optimistic future for the firm. Altria, however, still faced numerous legal challenges.[5] In 2011, thinking that the air had finally cleared, Camilleri claimed that cigarettes, though harmful and addictive, are "'not that hard' to quit."[6] His comment caused an uproar with shareholders because it followed a statement on ABC News by a nurse within the tobacco industry that "tobacco kills more than 400,000 Americans and 5 million people worldwide each year." Many believed it was a questionable statement to make given that some studies showed it may be just as hard to quit smoking cigarettes as it is to quit certain illegal drugs. Camilleri in his statement also noted that the company was working toward making tobacco products more regulated so that more Americans can quit easier; yet many challenged this statement in light of continued cigarette advertisements indirectly targeting adolescents.

The following questions are related to the Philip Morris case. Answers can be found within the chapter.

1. Describe Altria Group's (PM's) approach to management as presented in this case; is it stockholder or stakeholder?
2. Who are some of the strategic/critical stakeholders in this case?
3. How does PM interact with its stakeholders in this case?
4. What are the key issues in this case for PM?
5. What stage of the issues life-cycle model does this case reflect?
6. What are the market reaction and consequences of PM's nonmarket strategy of continuing to directly fight lawsuits in the courts and in the news media?

The Strategic Stakeholder Approach to Management and Ethics

In this section, we discuss the change from the stockholder to stakeholder approach to management, explain what stakeholder management is, and describe the need to ethically balance owner and other stakeholder interests.

From the Stockholder to the Stakeholder Approach

The traditional *stockholder* a*pproach* to management focused on meeting the needs of the owners/stockholders and maximizing profits, without regard for other business stakeholders described in Chapter 1. The power of various stakeholders has risen over the years,[7] and the paradigm has shifted from the stockholder to the stakeholder approach to management.[8] The stakeholder approach of trying to create a win-win for all stakeholders has been justified as a necessary precondition to stockholder value maximization.[9] However, with multiple stakeholders with different interests, it is often difficult to create a win for all stakeholders. But a win-win is the ultimate goal.

Today, managers realize that generating long-term value depends on responding to critical stakeholders, so they are developing a stakeholder orientation.[10] Thus, to be successful and maximize profits, businesses are focusing on being ethical with critical stakeholders that directly affect business performance.[11] Stakeholder theory is a popular area of research.[12] In fact, research provides evidence that businesses using the stakeholder approach are more successful than those using the stockholder approach, and most successful large businesses use a stakeholder approach.[13] For example, **Shell Oil Company** integrated the stakeholder management approach into its business practice worldwide as a long-term comprehensive strategy.[14]

Personal and Professional Applications

1. The CEO of Land O' Lakes suggests that you should help others to get ahead in their career. Do you agree?

> Philip Morris Case Question 1: Describe Altria Group's (PM's) approach to management as presented in this case; is it stockholder or stakeholder?
>
> PM appears to be employing a stockholder approach by focusing on the needs of the owners/stockholders and maximizing profits without regard for any other business stakeholders, especially their customers who claim to have been injured by their products and lured into smoking light cigarettes through false advertising. Rather than discontinue manufacturing these products and/or settling injurious claims, PM chose to confront their consumers and detractors through the court system and in the media.

Learning Outcome 1: Describe stakeholder management and the need to balance stockholder and other stakeholder interests.

Stakeholder Management and Ethics

***Stakeholder management** is based on making decisions on specific issues in an ethical manner in ways that provide value to strategic stakeholders.* Thus, stakeholder management includes being ethical by trying to create a win-win situation for strategic stakeholders.[15] It is common to differentiate between primary and secondary stakeholders. Thus, we refer to strategic stakeholders as primary, and other stakeholders as secondary. ***Strategic stakeholders** are critically affected by firm action, and/or they can affect firm performance.* Recall (Chapter 1) that stakeholders are affected by the business and can affect firm performance. The difference between primary and secondary stakeholders is the word "critical."

Critical refers to those stakeholder interests that have direct financial impact on the business (benefit or loss). Advocate interest groups and the government are critical stakeholders when they protect or hurt other stakeholders. All other stakeholders indirectly affected are stakeholders for the issue in question. So the business must focus more on strategic stakeholders because of their ability to help or hurt the firm, than on secondary stakeholders who have less impact.

Strategic also refers to developing a nonmarket strategy that can be integrated with the market strategy. Managers and firms can't give all stakeholders whatever they want because resources are limited, thus requiring the business to make choices as to which stakeholders' requests will be fulfilled and which will not. Sometimes the strategic answer to a specific stakeholder group's request, therefore, has to be no, especially when the stakeholder is a limited special interest person or group whose demand is not supported by the majority of the business stakeholders. Thus, strategic planning considers stakeholders.[16]

Personal and Professional Applications

2. Select a business you work(ed) for. Does it use a stockholder or a stakeholder approach?

> Philip Morris Case Question 2: Who are some of the strategic/critical stakeholders in this case?
>
> Besides the stockholders (including mutual fund managers), strategic/critical stakeholders include consumers (especially those engaged in class action suits), other litigants (the 48 states that settled), the tobacco industry, the various court systems, the Department of Justice, and the news media.

Balancing Owner and Other Stakeholder Interests

Managers, who are paid employees, are agents of owners/stockholders and they must look out for owners/stockholders' interests and make a profit; if they don't, they are often fired. Owners are usually strategic stakeholders, but other stakeholders vary by issue. Thus, managers need to balance the needs of owners and other stakeholders, attempting to ethically create value for both.[17] Notice that we said "try" to create value and win-win situations.

In reality, managers must make decisions that benefit (that is, produce positive circumstances while preventing negative consequences) business but don't necessarily benefit other stakeholders. For example, when a business or one of its units is not profitable, managers may implement layoffs, which is not beneficial to the employees and the community.

Successful top-level managers use the stakeholder approach to create a culture in which everyone in the organization focuses on stakeholders. Thus, they create a stakeholder corporation.[18] Successful companies today are assessing stakeholder management performance and so are organizations, including the **Dow Jones** Sustainability Indexes.[19]

Personal and Professional Applications

3. Give an example of a specific decision a business you work(ed) for that did *not* create value and a win-win situation for stakeholders. Be sure to identify the stakeholders and how they were hurt by the decision.

Public Affairs and Issues Management

This section broadens the discussion of stakeholder management and applies it to public affairs and issues management. We first discuss public affairs activities and functions, then managing public affairs, followed by issues management, which is part of public affairs management. We end by explaining how issues management helps the business prevent and prepare to manage crises.

Public Affairs Activities and Functions

***Public affairs* (PA)** *refers to how business interacts with stakeholders.* It is also about firm stakeholder relationships.[20] PA is about dealing with relevant stakeholders regarding a current issue that needs to be addressed through nonmarket strategies. Many terms are used to refer to public affairs, which can make PA somewhat confusing. Different companies that perform the same PA activities and functions may use different terms, such as public relations, corporate relations, external affairs, public policy, corporate communications, or corporate social responsibility. Issues management and crisis management also refer to PA. See Figure 7.1.1 for a list of the PA activities and functions of 250 large and medium-sized U.S. companies ranked by use. Many firms hire public relations agencies to help them perform their PA functions; public relations firms offer, among other benefits, contacts and an independent view of the firm and its issue. During all PA functions, managers must be ethical; unethical behavior should be reported through whistle blowing, which we discuss in the next chapter.

Activity/Function	% using	Activity/Function	% using
Political action committee (PAC)	89	Employee volunteer programs	66
Issues management	84	Media relations	64
State government relations	84	Public relations	61
Local government relations	77	Employee communications	59
Community relations	75	Strategic philanthropy	55
Direct corporate contributions	75	Regulatory affairs	43
Business/trade associations	73	Educational relations	34
Public policy group relations	73	International public affairs	32
Grassroots communication	71	Environmental affairs	23
Corporate foundation	71	Stockholder relations	21

FIGURE 7.1.1 Public affairs activities and functions

Source: Adapted from D. C. Richards, "Corporate Public Affairs: Necessary Cost or Value-Added Asset?" *Journal of Public Affairs* 3(1) (2003): 41.

Personal and Professional Applications

4. Select a business you work(ed) for and describe the public affairs activities and functions it performs.

> Philip Morris Case Question 3: How does PM interact with its stakeholders in this case?
> Although the case is not inclusive of all public affairs activities at PM, it does document the use of the news media, state government interactions (settlement with states), business/trade associations (industry settlement), stockholder relations (investor conference), and legal/regulatory affairs.

The scope and complexity of PA increased to address social activist concerns and significant federal laws in the early 1970s and included issues of discrimination, environmental protection, occupational health and safety, and consumer safety. Today, PA is broader in scope than public relations, but PA continues to include public relations, which is now often referred to as media relations. The use of PA communications is changing with the use of information technology and the Internet.[21]

Just as personnel management evolved to become human resources management, PA evolved from public relations. Thus, public relations executives have changed their title to "public affairs" executive. But whatever the title, PA practitioners formulate strategies to interact with stakeholders.[22]

The use of the term *public affairs* is illustrated in the title of **National Association of Schools of Public Affairs and Administration** (NASPAA) that accredits PA programs. Public affairs is a major focus of the master of public administration (MPA). The **Public Affairs Council** (**PAC**), based in Washington, D.C. (www.pac.org), is the leading international association for public affairs professionals. PAC is a nonpartisan, nonpolitical association whose mission is to advance the field of public affairs and to provide members with the training and information resources they need to achieve success while maintaining the highest ethical standards.[23]

Learning Outcome 2: Differentiate public affairs management from issues management.

Public Affairs Management

Public affairs management *is the process of developing corporate public policies and strategies regarding how the business will interact with stakeholders in the business, social, and government environments; it includes issues management, crisis management, and strategic analysis.*

Corporate public policies are general guidelines to influence how employees will interact with stakeholders. **Ford's** "Quality is job one" slogan reminds all employees to do quality work regardless of their position. Part of **JC Penney's** Statement of Business Ethics says it will "not seek an unfair advantage over our competitors," this is also a PA policy.

Why do businesses engage in PA management? Researchers find that PA has many activities and functions that must be managed effectively for the business to be successful. Firms that are more likely to be active in PA management are those that are significantly affected by government. To be more specific, firms highly dependent on government regulation or contracts for economic success, large firms, and those operating in more highly concentrated industries are more politically active.[24]

PA management policies and strategies are part of the overall nonmarket strategy, which, again, must be integrated with market strategies. For a review of nonmarket strategies, which are also called PA strategies, see Figure 7.1.4 (p. 248). The nonmarket strategies will be discussed in detail in later chapters.

With the increasing complexity of PA, many companies have created specialized departments, with titles such as Public Affairs Department, to manage it. With the emergence of PA departments, it is tempting for line managers to think that they are not responsible for PA. However, this is not the case. Line managers and employee actions are an integral part of PA management. For example, in 2010 when **Apple** came out with the iPhone 4 with its antenna design that caused reception problems, when **J&J** had to recall a halfdozen medicines, when **Facebook** was accused of privacy violations, and even worse when people died because of the **British Petroleum** (**BP**) Deepwater Horizon disaster, PA had to respond to the negative press and angry consumers.[25] Thus, all employees need to view PA as part of their day-to-day work, rather than the job of PA professionals.

As stated in our definition of PA management, issues management, crisis management, and strategic analysis are part of PA. We will discuss issues management in this section, crisis management in the next section, and strategic analysis in the last section.

Personal and Professional Applications

5. State some public policies affecting a business you work(ed) for that guide employees in their interactions with stakeholders in the business, social, and government environments.

Learning Outcome 3: Identify the three-phase process of issues management.

Issues Management

Issues management *is a public affairs management approach to identifying, monitoring, analyzing, and selecting public issues that may warrant nonmarket strategies.* Thus, PA professionals develop and implement issues management. Issues managers may be members of the *Issue Management Council* (www.issuemanagement.org) professional association.

PA and issues management are different while being closely related. PA deals with current issues that need nonmarket strategies, whereas issues management deals with identifying future issues that may need nonmarket strategies—but may not. For example, you would want to know about potential new laws and regulations, so you use issues management. If the government begins to draft new laws or regulations, the issue would become a PA matter that calls for the development of current nonmarket strategies. As long as the government does not implement new regulations, the process of monitoring the issue continues as part of ongoing issues management. So PA nonmarket strategies often come from issues management, but not always. Sometimes the source is a crisis that requires immediate PA nonmarket strategies.

Opportunities and Threats. Issues management is used to anticipate and respond to both threats and opportunities. Business looks for trends that will benefit the company. For example, the aging population trend continues to create a large market for products and health care needed by older people. Threats are discussed next and throughout the book.

The Issues Management Process. The three steps commonly involved in the *issues management process* include: *(1) scanning the environment to identify issues and trends that will affect the business; (2) evaluating the impact issues will have on the firm and ranking issues by priority; and (3) conducting a strategic analysis to develop strategies for dealing with high-priority public affairs issues.* Issues management continues our focus on stakeholder interactions.

1. **Scanning the environment to identify issues and trends that will affect the business.** For example, new legislation or regulation is an issue of concern to business, such as the financial reform under the Dodd-Frank bill, requiring interaction with stakeholders. Issues develop over time and require that the monitoring process be ongoing. Employees scan publications, such as newspapers, magazines, and specialty publications, and the Internet to develop a list of issues. Several professional associations have publications that discuss issues facing the profession or trade group. Firms also pay scanning fees to experts who provide summaries of publications and offer consultation services. Businesses commonly develop a list of issues and may conduct surveys to determine stakeholder views and public sentiment on those and emerging issues.
2. **Evaluating the impact issues will have on the firm and ranking issues by priority.** With a list of issues compiled, the next step is to determine which ones can benefit or hurt the firm the most. Companies use different systems. For example, **Xerox** used a process of categorizing issues into three classifications: (1) high priority

issues that management must deal with; (2) nice-to-know issues that are interesting but not critical or urgent; and (3) questionable events or practices that may not become issues. **PPG Industries** groups issues by their level of importance: Priority A issues must be dealt with, Priority B issues warrant monitoring by line managers, and Priority C issues are monitored only by the PA department.

3. **Conducting a strategic analysis to develop strategies for dealing with high-priority PA issues**. Monitoring the results of strategic action is also part of the analysis. Strategic analysis to develop strategies for dealing with high-priority issues is the heart of issues management, so we discuss strategic analysis as a separate section, after crisis management.

Many firms use issues management software to measure PA efforts in all three steps. **Cymfony, Biz360, VMS,** and **Cision** (formerly **Bacon's Information**) now provide real-time updates on what all aspects of the media are saying about a company, its latest products, and its competitors. Most issues management software is a monthly or annual service, and its price depends on the number of issues or words the firm wants to monitor. The information is delivered in real time to the firm via a software dashboard that resides on the firm's computer desktop.

Some companies use blogs to provide information to the public regarding industry issues.[26] **Google**'s legal counsel and others have blogged about controversies, such as copying books, to state why it is engaging in such practices. Steve Langdon, senior manager of corporate PR, says blogs are a way of quickly providing information about complex topics to the general public. Thus, Google may have been the first company to bring blogs into the realm of issues management.[27] For a review of the issues management process, see Figure 7.1.2. Note that the issues process is not linear; you can work on more than one phase of the process and/or return to prior phases. The firm continually monitors the issue and makes appropriate changes in all three phases of the process. The business may also deal with multiple issues and phases at the same time.

Personal and Professional Applications

6. Select a business you work(ed) for and discuss its issues management process. Be sure to state any sources it uses/d to gather information on issues.

1. Scanning the environment to identify issues and trends that will affect the business ↔	2. Evaluating the impact issues will have on the firm and ranking issues by priority ↔	3. Conducting a strategic analysis to develop strategies for dealing with high-priority public affairs issues ↔

FIGURE 7.1.2 The issues management process

Issues Management Can Preclude Crisis Management

Of course, not all crises can be planned for and prevented, but many crises can be anticipated through effective issues management programs by identifying and managing risks before they become disasters.[28] Issues managers identify issues that can escalate into a crisis. The better managers deal with issues, the less likely they are to become crises. Effective issues management assists the firm in preventing crises and in planning for crises that may occur. While in recent years **BP** has been in crises, **Exxon** has managed to avoid a crisis.[29] Thus, issues management is a form of precrisis management. But crisis management goes beyond issues management. So let's discuss it separately.

Learning Outcome 4: Define *crisis* and discuss the four stages of crisis management, including the 3 As of crisis communication.

Crisis Management

Managers need to understand the difference between a problem issue and a crisis. A *crisis is a major unexpected event that has a large negative consequence.* Large negative consequences include injuries, deaths, and large financial costs. Cost is relative to the size of the firm; for example, $1 million would put most small firms out of business, whereas it is a less consequential amount to big businesses like **Toyota**. Recall the crisis in the auto industry and financial crises that led to the federal bailout to prevent **GM** and **Chrysler** and many of the large banks and financial houses from going bankrupt.[30] The crises of current times seem much more extreme than crises of the past.[31] The financial meltdown and other crises prompted some business schools to retool some courses to focus on crisis management.[32] **AIG**, needing a $130 billion government bailout, started offering crisis insurance to businesses in 2011.[33]

> **ETHICAL DILEMMA 2.1 Can American Airlines Fly Out of Turbulence?**
>
> AMR Corporation, the parent company to American Airlines, which has been experiencing financial problems, filed for Chapter 11 bankruptcy protection in February of 2011. Company financials indicated that from 2007 until 2011 revenues went from $22.94 billion to $23.98 billion (its lowest revenue of $19.92 billion occurred in 2009) with net income going into a nose dive in 2008 all the way down to $1.98 billion in 2011.[34]
>
> According to a *New York Times* article the purpose of filing for bankruptcy protection was to "reduce labor costs and shed a heavy debt burden," copying

the tactic of other airline companies who had already successfully filed for bankruptcy. AMR's CEO also stated, "Our board decided that it was necessary to take this step now to restore the company's profitability, operating flexibility and financial strength."[35]

Yet a *Forbes* article warned that this bankruptcy filing could lead to less frequency of service to airports and open renegotiations with labor unions, which could harm passengers and employees if not handled in the correct manner.[36] Potential bad press could result in a loss of faith among passengers and employees of AMR, and therefore loss of quality personnel, service, and revenues (profits).

With a depressed economy, rising competition driven by Internet sales, increasing partnerships and alliances between airlines, limited airplane suppliers (Boeing and Airbus), rising oil prices, lack of capital, and now bad press, AMR is clearly flying through stormy weather.[37] Can AMR figure out how to steer its AA into clear skies and avoid further turbulence?

Questions

1. How would an understanding of PA and issues management help AMR better understand the problems they are facing?
2. What steps should AMR take in addressing this issue?
3. Who would be helped or hurt by the board declaring bankruptcy?
4. Given your answer to question 3, if you were on the board, would you have voted for bankruptcy? Why or why not?

We tend to have the mentality that a crisis will not happen to our business because crises tend to have a low probability of occurrence. But crisis can happen in any organization, such as violence (workers or outsiders killing employees and customers—**9/11/01 terrorist attacks** and **Virginia Tech**), accidents (oil spills—**Exxon Valdez** and **BP**), and natural disasters (hurricanes—**Katrina** and **Rita**, floods, fires). One event often causes a crisis in many organizations, and the firms can be far from the initial events.[38]

A crisis can also have long-term negative effects on brands, managers, and company reputations.[39] For example, **BP** (oil spill), **Tiger Woods, Inc.** (affair), and **Toyota** (safety problems) all are working to turn around negative situations.[40] In this section, we discuss a four-stage crisis management process.[41] **The crisis management stages** include: (1) *developing the crisis team;* (2) *planning;* (3) *managing the crisis—communication;* and (4) *analyzing post crisis.*

1. Developing the Crisis Team

The crisis leader must be supported by a strong team. A crisis management team is usually led by a senior-level executive, often the CEO when the event actually happens.[42] The team has a mix of representatives from all sectors of the organization along with external members, such as a trauma team. The team should work together, not simply divide the tasks, which leads to politics. Members can challenge one another's ideas without resorting to personal attacks, engage in debates without coercion or blame, and unite behind decisions once they are made. Members don't seem to circumvent or undermine each other, instead they work cooperatively, sharing information and encouraging teamwork.

2. Planning—Risk Assessment, Monitoring, and Crisis Prevention

Management at all levels needs to identify and manage risks before they become crises.[43] Good crisis management requires planning.[44] In many events, there are warning signs of the potential crisis. For example, it was known that **BP** had safety problems and the captain of the **Exxon** *Valdez* was repeatedly drunk on the job. People complained about **Toyota** safety problems at least a year before the recalls. Yet, nothing was really done until the oil spills and auto recalls. Most employees who kill people at work start with other acts of violence. Before a crisis some employees warn of the disaster to come. Natural disasters, like floods, are often predicted, giving some time to prepare and evacuate. Risk assessment and planning includes four parts:

- **Risk assessment and ranking**. The crisis team identifies potential events that could happen, determines the organization's necessary level of preparedness, and then makes plans to mitigate future risks.[45] They answer the question, Where are we vulnerable?, by engaging in "what-if" scenario analysis that focuses on creating realistic incidents under each crisis category. How likely is each crisis? **US Airways** and others, for example, recognize the risk of plane crashes.[46]

- **Risk monitoring**. The crisis management team needs the authority to require individuals and departments to keep logs of complaints, warnings, and incidents. It needs to look for increased activity and patterns. Will the event get worse? The crisis team needs to review the events and have a plan to take action when necessary.

- **Risk prevention and damage reduction strategies**. How can the crisis be prevented? What are the warning signs? How can damage be reduced if a crisis occurs? The best-case scenario is to prevent the crisis, followed by limiting the damage of a crisis. Identifying risk prevention and reduction strategies is great, but the plan must be followed up with monitoring, preventing, and limiting actions.

- **The crisis plan**. What is the plan to respond quickly to a crisis? **Exxon Mobil** maintains its own oil spill response teams and equipment stockpiles. It also has supported the establishment of a network of worldwide, industry-supported oil spill response organizations. **US Airways** has a crash playbook and has "dry run" emergency exercises at least three times a year at each airport it serves and has a network of employees who double as "Care Team" members who are dispatched to emergencies at a moment's notice. As a result of good crisis planning and implementing, it has been said that Flight 1549's water landing in the Hudson River in New York may become a model for crisis management.[47]

3. Managing the Crisis—Communication

Proper communication can help to maintain a positive company and brand reputation.[48] Once a crisis happens, the crisis leader and the crisis team must act immediately deal with it. The crisis leader needs to work with the crisis team, not go it alone, which includes putting into motion the crisis plan, adjusted to the situation. The communication plan must be implemented with good public relations,[49] as discussed next.

- **Selecting the spokesperson**. During the actual crisis, the CEO generally is the chief crisis officer,[50] but the CEO doesn't have to be the spokesperson. Companies need to select the right person to be the central voice. Don't throw the CEO in the middle of every story. In the **BP** crisis, former CEO Tony Hayward underplayed the gravity initially, and then he arguably overplayed it because he was on the defensive.[51] The crisis spokesperson should stay engaged, get out and communicate—not hide as Tiger Woods did—and send the message that there is nothing to hide.[52]

- **The crisis spokesperson should follow the "three As" of communicating during a crisis**. Before talking or writing about the crisis, a crisis team needs to plan what a spokesperson will say; using the 3 As helps. *The 3 As of crisis communication are: Acknowledge the crisis, state the Action to deal with the crisis, and state how the crisis will be Avoided in the future.*

    1. **Acknowledge**. Admit to the crisis. Be honest and straightforward. Tell the truth and don't lie or cover for the boss or the organization. But if a company is innocent, go on the offense and don't apologize.[53] **BP** tried to blame at least part of the Gulf oil spill on its partner **Transocean**, the company that owned and ran the vessel that exploded killing 11 men (9 Transocean employees and 2 BP workers) and causing the largest offshore oil spill, but Transocean will not admit even a portion of liability.[54]

2. **Action**. Tell what is being done to contain or repair the crisis damage. **Toyota** recalled more than 8 million vehicles because of several safety problems.[55] Handle those affected with utmost sensitivity; go the extra mile beyond the requirements of the situation. Following the plane crash, "Miracle on the Hudson," **US Airways** was cited as doing so. For example, staffers met the passengers with cash, dry clothes, and prepaid cell phones. Employees escorted each passenger to a new flight or a local NY hotel. They also arranged train tickets and rental cars for those who didn't want to fly.[56]

3. **Avoid**. Establish a plan to avoid a repeat crisis in the future. Although it was slow to acknowledge the safety crisis and take action, **Toyota** is working to regain market share by repairing its image with the help of ads that talk about its Star Safety System and showing that they are changing some processes on new models.

- **Communication**. A company today may have only minutes, not hours, to contain a crisis. With the Internet and cable television, the world often knows about a crisis before some managers and the employees. An organization should make itself accessible as quickly as possible. It is generally believed that "within an hour" of becoming aware that a crisis situation may exist, company officials must be prepared to issue an initial statement to the media and other key stakeholder groups, providing facts as they are known, and an indication of when additional details will be made available. However, it is important to balance the desire to say something right away with the need to get the facts. Managers typically speak too soon and have to eat most of what they said.[57] So again, plan the 3 As before speaking or writing about the crisis.

4. Analyzing Post Crisis

Top management should launch an evaluation (preferably conducted by an objective third party) of the organization's effectiveness in managing the crisis, with an assessment of its effectiveness in communicating with key stakeholder groups. The analysis should focus on questions pertaining to how effective the crisis team and the crisis management plan performed, how effectively the organization handled victims and family members, and what worked the least in mitigating the problem. This information is relevant for many reasons, the most important of which are the lessons learned that can help in preventing and minimizing future crises.

The **Institute for Crisis Management** (www.crisisexperts.com) is an excellent source of additional information on this topic. See Figure 7.1.3 for a review of the four crisis management stages, which, like issues management, is a continuing process.

1. Developing the crisis team
2. Planning—risk assessment, monitoring, and crisis prevention
3. Managing the crisis—communication
4. Analyzing post crisis

FIGURE 7.1.3 The crisis management stages

Personal and Professional Applications

7. Give an example of a business that did a good or poor job of handling a crisis. What did management do right or wrong?

Learning Outcome 5: List and briefly describe the 5 Is of strategic analysis.

ETHICAL DILEMMA 2.2 Susan G. Komen Foundation: Could a Painful Funding "Mastectomy" Have Been Avoided?

The Susan G. Komen for the Cure® is the global leader of the breast cancer movement, having invested more than $1.9 billion since inception in 1982. As the world's largest grassroots network of breast cancer survivors and activists, they are working to save lives, empower people, ensure quality care for all, and energize science to find the cures. They have become the largest source of nonprofit funds dedicated to the fight against breast cancer in the world.[58]

At the end of January 2012 Planned Parenthood announced that its preventive breast cancer funding from the Susan G. Komen foundation had been cut, and women's health advocates were immediately taking to the airwaves to make their dissatisfaction known, decrying the decision as a crass political calculation and urging Komen to reverse the decision. The organization defended its decision as part of an ongoing effort to exact "stronger performance criteria for our grantees," but many Planned Parenthood supporters have accused Komen of caving in to pressure from the political right in what they cast as an ongoing assault on abortion rights. Immediately after the announcement 26 Democratic senators had attached their names to a letter urging Komen to reverse its decision.

Many have pointed to Karen Handel, a new vice president to the Komen foundation, as a possible force behind the decision to cut off grant money to Planned Parenthood. Handel, who ran for governor of Georgia in 2010, describes herself as "staunchly pro-life" and frequently called for an end to abortion during her gubernatorial bid. At least one high-profile Komen staffer, Mollie Williams, resigned in protest over the decision to defund Planned Parenthood.

Regardless of whether the decision was borne out of political motivations, however, its impact has been to dramatically mobilize Planned Parenthood donors. Within 24 hours of the announcement Planned Parenthood had raised more than $400,000 online, mostly from small donors. Additionally, the Fikes Foundation gave Planned Parenthood a $250,000 grant toward starting the Emergency Breast Health Fund in the aftermath of the Komen decision. New York City Mayor Michael Bloomberg announced that he would match up to $250,000 donations from his personal wealth.[59]

1. How might the Komen Foundation have avoided this dilemma surrounding the funding cut before the decision was made?
2. Was the decision to cut Planned Parenthood funding an ethical one given the fact that Planned Parenthood provides other more controversial services besides breast cancer prevention?
3. How should the Komen Foundation handle this public relations crisis? What would you do?

Strategic Analysis: The 5 Is

Public affairs management is broad in scope and includes issues management and crisis management, and the heart of all three is strategic analysis. In other words, the analysis is used to determine strategies for interacting with stakeholders—PA. Strategic planning is important to businesses,[60] and businesses need to focus on stakeholders when developing strategies.[61]

Integrating market and nonmarket strategies is the primary focus of this entire book, and the text presents nonmarket concepts as integral to stakeholder management. Through a strategic analysis process, individuals develop and use critical thinking skills to analyze business issues and make better decisions in their personal and professional lives.

Researchers have suggested a methodical approach for analyzing stakeholder management. Among the many methods, with some variations, we have developed a detailed process for this text, which your professor may adapt to his or her preference. *The 5 Is strategic analysis* stages include: (1) issue identification; (2) interested strategic stakeholders; (3) incentive of *stakeholders; (4) information—objectives; and (5) interaction strategies.* A structured framework based on the 5 Is uses a table in case analysis. See the Appendix for a discussion of different case analyses methods and the option of using the Table. In this section, we discuss each of the 5 I stages.

1. Issue Identification

Logically, we need to start our analysis by knowing what the issue is. The sooner the issue is identified (often through issues management), the more time the business has to plan for and deal with it. Some businesses are good at issues management, are proactive, and take nonmarket strategic action to prevent the issue from being brought to the firm. But once the issue affects the business, a PA nonmarket strategy must be developed to deal with the stakeholder issue, even if the strategy is to take no action and monitor the issue. *Issues to business are usually brought to the company by any of its stakeholders because the firm is not meeting expectations and the stakeholder is pressing the firm to take action to meet its special interest.* Thus, PA management is often about solving problems under pressure from stakeholders.[62]

> Philip Morris Case Question 4: What are the key issues in this case for PM?
>
> Several of PM's stakeholder groups (consumers, state governments, and the Justice Department) have accused the firm (as well as the industry) of knowingly producing a harmful product and then falsely advertising that product. The situation has been exacerbated by recent public statements by the CEO. The issue for PM is how to minimize the economic damages that may directly (through fines) and indirectly (through depreciated stock prices) affect their stockholders.

Learning Outcome 6: Categorize the issue life-cycle stages with the strategic focus for each stage.

The Nonmarket Issues Life Cycle

Issues go through a life-cycle, as shown in Figure 7.1.4. *The **issues life cycle** includes: (1) identification and formation of the issue and public sentiment; (2) interested stakeholder formation; (3) issue brought to business for voluntary action; (4) legislative and regulation formation; and (5) enforcement and litigation.* The issue may be identified through the news media, and the issue may or may not be brought to business.

Stage 1	Stage 2	Stage 3	Stage 4	Stage 5
ISSUE				
Identification and formation of the issue and public sentiment (possibly news media coverage)	Interested stakeholder formation	Issue brought to business for voluntary action (may be skipped)	Legislative and regulation formation	Enforcement and litigation
STRATEGY				
Informational and *societal* strategies to influence the development of the issue	*Informational* and *societal* strategies, developing coalitions	Varies based on the issue and who brings it	*Political* lobbying to prevent or support change	*Legal*—comply with changes and avoid or bring lawsuits
Issue impact on the business increases with time and stages as managers have less ability to influence the stakeholders involved →				

FIGURE 7.1.4 The issues life cycle and strategy focus

Personal and Professional Applications

8. List some business issues and explain the stage of the life cycle each issue is in.

Strategies Change Over the Nonmarket Life Cycle. Note that the following strategies are from Figure 7.1.4 (p. 248). During the identification and formation of issues and stakeholders, stages 1 and 2, informational and societal strategies focus on affecting the development of the issue including developing coalitions to influence stakeholders for the issue. When the issue is brought to the business, stage 3, strategies vary based on the issue and who brings it to the firm. At the point of legislation and regulation formation, stage 4, political strategies focus on preventing or supporting the changes, primarily through lobbying. Once the law or regulation for the issue has been passed and is enforced, stage 5, the strategic focus is on legal compliance, damage control, and avoiding or bringing lawsuits.

> Philip Morris Case Question 5: What stage of the issues life-cycle model does this case reflect?
>
> This case describes a stage 5 litigation situation in which PM is trying to minimize the damages caused by a series of lawsuits brought by consumers and numerous state governments.

Issue Questions. The two major questions that you must answer during this first step of the analysis are: (1) What is the issue? (2) At what stage of the life cycle is the issue? With this information, you proceed to the second step of the strategic analysis. If you are conducting a case analysis using the Table in the Appendix, this first I analysis goes in column 1.

2. Interested Strategic Stakeholders

Developing stakeholder public policies requires an understanding of stakeholders.[63] A good approach is to first identify the category of stakeholder using Model 1.1. Next, specifically list subgroups by name. For example, which competitors, suppliers, societal interest groups, or government agencies are interested, or have a stake, in the identified issue? If the issue is in life cycle stages 1 or 2, it is not as easy to identify the strategic stakeholders that are critically affected by or that can affect firm performance, as it is in stages 3–5.

Identify Strategic Stakeholders that Are For and Against the Firm. The second part of strategic stakeholder interest is determining which stakeholders can benefit through opportunities the issue presents, and which stakeholders can lose something through the threat of the issue, Will the specific strategic stakeholders be for or against the firm's stance on the issue? For example, if the **Food and Drug Administration** (**FDA**) wants to make it more difficult for pharmaceutical companies to bring new drugs to the market, several specific societal interest groups and public sentiment may be in favor of the FDA's efforts. However, the industry competitors will be against it, and will likely use the help of industry associations and/or form a coalition to fight new regulations. Business needs to determine which stakeholders it is up against and which stakeholders may support it.

Interest of Strategic Stakeholders Questions. The two questions you must answer are: (1) Who are the specific strategic stakeholders and will they be for or against your firm's stance on the issue?; (2) What do they have to gain or lose by helping or opposing your business? Once you have identified the interested strategic stakeholders, and whether they may help or hurt the business with regard to the issue, the next step is to identify each one's incentive to take action on the issue. […] Don't forget to use Model 1.1.

Personal and Professional Applications

9. Select a business issue and list the strategic stakeholders and their interests.

3. Incentive of Stakeholders

Even within the business, society, and government categories, different stakeholders can have different expectations, concerns, and requests for firm action to meet their special interest. Thus, you want to determine stakeholder legitimacy, power, and urgency and the likelihood of their taking action to help or oppose the business on the issue.

Legitimacy. What is the firm's responsibility to the stakeholder, and what is appropriate strategic action based on the issue? Regardless of the stakeholder group's legitimacy, the business's decision is often based on stakeholder power and situational urgency.

Power. If stakeholders do take action against the business, how much pressure can they exert? Can stakeholders really affect the performance of the firm? Or if stakeholders do take action to help the business with an issue, how much can they really contribute? Power is more important than legitimacy, because even if you believe stakeholders' issues are not legitimate, if they can hurt or help the firm, the firm needs to take action.

Urgency. If the issue is legitimate and the stakeholder has power, how quickly does a non-market strategy need to be developed and implemented? Figure 7.1.4 can help you answer this question. Generally, the more advanced the stage is, the more urgent the issue.

Likelihood of Stakeholder Action—Costs vs. Benefits. Although stakeholders may be legitimate and have power, the next question is whether the strategic stakeholders will take action to help or oppose the firm on the issue. One popular method in answering this question is the costs vs. benefits approach, which measures the consequences of issue action. Stakeholders weigh the costs and benefits of becoming active by taking action to help or oppose the firm, which may be a conscious or unconscious decision process. Financial incentives often drive action. Economic benefits can come from gaining something new, keeping what one has, or preventing loss, such as having to incur new costs. These benefits are strong motivators to take action, which means that the greater the benefit, the more likely the stakeholder will become active, and conversely, the greater the cost, the less likely. For large businesses, the benefits and costs can be in the millions of dollars. See Figure 7.1.5 for a list of stakeholders with their incentive measure of costs vs. benefits and powers. (Note that the stakeholders are presented in Model 1.1, p. 00.)

Potential Action, Consequences, and Preferences. Once you have determined the stakeholders that most likely will take action, the next question is what action they will take. Figure 7.1.5's last column, Power, lists the actions each stakeholder group might take. These stakeholder strategies will be explained throughout the book. You need to determine the consequences of potential alternative courses of action and the preferences of those stakeholders that are concerned about the issue.

Thus, putting the first three Is together, ***strategic stakeholders with incentives*** *can benefit or be hurt by the issue, will be for or against the firm's position on the issue, or may have an incentive (benefit greater than the cost) and will most likely take action to help or oppose the firm on an issue.* Thus, if the cost is greater than the benefit of taking action on an issue, stakeholders

Stakeholder	Incentive—Measure of Costs vs. Benefits	Power—Strategic Action Stakeholder Might Take
Market Environment		
Stockholders	Sales and profits Fair return on investment—dividends Increased value of stock	Vote for board of directors Pressure board and managers
Managers/Employees	Compensation (wages and benefits) Job security and opportunities Working conditions	Union/collective bargaining Work slow down—call in sick Strike
Customers	Price Quality Safety	Buy from competitors Boycott if products or policies don't meet expectations
Suppliers	Gain, or lose, sales to firm Payment, in full and timely Relationship, ethical	Provide needed products Refuse to sell to firm Slow down delivery Sell to competitors
Competitors	May face same issue Fair competitive practices	Complain to regulators File lawsuits
Nonmarket Society Environment		
Societal Interest Group	Monitor firm to ensure compliance with its interest	Picketing Organize demonstrations and rallies Boycott Appeal to press Appeal to government File law suits
Business Associations Community and Consumerism	Provide research and information Business creation of value Not hurting environment	Provide staff and resource help Provide political and legal help People are part of other stakeholder group power
News Media	Inform community of issues Shape public sentiment Shape nonmarket agenda	Provide positive news coverage Provide negative news coverage
Nonmarket Government Environment		
Legislative	Make the laws to help business and society	Make firm practices legal (can do) or illegal (can't do)
Executive	Enforce laws Make and enforce regulations to help business and society	Tell firm what practices it can and can't perform and make firm comply Can close down business
Judicial	Interpret the law Determine litigation outcome	Can change laws Decide who wins lawsuits

FIGURE 7.1.5 Stakeholder incentives and powers

do not have an incentive to do so, and nonmarket strategic action may not be needed with these stakeholders.

This process is relatively easy if the business only has one issue with only one stakeholder. Business situations, however, may involve many issues and are usually more complex due to multiple stakeholders who often have differing interests and conflicting incentives and therefore may make incompatible requests of the firm. Businesses need to know what stakeholders want, what action they might take to pressure the firm to give it to them, and what the consequences are to the firm if it does not meet the stakeholders' requests.

Incentive of Stakeholders Questions. The questions for managers include: Are the stakeholders' interests legitimate? Do the stakeholders have power? Is action urgent? At that point, the ultimate questions become Will the stakeholders take action to help or oppose the business on the issue? and, If so, what action might they take? The business must consequently conduct its own costs vs. benefits analysis to predict which stakeholders will become active and take action on the issue. Another consideration is whether stakeholders will join together to form a coalition to help or hurt the business. Nonmarket strategies must be developed and implemented for the stakeholders that have higher benefit/cost ratios and will more likely take action on the issue. If you are doing a case analysis using the Table in the Appendix, this third I analysis goes in column 3. First, be sure to state what the firm can gain or lose. Secondly, state whether the benefit is greater than the cost (B >C), or if C >B, which means the firm will, or will not, get involved to help or oppose the firm.

Personal and Professional Applications
   10. Using the stakeholders from application 9, identify their incentives and power.

4. Information—Objectives

The fourth I is information. *Information* is what people know or believe about the issue and the forces affecting the issue's development. To this point, we have used information to determine what the issue is, who the strategic stakeholders are, and what incentives and strategic action the stakeholders are likely to take. The information we are now considering is used to present the business's side of the issue to stakeholders. Before presenting the business's side of the issue, however, you should write objectives.

Objectives. Without an objective, how do you know what you want to accomplish and whether you have achieved it? ***Objectives*** *state the end result the business wants to achieve in trying to create value for the stakeholders of the issue.* Writing objectives clarifies what you want to accomplish for the business, and using the writing objectives model helps you write effective objectives to deal successfully with the business issue.

The ***writing objectives model*** is: *To + action verb + singular, specific, and measurable result to be achieved + target date.* The action verb specifies the end result, such as to "increase" sales, "decrease" cost, or "stop" the strike. Singular means only one end result should be in the objective, or have a new objective for each result you want to achieve. Specific means to state things quantitatively, whenever possible, such as to increase sales by $100,000 and to decrease costs by $50,000. Measurable means that you have a system or process of determining whether you achieved the end result. If your objective for this course is to learn a lot, how do you know if you did? If your objective is to get an A in the course, you'll find out if you met that objective by examining your end-of-semester transcript. The target date tells you at what point you should accomplish the objective. Remember to try to create value for stakeholders when writing objectives.

For example, your course objective would be, "To receive an A in Business, Government, and Society at the end of this Fall 20XX semester." A business objective could be, "To end the strike by midnight July 24, 20XX." In some cases, objectives are ongoing and don't require a date. For example, to keep reject rates to fewer than 2 percent, or to prevent a strike.

Personal and Professional Applications

11. Write at least five personal (i.e., school, diet, health, exercise) and professional (job/career) objectives using the writing objectives model.
12. Select a business issue and write the firm's objective using the writing objectives model.

Information. Now that you have a written objective for an issue, you need information to back it up or help you meet it. Let's discuss how to classify information, the difference between primary and secondary information, what supportive information is, and what information strategies entail, and how to present the business side of the issue.

Classifying Information: Facts, Assumptions, and Sentiments. Information can be classified as facts, assumptions, or sentiments. These classifications are critical for both understanding the issues surrounding a particular business situation (the foundation of a case summary) as well as for providing information that supports a business's nonmarket strategies. Data can be broken down into facts and assumptions and sentiments (feelings derived from facts and assumptions).

Facts. A fact can be proven, whereas an assumption can't. Good PA management is based on facts. Therefore, when analyzing a situation, in order to assert that a piece of information is a fact, you need to examine the source of the information and whether the information can be confirmed from another source. Unfortunately, although facts can be proven, some people will not believe facts due to their biased perception of the information because it doesn't support what they want to hear.

The process starts with examining the source of the information. You first need to determine whether this source is a *strategic stakeholder, a stakeholder, or a disinterested party*. It is usually understood that the more disinterested the party, the more factual the information is from that party, such as an outside source who is an expert on the issue.

Second, once the source of the information has been identified and its level of interest in the business situation determined, its *reputation for veracity and accuracy* must be examined. *The* **New York Times** (**NYT**) slogan is "all the news that's fit to print," yet even the NYT has come under attack on numerous occasions for being a "liberal" newspaper.[64] Although no source of information is truly objective or always accurate, some sources of information can be considered better than others. An article published in the NYT certainly would be considered far more factual in nature than an article published in **People** magazine; both would be deemed more factual than gossip heard at the local barber's shop. As a rule of thumb—always try to determine the relative expertise of the source of information (high, medium, low).

Third, use *data triangulation*—confirming the information presented through a second source of information. The more sources you can locate that present the same data, the more probable the data are factual in nature, especially if the data come from sources with differing interests and agendas. Make sure to determine both the interest and reputation of these sources as well. With all this information gathered about the data sources, you can then make a determination as to whether the information is factual. Figure 7.1.6 outlines the fact-determination process.

Information Source	Source Interest	Reputation/ Expertise	Data Confirmation	Data/Fact Determination
Stakeholders with subgroups 1. Business 2. Society 3. Government	1. Strategic stakeholder 2. Stakeholder 3. Disinterested party	1. High 2. Medium 3. Low	List other sources with interest and expertise ratings	*Guaranteed Fact* Nonmarket sources, disinterested parties, high reputation, multiple sources *Probable Fact* Mixed sources, stakeholder, medium, reputation single or double source *Questionable Fact* Market source, critical stakeholder, low reputation, no confirmation

FIGURE 7.1.6 Determining whether information is factual in nature[65]

Assumptions. If information is not a fact, it is an assumption. FreeDictionary.com defines an assumption as "the act of taking for granted ... something taken for granted or accepted as true without proof; a supposition."[66] If information is evaluated to be at best a questionable fact, as determined using Figure 7.1.6, then it is an assumption. Firms or stakeholders who act on assumptions as if they were facts tend to create market inefficiencies that negatively impact the stakeholders in a situation—the old adage that when you assume, you make an "ass" out of "u" and "me" can be quite accurate.

Sentiments. Unlike facts and assumptions, sentiments are based solely on the stakeholders' *feelings* about the issue as defined by the facts and the stakeholders' assumptions. Sentiment is the driving force behind stakeholders' actions and interests. The more important the issue is to a broader segment of people, the less likely the business will be able to advance its own interests and ignore stakeholder pressure on that issue.[67]

Ironically negative sentiment (being against something) tends to be a stronger driving force than positive sentiment (being for something), partly because pain avoidance is a stronger lower-level psychological need than pleasure acquisition. Putting it another way, it is human nature to act in opposition to something rather than to support it. (To quote Groucho Marx in the film *A Day at the Races*, "Whatever it is, I'm against it.")

It is essential for business to understand the power inherent in negative sentiment. The business's first priority should be to discern which stakeholders oppose a particular situation and then to develop objectives for dealing with the opposition—in strategic language, deal with threats to the business by taking action, not by inaction, and then build your strategic alliances with supporter stakeholders. Stakeholders that have minimal sentiment toward an issue, on the other hand, will tend to take no position and may be discounted and dropped from a firm's nonmarket strategy.

A Final Word on Classification. As mentioned earlier, business will use information in order to create nonmarket and market strategies so as to ethically create a win-win situation for stakeholders. This information can now be classified into facts, assumptions, and sentiments with the understanding that business will utilize each type of information to implement the strategy and obtain the objectives.

Personal and Professional Applications

13. Select a business issue and classify the information about the issue as facts, assumptions, and sentiments.

Primary and Secondary Information. Information can be primary, you gather data yourself, or secondary, other people gather data and provide information to others. Some view primary data as data gathered for your specific interests.[68] Businesses commonly use primary information from within the firm, such as profits and number of employee accidents. Annual reports and company websites are full of their primary data. Businesses also use secondary information that can be obtained from outside sources directly and through business professional/trade associations, libraries, and over the Internet.

Supportive Information. Good *supportive information contains accurate facts and figures and is stronger when gathered or supported by outside sources.* People trust facts and figures over generalizations. For example, to say that lots of people watch our show isn't supportive. People also trust outside sources of information over inside sources. When a business references outside sources of information, it is supporting its case (e.g., saying, "According to the **Neilsen Ratings**, 100,000 viewers watch our show each week"). Here is an example of how supported information can benefit a business. The late Dr. **Atkins** started his low carbohydrate diet some 30 years ago, with some following. Dr. Atkins consistently claimed it was a healthy diet. However, researchers at **Duke University** conducted a study using facts and figures; the results of the study supported Dr. Atkins' health claims, and the diet became a fad.

Information Strategies. *Three **information strategies** include outside sources conducting research, getting expert testimony, and getting stakeholder support.* The more detached the business is from the generator of supportive information, the stronger the supportive information.

1. **Outside Source Research Strategy.** The federal, state (and sometimes local) governments, conduct research studies and financially support others to conduct studies, such as the U.S. Census. *Professional and trade associations* also provide information to members, who pay membership fees and sometimes a fee for special reports. Secondary sources often provide generic types of information, such as a review comparing all diets. Consequently, businesses sometimes hire outside specialists to conduct research studies to provide specific information relevant to them, which can be expensive. You can hire outside experts, such as university professors, lawyers, certified public accountants (CPAs), and others to conduct research for your company.
2. **Expert Testimony Strategy.** Businesses also get experts, usually for a fee, to give testimonies. For example, **Merck & Co.** retained well-known doctors to state that its painkiller drug VIOXX does not cause a patient to die. On the other hand, the stakeholder lawyer who took Merck to federal **U.S. District Court in Houston**, accusing that VIOXX did cause a patient to die, videotaped a deposition from Dr. Eric Topol, a

top U.S. cardiologist, and Edward Scolnick, a former top Merck scientist, who claimed that VIOXX may lead to heart problems. Thus, you may obtain expert testimony, but you also need to be prepared to counter expert testimony against your business.

3. **Supportive Stakeholder Strategy**. Businesses also use the expertise of supportive stakeholders, usually for free. Consequently, determining who is for and against you on an issue is important. Even stakeholders who are against you on some issue may be supportive on another issue when asked. For example, when **Staples** and **Office Depot** wanted to merge, the CEO of **Office Max** went on record stating that the merger would be good for competition. As discussed, information strategies are critical to PA management.

Personal and Professional Applications

14. Describe the information strategy used by a business to achieve an objective.

The Business Side of the Issue. As you know, every issue has at least two sides. Stakeholders commonly contest an issue because they have different information supporting their side. So another important part of information strategy is to predict the information your strategic stakeholders may use against you, and to be prepared to defend your side of the issue with supportive information. Sometimes, stakeholder information is not accurate, and when the business provides its supportive information (facts), the issue is resolved or the interest demand may change.

A business develops its objectives for the issue in an attempt to create value for stakeholders. However, it is not uncommon for the business to believe its actions are legal, ethical, and appropriate, yet stakeholders don't agree. When contested, you present the business side of the issue by focusing on the information that will support that position. The stakeholder approach to business does not mean that you give a balanced presentation supporting the stakeholder against you. Think of it like a court case or a debate. Your lawyer or your side of the debate presents only your position, while trying to discredit others' information, in an effort to persuade the listeners (judge and jury) that your position has the most merit.

Objective and Information Questions. The questions for managers are: What do we want to accomplish, or what is our objective?, What are the facts, assumptions, and sentiments regarding the issue, interest, and incentives?, and What supportive information should we get to present our side of the issue? When dealing with the government, a key message is that your business creates jobs—that's a story that needs to be told.[69] When analyzing cases, be sure to look for supportive information for and against the business you are analyzing and use it to defend/oppose the firm's side of the issue. [...]

5. Interaction Strategies

The reason for strategic analysis is to formulate and implement strategies, which reflect a stakeholder orientation.[70] Based on your analysis of the issue, the interest and incentives of stakeholders, and on having set objectives, with information supportive of your side of the issue, it's time to develop strategies to deal with the issue—the fifth I. PA managers formulate nonmarket strategies that must be integrated with market strategies to coordinate social issues and business goals. *Developing* **interaction strategies** *includes generating alternative strategies to meet the objective, forecasting the market and nonmarket reactions and consequences of each alternative, selecting strategies, and implementing and evaluating strategies.*

Generate Alternative Strategies to Meet the Objective. Here you want to be creative and brainstorm several ways to meet the objective. When brainstorming, the major rule is *not* to evaluate the alternatives as you develop them. Just list any strategy that can be used to meet the objective. For a list of nonmarket strategies that may be used, see Figure 7.1.4 (on p. 248), which includes information strategies. [...]

Forecast the Market and Nonmarket Reactions and the Consequences of Each Alternative. Now you evaluate each alternative to estimate public sentiment, or how the market and the nonmarket stakeholders will react if the business takes the strategic action. A simple method is to classify the reaction as being positive, neutral, or negative (+, =, –); the stakeholders are expected to like the action, not care one way or the other, or not like the action. If the anticipated reaction is not going to be positive, the business will need to deal with the opposition. [...]

> Philip Morris Case Question 6: What are the market reaction and consequences of PM's nonmarket strategy of continuing to directly fight lawsuits in the courts and in the news media?
>
> The confrontational approach employed by PM has, at least to the current point in time, deflated the price of the stock. The stock is still considered undervalued and a good buy, yet many investors are hesitant to purchase the stock given the inherent risks associated with continuing court battles and the most recent statements made by the CEO. Only time will tell whether mutual funds managers and individual investors will shake off their hesitancy about this stock or whether the analysts' prediction of a rosier future comes to pass.

Select Strategies. After generating and analyzing each alternative, the next thing to do is select the most feasible alternative or combination of alternatives that will meet the business objective for the issue. When selecting alternatives, it is important to make sure that the alternatives are legal and, in your opinion, ethical; if they are not, don't select them. You also need to consider the power of the stakeholders involved with each strategy. If the stakeholder is powerful, you may need to select some alternative to meet the firm's objective and appease the stakeholder. Strategies should also be consistent with the company's policies, procedures, and rules. Your three select options are: yes, no, or wait. If yes, you go on to develop a strategic plan, and, if no, you don't. Selecting to wait is a contingency plan, with what-if scenarios. For example, wait and see if you get sued, and if so settle. [...]

Plan, Implement, and Evaluate Strategies. After selecting strategies, you need to develop strategic plans to achieve the objective. Then, you implement the strategies. When determining the time frame of strategy implementation, the more details you can provide in your planning, the better off you are. [...]

The last part of the strategic analysis is to evaluate the strategy implementation. PA professionals are responsible for evaluating progress in developing and implementing issues management strategies. However, no universal approach to evaluation is available. Most businesses view their issues or environment as unique, calling for their own assessment approach. However, PA managers should base their methods of evaluation on best practices of other firms. Also, evaluation is usually not possible when completing case studies because the focus is on developing "your" strategic plan, not evaluating it after its implementation. However, an evaluation plan should be discussed as part of the implementation plan. If the strategy is successful, the issue should be resolved. If not, you may have to return to prior stages. Strategies also need to change over time, as discussed in the section on the nonmarket issues life cycle.

You may need to redefine the issue, interest, and incentives; change objectives; get more information or change information strategies; reassess market and nonmarket reactions and consequences; select new strategies; or do a better job of implementing strategies. And when you change strategies, you need to assess their success at achieving the objective.

Interaction Strategies Questions. Interaction strategies questions include: (1) What alternatives are there to meet the objective?; (2) What will be the market and nonmarket reaction and consequences of each alternative?; (3) What strategies should we select?; and (4) How do we plan, implement, and evaluate them?

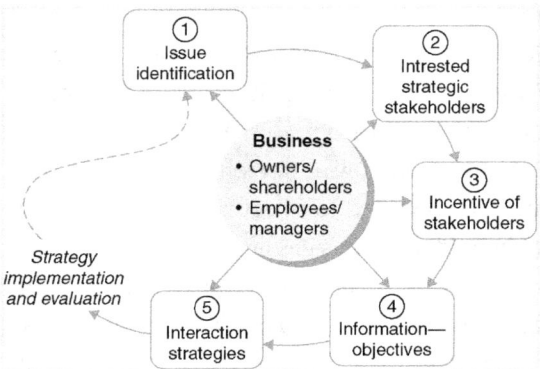

FIGURE 7.1.7 The 5 Is strategic analysis steps

See Figure 7.1.7 for a review of the 5 Is strategic analysis steps. Note that although the process includes five stages, the analysis is not simply linear; in other words, you may work on multiple stages at the same time and return to any stage at any time.

Where Do We Go from Here? The 5 Is strategic analysis is the model to use when analyzing business issues to determine how to strategically deal with stakeholders. However, the rest of this book provides you with more details on how different issues and various strategic stakeholders require different strategies. […]

Case Studies. The case studies in each chapter give you the opportunity to develop your critical thinking skills and your ability to successfully interact with stakeholders. We recommend reviewing this strategic analysis and applying it when conducting case studies, as directed by your professor, to develop your critical thinking skills. […] You should utilize the 5 Is analysis in your personal life when thinking about business news, and in your professional life as you work and make decisions.

Summary

The chapter summary is organized to answer the learning outcomes for Reading 7.1.

1. **Describe stakeholder management and the need to balance stockholder and other stakeholder interests.**
   Stakeholder management is based on attempting to make decisions on specific issues that provide value to strategic stakeholders. Managers have a responsibility

to make a profit to give stockholders a return on their investment. However, at the same time they must operate in a legal and ethical manner and not take advantage of other stakeholders. Thus, managers attempt to create a win-win situation for all stakeholders.

2. **Differentiate public affairs management from issues management.**
Public affairs (PA) management is the process of developing corporate public policies and strategies regarding how the business will interact with stakeholders in the business, social, and government environments when dealing with a current issue needing nonmarket strategies; it includes issues management and crisis management. Issues management is a public affairs management approach to identifying, monitoring, analyzing, and selecting public issues that may warrant nonmarket strategies. Thus, PA management is broader in scope and provides general guidelines. It also encompasses issues management, which has a specific three-phase process for dealing with PA issues.

3. **Identify the three-phase process of issues management.**
The three phases of issues management are: (1) scanning the environment to identify issues and trends that will affect the business; (2) evaluating the impact issues will have on the firm and ranking issues by priority; and (3) conducting a strategic analysis to develop strategies for dealing with high-priority public affairs issues.

4. **Define *crisis* and discuss the four stages of crisis management, including the 3 As of crisis communication.**
A crisis is a major unexpected event that has a large negative consequence.

The four stages of crisis management include:
1. Developing a crisis team with a mix of representatives from all sectors of the organization to deal with the crisis.
2. Conducting a risk assessment to determine potential crises, monitoring events to prevent them from becoming a crisis, and planning how to deal with a crisis if it occurs.
3. Managing the crisis by implementing the plan and communicating to: (a) *acknowledge* or admit to the crisis; (b) state the *action* you are taking to contain or repair the crisis damage; and (c) state how you plan to *avoid* a repeat crisis in the future.
4. Analyzing the organization's effectiveness in managing the crisis, with a focus on doing a better job of preventing and managing future crises.

5. **List and briefly describe the 5 Is strategic analysis.**

The 5 Is strategic analysis stages include:
1. **Issue identification.** The business identifies issues of stakeholders who want the firm to take some action to meet their special interest. The business identifies which stage of the life cycle the issue is in to determine the strategic focus.
2. **Interested strategic stakeholders.** The firm determines which specific strategic stakeholders will be for and against its stance on the issue.
3. **Incentive of stakeholders.** The business determines stakeholder: (a) legitimacy (What responsibility does the firm have to the stakeholder?), (b) power (Can the stakeholder help or hurt firm performance?); (c) urgency (Is quick action needed?); and predicts the (d) likelihood (costs vs. benefits) of their taking action, and (e) what action they will take to help or oppose the business on the issue.
4. **Information—objectives.** The firm states the end result it wants to achieve in trying to create value for the stakeholders of the issue. Information is classified as fact (can be proven), assumption (not factual), or sentiment (feelings about the issue). The firm presents its side of the issue, using information facts and figures to meet its objective through information-gaining strategies—outside sources conducting research, expert testimony, and using information of supportive stakeholders.
5. **Interaction strategies.** Developing interaction strategies involves: (a) generating alternative strategies to meet the objective; (b) forecasting the market and nonmarket reactions and the consequences of each alternative; (c) selecting strategies; and (d) implementing and evaluating strategies.

6. **Categorize the issue life-cycle stages with the strategic focus for each stage.**

The five stages of the life cycle with their strategy focus are:
1. Identification and formation of the issue and public sentiment. *Informational* and *societal strategies* are used to influence the development of the issue.
2. Interested stakeholder formation. The focus is on *informational* and *societal strategies* including developing coalitions.
3. Issue brought to business for voluntary action. The strategic focus varies based on the *issue and who brings it to the firm.*
4. Legislative and regulation formation. *The political strategic* focus is on preventing or supporting change, primarily through lobbying.
5. Enforcement and litigation. The *legal strategic* focus is on complying with changes and avoiding or bringing lawsuits.

7. **Fill in the blanks with the appropriate key terms (in order of appearance in the chapter):**

   _____ is based on making decisions on specific issues in an ethical manner in ways that provide value to strategic stakeholders.

   _____ are critically affected by a firm's actions, and/or they can affect firm performance.

   _____ refers to how business interacts with stakeholders.

   _____ is the process of developing corporate public policies and strategies regarding how the business will interact with stakeholders in the business, social, and government environments; it includes issues management, crisis management, and strategic analysis.

   _____ is a public affairs management approach to identifying, monitoring, analyzing, and selecting public issues that may warrant nonmarket strategies.

   _____ includes: (1) scanning the environment to identify issues and trends that will affect the business; (2) evaluating the impact issues will have on the firm and ranking issues by priority; and (3) conducting a strategic analysis to develop strategies for dealing with high priority public affairs issues.

   _____ is a major unexpected event that has a large negative consequence.

   _____ include: (1) developing the crisis team; (2) planning; (3) managing the crisis—communication; and (4) analyzing post crisis.

   _____ consist of acknowledging the crisis, stating the action to deal with the crisis, and stating how the crisis will be avoided in the future.

   _____ stages include: (1) issue identification; (2) interested strategic stakeholders; (3) incentive of stakeholders; (4) information—objectives; and (5) interaction strategies.

   _____ are usually brought to the company by any of its stakeholders because the firm is not meeting expectations, and the stakeholder is pressing the firm to take action to meet its special interest.

   _____ includes: (1) identification and formation of the issue and public sentiment; (2) interested stakeholder formation; (3) issue brought to business for voluntary action; (4) legislative and regulation formation; and (5) enforcement and litigation.

   _____ can benefit or be hurt by the issue, and will be for or against the firm's position on the issue, or may have an incentive (benefit greater than the cost) and will most likely take action to help or oppose the firm on an issue.

_____ state the end result the business wants to achieve in trying to create value for the stakeholders of the issue.

_____ follows the formula: to + action verb + singular, specific, and measurable result to be achieved + target date.

_____ contains accurate facts and figures, and is stronger when gathered, or supported by, outside sources.

_____ include outside sources conducting research, getting expert testimony, and getting stakeholder support.

_____ include generating alternative strategies to meet the objective, forecasting the market and nonmarket reactions and consequences of each alternative, selecting strategies, and implementing and evaluating strategies.

Key Terms (In Alphabetical Order)

3 As of crisis communication (p. 243)
5 Is strategic analysis (p. 246)
crisis (p. 240)
crisis management stages (p. 241)
information strategies (p. 256)
interaction strategies (p. 258)
issues life cycle (p. 247)
issues management (p. 237)
issues management process (p. 238)
issues to business (p. 247)
objectives (p. 252)
public affairs (PA) (p. 235)
public affairs management (p. 236)
stakeholder management (p. 233)
strategic stakeholders (p. 233)
strategic stakeholders with incentives (p. 250)
supportive information (p. 256)
writing objectives model (p. 253)

Review Questions

1. In the definition of strategic stakeholders, what do *critical* and *strategic* mean?
2. What is the relationship between issues management and crises management?
3. What is the difference between problems businesses face and a crisis?
4. What is the role of the crisis management team?
5. Why are the 3 As of communication so important to crisis management?
6. Why is it important for a business to know in what stage of the life cycle an issue is?
7. Why is it important for a business to understand the power of stakeholders?
8. Should a business present both the stakeholders' and its own side of the issue?
9. What is the purpose of a strategic analysis?
10. Why should generating and evaluating alternative strategies be done sequentially?

Discussion/Critical Thinking Questions

Be sure to give a detailed explanation for your answer to each question.

1. Is the stakeholder approach to management appropriate only for big corporations run by professional managers? After all, professional managers, for the most part, don't take the risk of ownership. Unlike the owners, professional managers get a salary even if the business loses money. If you start your own sole proprietorship business, or already own a business, will you look out for the interest of stakeholders, rather than your own profits?
2. Will the stakeholder approach to management become more or less commonly used in the future?
3. What qualities should public affairs managers possess?
4. How can all managers incorporate public affairs into their job on a daily basis?
5. There are two primary ways to increase profits—increase revenues and decrease costs. Large corporations spend millions on public affairs activities and employees. Doesn't it make sense to dramatically reduce PA spending to increase profits?
6. Issues management is about identifying, monitoring, and analyzing trends and issues that "might" affect business, which is costly. Why not just wait until issues actually do affect the business?
7. Many large corporations spend a lot of time and resources planning to prevent crises, yet they still have crises. So is it really worth having a crises program?
8. The terrorist attack of September 11, 2001, was clearly a major national crisis. Can business, society, and government really be effective in terrorist crises management? Should business focus on terrorist crises management or leave it to the government?
9. Why is it valuable to learn how to conduct a strategic analysis, and who benefits?

Application Exercises

For these two application exercises, try to use a business you work(ed) for or one you would like to work for.

2.1 Crisis Management

Select a business that has gone through a crisis. Identify the crisis and describe how the business managed the crisis. Be sure to state its 3 As of communicating during a crisis. Could the business have done anything to prevent the crisis? If so, what? How could the business have better handled the crisis?

2.2 Conducting a 5 Is Strategic Analysis

Select a firm that has an "issue to business" as described in the issue identification section. Conduct a complete 5 Is strategic analysis for the issue. Be sure to clearly label each of the 5 Is, including the objective. In essence, you are doing your own selected case study, similar to the case studies at the end of the chapters, without case questions.

Alternative: If your professor is assigning the BSG case analysis table in the Case Analysis approaches, you should study it and follow the analysis format as per the instructor's guidelines.

Before doing a case analysis for this chapter, you may want to read Case Analysis Approaches in the Appendix for ideas on how to conduct a case analysis. Your professor may require a specific case analysis approach.

Case 2.1

As If Your First Life Wasn't Bad Enough: Suing Your Virtual "Second Life" in Reality

Usually people go into a virtual reality game to get away from their day-to-day problems and to live a different, more carefree lifestyle. Fighting dragons (or each other), going on quests, having virtual dates, this would seem to be the formula for fun in the virtual world. Now, consider the world of Second Life where some residents have taken the game far too seriously and filed real-life lawsuits against one another for actions taken in this virtual world.

Second Life, an online virtual world created by Linden Lab, mimics real life. In this online computer game, users click to accept the Terms of Agreement, create their own avatar (called residents), and then explore the world (known as the grid) to meet other residents, socialize, participate in individual and group activities, and potentially create and trade virtual property and services with one another.[71]

An avatar named Richard Minsky filed a real lawsuit against another avatar in the game as well as two directors at Linden Labs because Keegan (the avatar being sued) opened up an art gallery in Second Life called "SLart," a name that Minsky had originally trademarked in 2008. Minsky felt that his trademark had been violated regardless of the virtual nature of the gallery in question.

Interestingly enough, Minsky's lawyer is someone he met through Second Life and has an avatar himself. Reportedly the lawyer's avatar sent Keegan's avatar a "cease and desist" order and also sent the same orders to the directors of Second Life. In his own defense, Keegan stated, "A Second Life neighbor actually living in Australia did it for me. As a logo I just put SL in capitals followed by art. I may have thought of 'SLart' around the same time as Minsky. But that doesn't matter in U.S. trademark law: who gets there first wins."[72] Since the suit, the sign was officially taken down by Second Life and the trademark was officially given to Minsky in the game's virtual reality as well. This case was considered a bench test of whether real courts can get involved in virtual world disputes.

Second Life has been in other lawsuits as well. The most recent is a class action lawsuit filed by several users accusing Linden Labs of changing the terms of virtual property ownership. Residents claimed they were forced to agree to new terms that eroded their ownership rights to virtual property and goods.[73] They claimed that the promises of ownership were empty and that the company falsely advertised these rights so that they could add new people from around the United States.

Questions:

1. How many critical issues are discussed in this case and what are they?
2. Identify the facts, assumptions, and sentiments (FAS) for each issue of the case.
3. Who are the interested stakeholders for each issue?
4. Choose one issue. What are the stakeholders' incentives?
5. As a director of Linden Labs, you have been asked to testify in court for a lawsuit similar to the ones in the case. Present an argument that can serve as a defense for Second Life.
6. What strategy would you use as director of Linden Labs for accomplishing one of your issue objectives?

References and Notes

1. R. F. Hartley, *Management Mistakes and Successes*, 8th ed. (New York: John Wiley & Sons, 2005).
2. V. O'Connell, "Future of Altria Hangs on Ruling in Tobacco Suit," *Wall Street Journal* (December 14, 2005): B1.
3. G. Zuckerman, "Altria Soars, Doubters Say: 'D'oh!'" *Wall Street Journal* (December 16, 2005): C1.
4. W. Civils and P. Lattman "Analysts React to Altria Ruling," *Wall Street Journal* (December 15, 2005). http://online.wsj.com/article/SB113466843615923619.html?mod=us_business_whats_news.
5. V. O'Connell, "Philip Morris Gets Big Legal Victory," *Wall Street Journal* (December 16, 2005): A3.
6. L. Salahi, "Philip Morris CEO: Smoking 'Not That Hard' to Quit," ABC News (May 12, 2011). http://abcnews.go.com/Health/Wellness/philip-morris-ceo-smoking-hardquit/story?id=13589835#.T3lLzGFAu8A.
7. A. Armenakis and J. Wigand, "Stakeholder Actions and Their Impact on the Organizational Cultures of Two Tobacco Companies," *Business and Society Review* 115(2) (2010): 147–171.

8. M. Van Huijstee, and P. Glasbergen, "NGOs Moving Business: An Analysis of Contrasting Strategies," *Business & Society* 49(4) (2010): 591–618.
9. R. G. Castro, M. A. Ariño, and M. A. Canela, "Over the Long-Run? Short-Run Impact and Long-Run Consequences of Stakeholder Management," *Business & Society* 50(3) (2011): 428–455.
10. P. C. Godfrey, N. W. Hatch, and J. M. Hansen, "Toward a General Theory of CSRs: The Roles of Beneficence, Profitability, Insurance, and Industry Heterogeneity," *Business & Society* 49(2) (2010): 316–344.
11. S. Sorenson, J. E. Mattingly, and F. K. Lee, "Decoding the Signal Effects of Job Candidate Attraction to Corporate Social Practices," *Business and Society Review* 115(2) (2010): 173–204.
12. H. J. Van Buren III, "Taking (and Sharing Power): How Boards of Directors Can Bring About Greater Fairness for Dependent Stakeholders," *Business and Society Review* 115 (2010): 205–230.
13. J. P. Walsh, "Taking Stock of Stakeholder Management," *Academy of Management Review* 30(2) (April 2005): 426–439.
14. J. Wei-Skillern, "The Evolution of Shell's Stakeholder Approach: A Case Study," *Business Ethics Quarterly* 14(4) (October 2004): 713–729.
15. B. Dyck, K. Walker, F. Starke, and K. Uggerslev, "Addressing Concerns Raised by Critics of Business Schools by Teaching Multiple Approaches to Management," *Business and Society Review* 116(1) (2011): 1–27.
16. C. H. Amato and L. H. Amato, "Corporate Commitment to Global Quality of Life Issues: Do Slack Resources, Industry Affiliations, and Multinational Headquarters Matter?" *Business & Society* 50(2) (2011): 388–416.
17. M. D. P. Lee, "Configuration of External Influences: The Combined Effects of Institutions and Stakeholders on Corporate Social Responsibility Strategies," *Journal of Business Ethics* 102(2) (2011): 281–298.
18. B. Dyck, K. Walker, F. Starke, and K. Uggerslev, "Addressing Concerns Raised by Critics of Business Schools by Teaching Multiple Approaches to Management," *Business and Society Review* 116(1) (2011): 1–27.
19. C. Walker, "Long-Term Outlook: Corporations in the Dow Jones Sustainability Indexes Reflect on How They Rely on Sustainable Strategies to Boost Performance and Generate Growth for Investors Over Time," *Research* 28 (May 2005): 80–82.
20. S. Vranica, "Public Relations Learned the Hard Way," *Wall Street Journal* (December 30, 2010): B6.
21. N. I. Torres, "Dealing with a PR Disaster," *Entrepreneur* (February 2009): 70.
22. A. Armenakis and J. Wigand, "Stakeholder Actions and Their Impact on the Organizational Cultures of Two Tobacco Companies," *Business and Society Review* 115(2) (2010): 147–171.
23. The Public Affairs Council, www.pac.org (accessed October 27, 2011).

24. J. P. Bonardi, M. J. Hillman, and G. D. Keim, "The Attractiveness of Political Markets: Implications for Firm Strategy," *Academy of Management Review* 30(2) (2005): 397–413.
25. S. Vranica, "Public Relations Learned the Hard Way," *Wall Street Journal* (December 30, 2010): B6.
26. N. I. Torres, "Dealing with a PR Disaster," *Entrepreneur* (February 2009): 70.
27. "Analysis: The Blogosphere—Google Carves New Path by Blogging to Confront Issues," *PR Week* (October 10, 2005): 11.
28. G. Colvin, "What Makes a CEO an MPV?" *Fortune* (June 13, 2011): 27.
29. B. George, "How Do I Keep My Company's Reputation Intact When Our Industry Has Been Tainted by Bad News?" *Fortune* (March 16, 2009): 30.
30. B. O'Connor, "Donor Profile," *Salem Statement* (Fall 2011): 8.
31. J. Collins, "How Great Companies Turn Crisis into Opportunity," *Fortune* (2009): 49–52.
32. A. Lobb, A. Dizik, and J. Porter, "Lessons That Fit the Times," *Wall Street Journal* (August 20, 2009): B5.
33. E. Holm, "Got a Crisis? Tap AIG," *Wall Street Journal* (October 12, 2011): C1.
34. http://subscriber.hoovers.com.cwplib.proxy.liu.edu/H/company360/financialSummary.html?companyId=10021000000000.
35. M. De La Merced, "American Airlines Parent Files for Bankruptcy," *New York Times* (November 29, 2011). http://dealbook.nytimes.com/2011/11/29/american-airlines-parent-files-for-bankruptcy.
36. A. Bender, "American Airlines' Bankruptcy: Who Loses?" *Forbes* (November 29, 2011). http://www.forbes.com/sites/andrewbender/2011/11/29/american-airlinesbankruptcy-who-loses/.
37. H. Yousuf, "American Airlines CEO: 'We're Facing a Fuel Crisis,'" *CNN Money* (April 8, 2011). http://money.cnn.com/2011/04/08/news/economy/American_Airlines_fuel_crisis/index.htm.
38. V. M. Desai, "Mass Media and Massive Failures: Determining Organizational Efforts to Defend Field Legitimacy Following Crises," *Academy of Management Journal* 54(2) (2011): 263–278.
39. M. Rhee and M. E. Valdez, "Contextual Factors Surrounding Reputation Damage with Potential Implications for Reputation Repair," *Academy of Management Journal* 34(1) (2009): 146–168.
40. S. Vranica, "Public Relations Learned the Hard Way," *Wall Street Journal* (December 30, 2010): B6.
41. This section primarily adapted from L. Barton, *Crisis in Organizations*, 6th ed. (Mason, OH: South-Western/Cengage, 2010).
42. B. George, "How Do I Keep My Company's Reputation Intact When Our Industry Has Been Tainted by Bad News?" *Fortune* (March 16, 2009): 30.
43. G. Colvin, "What Makes a CEO an MPV?" *Fortune* (June 13, 2011): 27.
44. C. Wilson, "How Do I Keep My Company's Reputation Intact When Our Industry Has Been Tainted by Bad News?" *Fortune* (March 16, 2009): 30.

45. M. Rhee and M. E. Valdez, "Contextual Factors Surrounding Reputation Damage with Potential Implications for Reputation Repair," *Academy of Management Journal* 34(1) (2009): 146–168.
46. D. Foust, "US Airways: After the Miracle on the Hudson," *BusinessWeek* (March 2, 2009): 31–32.
47. D. Foust, "US Airways: After the Miracle on the Hudson," *BusinessWeek* (March 2, 2009): 31–32.
48. M. D. Groza, M. R. Pronschinkse, and M. Walker, "Perceived Organizational Motives and Consumer Responses to Proactive and Reactive CSR," *Journal of Business Ethics* 102(4) (2010): 639–652.
49. S. Vranica, "Public Relations Learned the Hard Way," *Wall Street Journal* (December 30, 2010): B6.
50. E. Dezenhall, "How Do I Keep My Company's Reputation Intact When Our Industry Has Been Tainted by Bad News?" *Fortune* (March 16, 2009): 30.
51. M. Penn, "Handle a Crisis," *BusinessWeek* (September 26–October 2, 2011): 104.
52. N. I. Torres, "Dealing with a PR Disaster," Entrepreneur (February 2009): 70.
53. E. Dezenhall, "How Do I Keep My Company's Reputation Intact When Our Industry Has Been Tainted by Bad News?" *Fortune* (March 16, 2009): 30.
54. P. M. Barrett, "Success Is Never Having to Say You're Sorry," *BusinessWeek* (July 4–10, 2011): 52–61.
55. S. Vranica, "Public Relations Learned the Hard Way," *Wall Street Journal* (December 30, 2010): B6.
56. D. Foust, "US Airways: After the Miracle on the Hudson," *BusinessWeek* (March 2, 2009): 31–32.
57. M. Penn, "Handle a Crisis," *BusinessWeek* (September 26–October 2, 2011): 104.
58. http://ww5.komen.org/AboutUs/AboutUs.html (accessed March 27, 2012).
59. http://www.cbsnews.com/8301-503544_162-57370867-503544/backlash-growsover-susan-g-komen-planned-parenthoodflap/(accessed March 27, 2012).
60. C. H. Amato and L. H. Amato, "Corporate Commitment to Global Quality of Life Issues: Do Slack Resources, Industry Affiliations, and Multinational Headquarters Matter?" *Business & Society* 50(2) (2011): 388–416.
61. M. D. P. Lee, "Configuration of External Influences: The Combined Effects of Institutions and Stakeholders on Corporate Social Responsibility Strategies," *Journal of Business Ethics* 102(2) (2011): 281–298.
62. M. D. P. Lee, "Configuration of External Influences: The Combined Effects of Institutions and Stakeholders on Corporate Social Responsibility Strategies," *Journal of Business Ethics* 102(2) (2011): 281–298.
63. M. Rhee and M. E. Valdez, "Contextual Factors Surrounding Reputation Damage with Potential Implications for Reputation Repair," *Academy of Management Journal* 34(1) (2009): 146–168.
64. http://www.fair.org/index.php (accessed November 11, 2011).

65. Adapted from H. Sherman, "A Model of Communication Processing," in E. Bewayo, J. Cross, B. Kaplan, C. Rodrigues, and H. Sherman (eds.), Selected Readings in *Management Process & Organizational Behavior*, 2nd ed. (Boston: Ginn Press, 1985).
66. http://www.thefreedictionary.com/assumption (accessed November 11, 2011).
67. M. D. P. Lee, "Configuration of External Influences: The Combined Effects of Institutions and Stakeholders on Corporate Social Responsibility Strategies," *Journal of Business Ethics* 102(2) (2011): 281–298.
68. Suggestion made by reviewer Professor William Matthews, William Patterson University, (July 24, 2012).
69. N. Easton and T. Demos, "The Business Guide to Congress," *Fortune* (May 11, 2009): 72–75.
70. A. Armenakis and J. Wigand, "Stakeholder Actions and Their Impact on the Organizational Cultures of Two Tobacco Companies," *Business and Society Review* 115(2) (2010): 147–171.
71. http://en.wikipedia.org/wiki/Second_Life.
72. U. Khan, "Second Life Lawsuit to Test How Much Jurisdiction Courts Have Over Virtual World." *The Telegraph* (November 25, 2008). http://www.telegraph.co.uk/technology/3517319/Second-Life-lawsuit-to-testhow-much-jurisdiction-courts-have-overvirtual-world.html.
73. C. McCarthy, "Class Action Lawsuit Targets Second Life," CNET (May 3, 2010). http://news.cnet.com/8301-13577_3-20004004-36.html.

Post-Reading Questions

1. Discuss the strengths of the stakeholder management concept in addressing external ethical challenges. What was the outcome? What do you think could have been done differently?
2. Define the concept of corporate crises and discuss the four stages of crises management. What are the strengths and weakness of each stage? Would this model be applicable to your organization? Why or why not?
3. Describe a corporate crisis situation. How would the five-stage analysis model have been of value to the organization? At what stage would ethics be most important?

Videos Retrieved from the Internet

"Business Is about Purpose"

https://www.youtube.com/watch?v=7dugfwJthBY&feature=emb_logo

This is a TED talk on topic by R. Edward Freeman.

"The Stakeholder Model"

https://www.youtube.com/watch?v=YJnQBUu-Ycc&feature=emb_logo

This is a corporate video on defining the stakeholder model.

Internet Sites on Ethics, Public Affairs, Crisis Management, and Stakeholder Management

"Crisis Management Strategies for Business Owners"

https://www.investopedia.com/articles/financial-theory/10/crisis-management.asp

This is a guide on "what to do" regarding a business crisis.

"Seven Critical Steps to Crisis Management"

https://www.inc.com/bruce-condit/7-critical-steps-to-crisis-management.html

This is an INC article on "how to" address a business crisis.

"Ethics in Crisis Management"

http://www.pcma.com/PDF/Ethics_in_Crisis_Management.pdf

This is a Professional Crisis Management Association presentation.

"How to Survive an Ethics Crisis"

https://chiefexecutive.net/how-to-survive-an-ethics-crisis/

This is a *Chief Executive* magazine article on the topic.

"The Underlying Role of Ethics in Crisis Management"

http://www.sagepub.com/sites/default/files/upm-binaries/28757_10.pdf

This is a book chapter on the topic.

"Crisis Communication Objectives"

https://pagecentertraining.psu.edu/public-relations-ethics/ethics-in-crisis-management/lesson-1-prominent-ethical-issues-in-crisis-situations/crisis-communication-objectives/

This is a Penn State University classroom presentation on the topic.

CPSIA information can be obtained
at www.ICGtesting.com
Printed in the USA
LVHW062126070421
683743LV00003B/5